HOME AUDIO

CHOOSING, MAINTAINING, AND REPAIRING YOUR AUDIO SYSTEM

HOME AUDIO
CHOOSING, MAINTAINING, AND REPAIRING YOUR AUDIO SYSTEM

Andrew Yoder

McGraw-Hill

New York San Francisco Washington, D.C. Auckland Bogota
Caracas Lisbon London Madrid Mexico City Milan
Montreal New Dehli San Juan Singapore
Sydney Tokyo Toronto

McGraw-Hill

A Division of The McGraw·Hill Companies

ISBN 0-07-065346-1 (HC)
ISBN 0-07-065347-X (PBK)

The sponsoring editor for this book was Scott Grillo, the editing supervisor was Sally Glover, and the production supervisor was Sherri Souffrance. It was set in Windsor Light through the services of Cabinet Communications (Editing, Design, and Production).

Printed and bound by Quebecor/Fairfield

 This book is printed on recycled, acid-free paper containing a minimum of 50% recycled, de-inked fiber.

McGraw-Hill books are available at special quantity discounts to use as premiums and sales promotions, or for use in corporate training programs. For more information, please write to the Director of Special Sales, McGraw-Hill, 11 West 19th Street, New York, NY 10011. Or contact your local bookstore.

CONTENTS

ACKNOWLEDGMENTS

Because of the scope of this book, it could not have been written without help from many people and organizations. Thanks to Richard and Judy Yoder, Angie Piwonka, Dave Benson, Scott Hepler, Dave Homan, Gary Matthews, Aaron Bittner, Paul Sanders, David McCandless, John C. Baker, Stephen Moore, and Lance Scott. Special thanks to Brad Robison for the last-minute tutorial on PageMaker and PhotoShop!

Thanks to Alasdair Patrick of Audioquest; Sam Fontaine of AudioControl; Ryne C. Allen of ESD Systems; James R. Lawson of Shure; Norman Rubin and Nathan Rahimi of Thorens America; Grant Lansdell of JVC; Eric C. Kreis of Kenwood USA; Laurie Bianchi; Anthony Federici of Mondial Designs; Mike Byrne of Madrigal Audio Laboratories; Rich Hering of Brookside Veneers; Ralph Nichols of Polydax; Joanne Mustaphich of Harman/Kardon; Craig Siegenthaler of Kiwa Electronics; Amy Stratton of Ramsey Electronics; Maria Horton of CD Technologies; S. Chiba of ELP; Doyle Albee and Lynne Wall of Maxtor; Stacey Pierson of Voyetra Technologies; Jeffrey L. Hipps and Stephanie Rojas of Sherwood; Laurie Compton of Sony Electronics; David Berkus of Sanyo Fisher; Rodney E. Beyl of Flexible Materials; Milan Hudecek of Rosetta Laboratories; Georgia Morgan of Drake; Joan McCarrell, Doan Hoff, and Marcia Walker of Yamaha; Justin Yamada of Morel Acoustics; Evelyn Sinclair of Theta Digital; Roksan; J. Winter of the Bellingham Antique Radio

Museum; Luke Manley of VTL; Roger Maycock of Tascam; and Wee Bee Audio.

Thanks to April Nolan for giving the first book in this series a chance. Also to Scott Grillo for acquiring this book, Sally Glover for the editing, and to Sherri Souffrance. Thanks to the rest of McGraw-Hill for getting this book out of the warehouse and onto peoples' bookshelves. Thanks to Michael O'Niel and Audrey Weilamb from Quebecor for help with the layout and production of this book.

Very special thanks to Yvonne for improving my writing quality and for always pushing me to do better.

INTRODUCTION

In the Introduction to *Auto Audio*, I said, "For years, music has inspired me to do more, faster, and more passionately. Music isn't just background Muzak; it's the soundtrack to my life." Now, I've decided that my analogy was incorrect—it isn't a soundtrack; it's fuel. It's a driving force that gets me started and keeps me going (no, it's not coffee!).

The problem is that you've got to have an audio system so that you can play back that music. And the obvious goal of any audio system is to reproduce the music as faithfully as possible. The ultimate is to sit in front of the system, close your eyes, and have no problem imagining that you're in the studio, hearing the performance firsthand.

This is a very simple goal and plenty of companies manufacture equipment capable of "taking you to the studio." But the problems that arise are those of electronics and economics. First, it takes special care—both in the design and the manufacturing—of electronic equipment in order for it to reach this level of fidelity. The extra time and more-expensive materials drive up the cost of the equipment. As a result, fewer people are willing to pay extra for the better equipment, further raising the costs. And this gives the companies in question a reputation for quality among the diehard. This reputation costs extra, too.

This is the beginning of the dilemma for anyone with interests in music. If your funds are unlimited, you can purchase an incredible-sounding audio system. Otherwise, your options are low-end equipment (which is also more prone to failure) or "mid-fi" (equipment that has been mass produced, but by companies with better reputations for quality).

The final question is: "What system is the best for you and your budget?" That's it. It has nothing to do with imaging, analog vs. digital, the "warmth" of the sound, the frequency range, or the total harmonic distortion.

At this point, many audio enthusiasts lose their primary focus—the music. Some of these people become so caught up in the fidelity of the system that it taints their overall perspective. I've seen some audio pundits make some rash statements, such as, "Any system under XXX amount of dollars isn't worth listening to." I would venture a guess that most of these people are more interested in listening to system fidelity than music.

Along the same lines, I've read and heard some statements from audio enthusiasts saying that it's a must to walk into a few audio test rooms at stereo shops, listen to everything you can, and choose whichever system sounds the best to you, regardless of the price! This is shockingly bad advice because a complete high-end audio system can cost anywhere from several thousand dollars to more than $100,000!

Home Audio was written because there's such a gap between low-end audio and the high end. You can go to any stereo store and pick up an inexpensive audio system. Or you can read a number of magazines that tout the ghastly expensive equipment. There's a huge gap between the two.

I have spent a considerable amount of time writing this book and making the information contained within as useful as possible. I certainly hope that you will find that it is useful as well.

I don't do equipment recommendations and I don't have the resources to respond to all of the questions about system designs, room acoustics, and equipment specifications. Read the audio magazines and newsletters for this information. However, if you would like to drop me a line concerning this book or your personal experiences with audio systems, feel free to contact me:

Andrew Yoder
P.O. Box 642
Mont Alto, PA 17237 USA
ayoder@cvn.net

Because of the volume of mail that I've been receiving, I can't guarantee a response, but I will try.

1

CHOOSING A SYSTEM

Most people don't bother researching audio component companies' prices; they just go to a store and choose whatever components are on sale. But if you're serious about your sound or your wallet, you'll have to do a bit of groundwork before you begin filling your rack. Possibly the toughest aspect of buying an audio system is just searching through piles of magazines, catalogs, and sale fliers to pick out the components that you want. There's a mind-boggling array of stereo equipment on the market, and it can be rather difficult to research all of it.

That route will most likely produce a mediocre system—one that's not worth the stack of bills that you will have to pull from your wallet. Or you might decide to buy a certain system because you read through a stereo magazine and found reviews of a few highly rated components. Once again, this is a great way to pay for much more than you are getting. The next option is to get nervous over all of the prices that you have seen in the magazines and audio shops and settle on something inexpensive from a discount department store. This method is somewhat different from the other two; you will get exactly what you pay for—a cheaply manufactured system. The last option is to search through stereo magazines and check out the prices from the mail-order companies. With a little work and some luck, you will wind up with a good system at a low price.

Fig. 1-1 Some of the major audio periodicals in North America.

If you love music enough to want your CDs to sound terrific, not just good, you'll probably try to buy the best system you can afford. Expect equipment manufacturers and dealers to take advantage of that desire.

BUYING NEW EQUIPMENT

Just about everywhere you look, someone is selling new stereo equipment. Getting a great system for a great price can be difficult.

FOLLOWING THE MAGAZINES

The audio magazines on the market are excellent sources of information for purchasing a system (Fig. 1-1). You can find information and specifications on most of the pieces of equipment that are currently on the market. *Audio* features a massive guide to stereo component prices and specifications in one of their issues. These listings are excellent if you are planning to become an active audio consumer. Aside from the listings, this magazine (as well as *Stereophile* and *Stereo Review*) features plenty of product reviews, new equipment glimpses, glossy manufacturer advertisements, and helpful tips.

On the other hand, the more narrowly focused *Speaker Builder* and *Amateur Audio* feature plenty of how-to construction projects and practical advice. These are great for the audio buff with some previous hands-on electronics or woodworking experience, but it can be a bit intimidating for the beginner. Still, the home-construction route is a great way to save some money and learn quite a bit about how your music is produced (both physically and electrically). Most of the projects in the construction magazines are high-end, but some of them (such as some of the projects in *Speaker Builder*) can be fairly inexpensive. For more information on speaker enclosure and construction basics, see Chapter 7.

Because each magazine's focus differs greatly from the others, there is a huge gap between the high-end audiophile with money and the high-end audiophile with skill. As mentioned, the general bias of the general-coverage audio magazines is toward expensive, high-end audio. The target audiences of these magazines appear to be college-educated men between the ages of 30 and 60— people with some extra cash and a comfortable lifestyle. Very few of the high-end magazines feature articles on how-to installation, troubleshooting, maintenance, or repair. You are more likely to find pages of frequency-response graphs than hands-on information about repairing your equipment. Also, most of the audio pundits don't leave any alternatives. For example, some might say that you must have a CD transport and a separate DAC (instead of a CD player in one unit). This system could easily cost a few thousand dollars. This particular pundit might say that a regular CD player isn't worth listening to, but what if I can't afford the separate units? Then what?

Although the advice given by the various stereo experts is very good, you also have to remember who pays the bills at the magazine office. Your subscription or newsstand price money is only part of the cash flow received by these magazines. The major source of revenue is generated by all of those beautiful, full-color, full-page advertisements throughout the magazine. As a result, the magazines are quick to push the expensive components and maxi-systems, whether they are necessary or not. Instead of finding test reports and reviews of average components or good deals, you will find test reports and reviews of the very best that the industry has to offer or you'll read about new, innovative technology that everyone else will be talking about in five years.

One bit of periodical advice that can help out is *Consumer Reports* and the *Consumer Reports Audio/Video Buying Guide*. This magazine rates a number of the readily available audio/video components. So, you won't find any of the high-end audio equipment in the guide, but it does include the best of the consumer models. Of course, look carefully at the *Consumer Reports* ratings—some of what they consider to be important isn't terribly valuable to audio enthusiasts. For example, when rating CD players, there is no rating for the sound quality—even though CD players are known to sound at least a bit different.

Because of the different directions taken by stereo magazines, the do-it-yourself magazines, and consumers reports, it's best to read as much as you can and determine what matches your own desires and capabilities. Make a checklist and get ready!

DISCOUNT DEPARTMENT STORES

If you get tired of running around, looking at ads, and researching, you might check out the stereo equipment at the local discount department store. After all, your "significant other" wants to try on some clothes and you want to look at the tennis racquets. There, you see equipment at great prices—complete minisystems for less than $149.95. Portable stereo systems (often called "boxes" around this part of Pennsylvania) are selling there for anywhere from $29.95 to $199.95. If you are lucky, they might even be selling some component stereo systems. If you have listened to the television advertisements from the discount department stores, you will know that the reason why their products are so inexpensive is because they have the "buying power" of thousands of stores; they don't just buy by the crate or even by the truckload!

All of these claims are correct; these stores buy in volume and they do pass the savings on to you. However, they only have enough room for a small quantity of stereo equipment, and you won't find much of a selection. As a result, plenty of equipment is vying for space in this department store. What is placed on shelf space in the store is not based on the quality, but on the number of units sold per month. This, in turn, is not based entirely on quality, but also on the price for the perceived number of features, size, and looks. The final judgment is decided by consumers (most of whom have not researched the market), not by audio professionals or hobbyists.

In general, the discount department stores attempt to give the consumer every feature possible for the least amount of money. This attitude is what sells products. You will see that the autoreverse cassette deck with Dolby C is much less expensive than the autoreverse cassette deck with Dolby C that you find in the stereo magazine advertisements. What you won't see is that the company that made the less-expensive deck probably skimped on the parts inside. Perhaps they saved a few cents per deck by using a less-sturdy PC board that will crack after a few years of use. Or maybe they used cheaper switches and knobs on the front panel that are much more likely to break. They almost certainly used cheaper heads, which means that the sound won't be as good and the heads will wear out quicker. The quality of the parts that go into a unit are much more important than the extra features and conveniences that you see on a deck. Nowhere is this more apparent than when comparing the equipment in discount department stores to that of higher-quality consumer-grade equipment.

CHOOSING A SYSTEM

Of course, there is a time and a place for everything. If you are on an extremely tight budget and you aren't serious about sound systems, you might want to try this route. When I was 14, my parents bought me a personal stereo. By audiophile standards, the fidelity was poor (still much better than the "slim" mono cassette players of the day), but I could actually listen to cassettes in stereo! I used this personal stereo until the cassette player's plastic drive gears stripped out about four years later. Overall, it was a great use of money because a good component system was well beyond my reach at the time (and that of my parents), and yet I was able to listen to plenty of music. In situations such as this, the el cheapo systems are worthwhile.

On the other hand, do not substitute cheap equipment for units that are well built if you plan to use the system for any length of time. Whereas the discount specials will reliably operate for maybe a few years, you can easily expect 5 or 10 years of good service from the better models. In the long run, researching the market and spending a few extra dollars on a solid system will be less expensive than buying inadequate systems that frequently break down.

One exception to the "cheap-equipment-at-national-chainstores" rule is Radio Shack. Although Radio Shack isn't a discount department store, it is basically a discount electronics department store. Because of its national-bargain nature, Radio Shack doesn't dig into the audiophile scene. They do, however, carry everything from low-grade to mid-grade consumer equipment, selling under the Optimus name. It can be rather tough to find comparison information on Radio Shack equipment in the stereo magazines. Evidently, Radio Shack has enough business from its own stores throughout the country and from the distribution of its sale fliers that it doesn't need to advertise in these magazines. In turn, the name Radio Shack is rarely mentioned in any of them. If you want to compare systems, you will have to look through *Consumer Reports* evaluations or check out the stereo section at the local

Radio Shack store yourself.

SPECIALTY STEREO SHOPS

If you live in or near a city, or live in a rural area and are very lucky, you will have a stereo shop nearby (Fig. 1-2). Most stereo shops are forced to carve a niche out of the audio market. Because most audio chain stores and department stores focus on inexpensive products for the mass market, most stereo shops sell anything from midrange to truly high-end equipment.

It's hard to say what type of stereo shop you'll have in your area. Many of those that I've seen were poorly stocked, but high priced. However, some have been fun to visit—well stocked and full of all sorts of new and used equipment. Often the best and biggest of the local stereo shops will branch out into mail-order sales.

Fig. 1-2 A very large local specialty stereo shop.

MAIL-ORDER COMPANIES

If you have done your background work, you will find your best price on any given piece of stereo equipment from one of the mail-order companies. Because these companies employ telemarketers, have computerized inventories, and sell thousands of units, they can afford to buy in huge quantities and, in turn, sell their equipment at a lower price than anyone else. Of course, this is just a generalization; some mail-order companies aren't at all inexpensive. Still, if you play the part of a smart consumer and shop around, you will probably be satisfied with the price (Fig. 1-3).

Fig. 1-3 The Internet Web page of Crutchfield—one of the world's largest stereo mail-order dealers.

Best of all, many of the high-end audio mail-order companies specialize in used equipment. You can't afford the new Conrad-Johnson amplifier, the McIntosh CD player, and the Thiel speakers, but you still have some money to play with? Start contacting the stereo dealers that also sell used equipment, you will find many components selling for as little as half of the typical asking price. The key to purchasing used equipment from dealers is whether the equipment is covered under warranty. The advantage of buying used equipment from a dealership, rather than from other audio enthusiasts (see the next section) is that the equipment is checked over and tested. If anything has failed, it will be replaced. In that respect, it is almost as safe as buying new equipment, yet you might save a considerable amount of money. The only audio equipment that you would expect to significantly degrade over five years or less are cassette decks and open-reel tape units. These tape player/recorders have numerous moving parts, and the heads will wear down with use. As a result, a used equipment dealer should have a warranty that lasts at least 90 days. If the money-back guarantee period lasts for only a week or so, avoid the dealer.

You can locate a number of large regional audio dealerships through different audio magazines and via the Internet. Both *Audio* and *Stereophile* magazines feature classified ads and a number of dealer ads. *Audio* even features a "Dealer Directory" in the back so that you can locate some of the larger mail-order stereo shops. *Stereophile*, on the other hand, prints a nice, big list of audio stores where you can buy *Stereophile*. The list only consists of cities and telephone numbers, but with a little bit of searching, you can locate a number of high-end audio stores. Unfortunately, many of the stores on the *Stereophile* list are retail only—no mail order.

Dig through these advertisements and make a list of phone numbers and addresses. Be sure to ask the salesperson if the store sells via mail order or is retail only. If you are only interested in a few particular models, call each company for price information. Always ask if they sell used, demo, or closeout equipment; you might find some excellent deals that aren't listed in the company's recent ads or catalogs. Compare the prices and go for the best deal.

In my opinion, it is best to make a list with a number of different components that would be satisfactory for your needs. Then, pick up their catalog or, if they don't have a catalog, ask the customer service representative for some of the recent sales. That way, if some mail-order company has a magnificent sale or closeout on a system that might be a little better than you thought you could afford, you can still be flexible enough to pick it up.

A peculiar, somewhat-related price discrepancy occurred whenever I was buying the head unit for my car. I only had one in mind because I wanted shortwave reception. After some searching, I found that one dealer had it for less than half of the list price. I called back a few days later and found that the price had gone up by nearly $100! The salesman said that the manufacturer had them on sale to the dealerships. He also said that at that point, they couldn't even buy those head units for the price that they had been selling them for. He might have been feeding me a line about the unit, but I haven't seen them anywhere for less than $50 over that original sale price since that time. The bottom line is: Be cautious and thorough when searching for cheap prices. A higher price might not be the fault of the stereo shop, the salesman, or the distributor, so please don't verbally abuse them!

Unfortunately, many mail-order companies don't have customer service representatives that are abreast of the current catalogs, like traditional showroom salesmen and saleswomen are. To make matters worse, it can sometimes be difficult to talk to the customer service representatives for more than a few minutes. You're usually lucky if you can get out more than name, address, credit card number, price, and catalog order number. To get a feel for what mail-order companies you can and can't talk to, call around, work with the companies that you like best, and write them a supportive letter or e-mail to let them know that you liked their customer service policy.

Of course, to order from one of the mail-order companies, you will either need to have a credit card out and ready or you will have to send a check or money order to the company's address.

Either way, the concept of sending hundreds or even thousands of dollars off to some address that you saw in a magazine isn't terribly appealing. What if that one million square foot warehouse that is packed with stereo equipment on the waterfront is actually just an empty apartment in Brooklyn with two telephones? You really have no way of knowing, unless you have visited the store's showroom or unless you know someone who has ordered from that company before. Although you can't be certain of the integrity of the company that you are ordering from, one good method to help you evaluate a company's performance is to check a few month's worth of magazines for advertisements. If you can find that a company has been in business awhile, it's a good sign. It's an even better sign if you can find advertisements from that particular company that are at least several years old—and the ads in question have gotten larger in size. That probably means that the mail-order company has performed well over the years and has, in turn, consistently built up a larger customer base.

Still, even after researching the mail-order company, you might have reservations about sending that much money. That's a natural reaction, and it is always better to be cautious than to risk your money. So, if you have found a company that you would like to order from, only order part of what you want—maybe only a relatively inexpensive set of speakers. That way, if the company sends everything quickly and you are satisfied with its service, you can order the more expensive components (such as amplifiers, CD players, speakers, etc.) later. If you are not satisfied with the service, write a letter to the company and to the Better Business Bureau, if necessary. Chances are that you will be very happy with the service that you receive from one of the mail-order companies. Personally, I don't know of anyone who has had any problems ordering from them.

BUYING USED EQUIPMENT

If you are daring and like to live life on the edge, then you might be game for stereo Russian roulette. Except, in this game, you win if you hit a hot component and get reamed monetarily if you pull a dud. Or you might be handy with a soldering iron and some test equipment and be perfectly capable of repairing your own equipment and saving a fortune. Either way, buying used equipment is not for the faint of heart.

As you might expect (especially if you frequent yard sales, auctions, or flea markets), you can find nearly any type of equipment in any condition for virtually any price. It's only a matter of looking to find what you want or need. Unfortunately, you probably will have to sift through hundreds of pieces of equipment until you find the right piece(s). Still, with patience and determination, buying used can be both rewarding and fulfilling.

WHERE TO BUY USED EQUIPMENT

If you are a "slave to convenience," you will quickly tire of the used equipment game and pick up your stereo components at premium prices elsewhere. This route is fine if you have at least $3,000 ready for an audio system; at least you won't have to take any risks or have any hassles this way.

CLASSIFIED ADS

One easy way to find the type of equipment that you want is to check out the classified advertisements in the local newspapers, in the shopper-type free classified papers, or on computer bulletin boards. It's much easier to sift through classified ads than it is to search through thousands of pieces of equipment at a flea market, electronics show, or auction.

The classified ads are excellent because they're a clearinghouse for audiophiles, technoids, and "sonic destroyers," who constantly buy new equipment and sell off their old components. The prices in the classified ads are often very good—usually about 1/2 to 3/4 of the price that the owner paid for the equipment. However, the prices are not quite as inexpensive as those at flea markets. Most people who will take the time and money to put a classified ad in a daily newspaper will expect to receive a price that is closer to what they originally paid for the components.

When scouring the classified ads for good prices, keep abreast of the discount prices from the stereo distributors. What sounds like a great deal might be a dud. The audiophiles and technoids commonly buy equipment with new features as soon as it hits the market. As a result, they pay the premium prices to be the first person around to have whatever it is that they have. When something new rolls around, they will buy it and sell off the old equipment. Even if they are selling the particular piece of equipment for 66% of what they paid for it, you might be able to find a stereo discount store that has a closeout on the same model—but is selling it for less than half of the original list price. For that matter, I picked up my present car amplifier for approximately 25% of the manufacturer's list price from a mail-order company that sells factory-serviced, discount, and closeout products. Chances are that I couldn't have found the same model in a classified ad for a price this low.

Another trap to beware of is people who purchase new equipment, raise the price, and resell it in the classified ads as new or almost new discounted equipment. This practice isn't common, but occasionally someone will try to make a few bucks off of an unknowledgeable person in this manner.

When you find a component that you are interested in buying, make a list of questions to ask the owner. In addition to the type-specific questions that you need to write down, ask:

* When did you buy it?
* Where did you buy it?
* Did you buy it new or used?

13

* Why are you selling it?
* Have you ever had any problems with it?
* Do you smoke?
* Do you have the manuals and the contact information from the manufacturer ?

Of course, not everyone will be honest with you, but some people will be. A few signs to beware of are physically damaged or dirty equipment. Physical perfection is not a must, but heavy wear can cause problems in some equipment. For example, an amplifier can usually get scratched and worn, yet still work perfectly. But a worn cassette deck might have more problems: heads can wear out; fragile buttons can wear out or become intermittent as a result of dust, smoke, or grease; and motors and gears can break down and strip. If the owner says that he or she doesn't smoke and that the unit was purchased new, but the front panel (in the case of a head unit or an equalizer) is yellowed from nicotine, then you know that the owner's answers are unreliable. If you know when the equipment was manufactured, you can figure out whether or not the owner is telling the truth about buying the unit new. Also, when checking the physical condition of the equipment, be sure to check the serial numbers or equipment part numbers. As mentioned in the previous section, beware of equipment that has the identification stickers ripped off, and do not buy any components that have the numbers scratched or etched out. This stuff is almost certainly stolen. Buying stolen equipment encourages thieves, and it could get you in trouble.

The best way to find out whether or not a component works is to test it. Few people will bother to try to sell an unworking system if you have a chance to test it; it's easy to see if it works and how well. If the component that you are checking is anything but a speaker, check to see if the power indicator (usually an LED) lights. Then, be sure that the wires are all connected. Otherwise, in the case of speakers or amplifiers, the owner might let you listen to the system, including the component that you want to buy. Check to be sure that the particular amp or speaker system is actually connected to the system that you're listening to.

Be sure to press all of the buttons and make sure that they work. Either a particular control system in the unit could be knocked out or a button could be broken or intermittent. You won't know if you don't check them. Don't just let the owner press a few buttons and say, "See, it works great. Are you going to buy it?" Hastiness and high-pressure sales are a warning sign that the system doesn't work as well as it should, that the price is too high, or that the owner is an impatient jerk. Beware in any case because if the owner is a jerk, he or she won't be reliable and won't help out if you run into any problems.

After all of these negative signs to avoid and potential reasons to distrust the owner, there is one very positive sign to be on the lookout for. It is an excellent sign if the owner has the original box, manuals, installation information, and/or receipts. For one thing, it rules out the possibility that the unit was stolen. Also, the component is less likely to have been bought second-hand by the original owner. One of the most important positive signs about having all of this information is that if the owner was so careful with the information that pertained to the component, he or she was probably just as careful (maybe more so) with the component itself.

If you are interested in buying a system from someone on the Internet (on one of the Usenet groups or on the classified section of an audio Web page), beware. There is no way for you to know if the seller is telling the truth or if he or she will take your money and disappear. On your side are the other users on the group, who will often alert everyone if someone with a bad reputation is offering something for sale. I witnessed a ripoff that occurred across country lines on an old BBS system that I used to frequent. The person who was ripped off told the story a few times after not being able to pursue the case across national borders. After a few months, a person from the other country checked in to say that he had read the posting, tracked down the offender, and somehow coerced him to return the money, plus some interest for the year and a half that he had it. Now that's cooperation! There are still some ripoffs via computer systems, but there are also a number of bargains. The only way for the system to work well is for the users to be honest and self-policing. If you plan to purchase a piece of equipment via this method, it is best to buy from someone who has had a lengthy presence on the system and has successfully sold items in the past. Also, it's best not to put your life savings on a whole system that you see adver-tised. Order only as much as you can afford to lose. If it works, you've got a great deal; if not, at least you won't have to sell your car to cover rent or a mortgage.

BUYING FROM MAIL-ORDER DEALERS OR LOCAL AUDIO SHOPS

Purchasing used equipment from mail-order dealers was lightly covered in the last section. Most of the mail-order dealers that sell used equipment also have one or more retail outlets. So, when you buy used equipment—even from the same shop—it could be via mail order or from the store itself. Most stores don't have different policies for mail order or for people who purchase locally, but you need to shop in a completely different manner.

If you have the ability to go into a shop and both see and listen to a piece of equipment, you can make a solid decision that is en-tirely based on your senses, not by putting your faith in what a salesperson described to you. Visiting a store, you can thoroughly look over equipment and make some subtle decisions to save yourself money or pick up some more expensive equipment for the money. For example, if your equipment isn't prominently displayed in your house, you might choose an amplifier that has a few scratches in the paint of the cabinet. Audiophiles tend to be incredibly particular about most everything, so because a unit is older and not cosmetically perfect, the sale price should drop significantly.

As mentioned in the previous section, the warranties and money-back guarantees are a major reason why many people purchase used audio equipment from stores, instead of from individuals. After all, it would be tough to sell any equipment at a high enough price to make a profit without some consumer insurance. As a result, the average installation shop or mail-order company that sells used equipment has anywhere from a one-week to a 30-day money-back guarantee. With this standard guarantee, you are usually able to return the stereo component for any reason and get all of your money back, less shipping costs (if applicable).

The average warranty on used equipment will last anywhere from 30 to 90 days. Generally, if the stereo component fails within the time of the warranty period, you can get your money back or have the unit repaired free of charge. These warranties are usually voided if you have opened the case or cabinet of the unit, physically damaged it, or if the unit was damaged because you connected it to a voltage or to an audio signal incorrectly. For any warranty or money-back guarantee, make sure that you have a hard copy of the signed agreement and be sure to read the specific terms. Some companies will void warranty agreements for reasons that might seem trivial to you. If you void a warranty and can't get your money back, it's your fault.

On the whole, buying used equipment from stereo shops and mail-order companies is a good move. Some shops don't like to bother with hiring a repair person to fix trade-in equipment, so you might have a few problems finding what you want, unless you live in a major city. Check your list of shops from the magazines and also check the yellow pages for stereo shops in your area and be sure to call first to find out if the shop sells used equipment. You shouldn't have any problems with buying used and repaired equipment from these suppliers.

PAWN SHOPS AND SECOND-HAND STORES

The flip side of buying equipment from shops or mail-order companies is scouring the pawn shops and second-hand stores. With pawn shops and second-hand stores, you trade a few extra dollars for the security of having a guaranteed unit. You might not need to shell out much money, but you are completely at risk.

The second-hand "thrift" stores are generally lousy places to look for stereo equipment. You might find something in one out of every five stores that you look through, but it will usually be an 8-track player from 1976 or something equally undesirable. Few people donate decent stereo systems to the Salvation Army.

Pawn shops, on the other hand, are great stores to look through for used stereo equipment or any other interesting electronics devices. It seems as though when financial hardships strike, the first things to be liquidated are the items of high technology. Likewise, it seems as though the people who need to quickly liquidate their possessions are those who dabble in high technology. If you are taxing your budget to buy your upcoming stereo system, beware of this warning sign! Don't overburden your budget or your beloved system could find a temporary home in a pawn shop!

The two big warnings about buying from a pawn shop are that you won't get a warranty or a money-back guarantee on your equipment and you could easily run across stolen equipment. Be sure to check the physical condition of the piece that you are interested in: Check all of the buttons, switches, and knobs to be sure that they all function. Also look for worn jacks, scratches, dents, oil or grease, burns, and melted areas. If one (or more) of these conditions exist, the price is less than 10% of the original sale price, and if you are good with repairing audio equipment, it might be worth your time and money to buy the component. Otherwise, avoid it! You will only lose money on it.

As stated previously, avoid stolen equipment. You can't be sure that anything is or isn't stolen, but if the component's serial number has been scratched or etched out, it has almost certainly been stolen. It is also best to avoid a piece of equipment if the serial number sticker or tag has been removed, painted over, or covered. If you find any equipment that has been altered in this way, complain to the store management and even complain to the proper state or local government bureaus. I have heard that some states have been working to organize and clean up the pawn shops within their boundaries and thus remove the stigma of pawn shops as being a clearinghouse for stolen goods. In these areas, you should have fewer problems with purchasing equipment.

Unfortunately, my location in Pennsylvania seems to be almost devoid of pawn shops. The closest ones to my present location are about 45 minutes away, in different states. But if you live in a city, you should have no problem finding several. One friend of mine regularly scopes out the bargains in three different pawn shops in his locale. If this is your situation, good luck!

HAMFESTS, COMPUTERFESTS, FLEA MARKETS, AND CONSUMER ELECTRONICS SHOWS

The flea market section at hamfests, computerfests, and consumer electronics shows are the best place to go for absolute minimum prices, with the trade-off of absolute maximum risk. Unfortunately, most people know nothing about these shows, and they are missing out on some great buys and interesting technology.

About half of the time when I mention to someone that I am going to a hamfest, the response is a joke, such as, "So, are you gonna eat a lot of pork? Ha ha." Yeah, real funny. A hamfest is an amateur radio gathering, where some large, open area (such as a county fairground) is filled with commercial amateur radio venders and another section (usually a section of the parking lot) is filled with a flea market. The flea market is filled with old shortwave and amateur radio parts that range anywhere from brand new to dating back to the turn of the century.

Just a few decades ago, nearly anyone with an interest or expertise in electronics was also an amateur radio operator. Of course, that was before the spread of personal computers and other electronic gadgetry. In many cases, the computer hobby overlaps the amateur radio hobby. Thus, most hamfests are also computerfests. Because of the overlap between computers and amateur and shortwave radio hobbies, you can also find other consumer electronics at these events. Some of the larger events are even advertised as "consumer electronics shows," and all sorts of electronic equipment is present, although the core is still amateur and shortwave radio and computers. The smaller hamfests usually have little more than just shortwave and amateur radio equipment. However, the larger events are really interesting; from antiques to junk to new merchandise, you have no idea what you might find (Fig. 1-4)!

Most of the fests that I have been at recently have been either radio or computer dominated. However, a few large fests that I went to a few months ago had a fair amount of stereo equipment in the flea market. One table featured a number of old tube McIntosh amplifiers. Another contained a big stack of 1980s-era cassette decks in various states of disrepair. One of my best hamfest purchases was a few years ago, when I picked up an Aiwa personal cassette player/stereo recorder in like-new condition with batteries for only $7. And even though not a lot of high-end audio equipment appears at hamfests, I've seen Carver and Marantz, in addition to the McIntosh table, at recent hamfests.

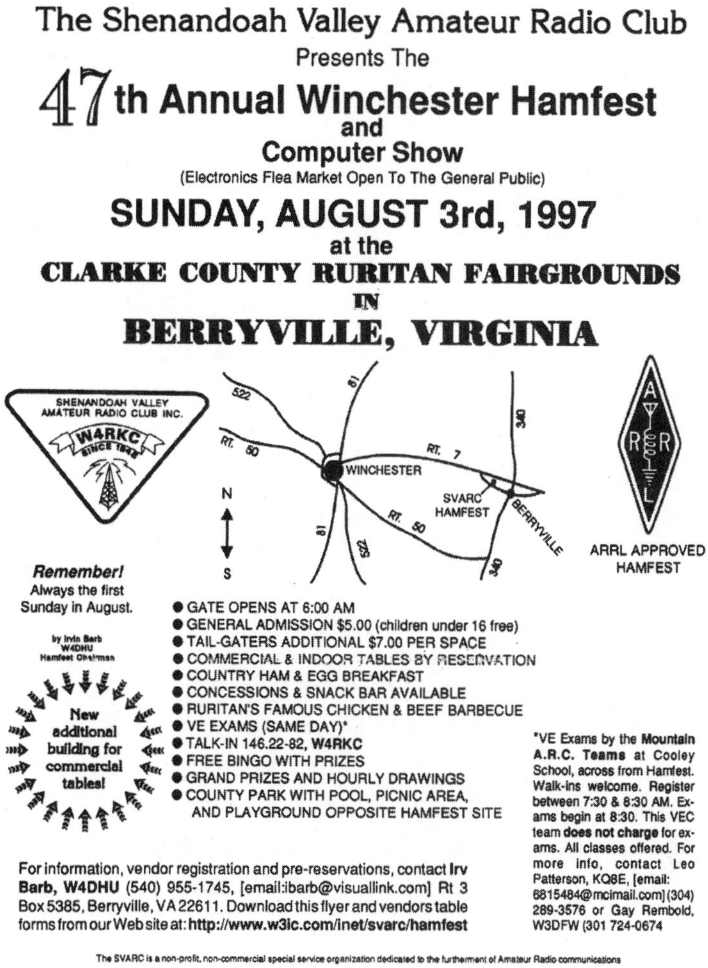
The Shenandoah Valley Amateur Radio Club
Presents The
47th Annual Winchester Hamfest
and
Computer Show
(Electronics Flea Market Open To The General Public)
SUNDAY, AUGUST 3rd, 1997
at the
CLARKE COUNTY RURITAN FAIRGROUNDS
IN
BERRYVILLE, VIRGINIA
SHENANDOAH VALLEY AMATEUR RADIO CLUB INC.
W4RKC
522
81
RT. 50
RT. 7
340
WINCHESTER
SVARC HAMFEST
BERRYVILLE
RT. 50
81
522
340
N
S
ARRL APPROVED HAMFEST
Remember!
Always the first Sunday in August.
by Irvin Barb W4DHU Hamfest Chairman
New additional building for commercial tables!
● GATE OPENS AT 6:00 AM
● GENERAL ADMISSION $5.00 (children under 16 free)
● TAIL-GATERS ADDITIONAL $7.00 PER SPACE
● COMMERCIAL & INDOOR TABLES BY RESERVATION
● COUNTRY HAM & EGG BREAKFAST
● CONCESSIONS & SNACK BAR AVAILABLE
● RURITAN'S FAMOUS CHICKEN & BEEF BARBECUE
● VE EXAMS (SAME DAY)*
● TALK-IN 146.22-82, W4RKC
● FREE BINGO WITH PRIZES
● GRAND PRIZES AND HOURLY DRAWINGS
● COUNTY PARK WITH POOL, PICNIC AREA, AND PLAYGROUND OPPOSITE HAMFEST SITE
*VE Exams by the Mountain A.R.C. Teams at Cooley School, across from Hamfest. Walk-ins welcome. Register between 7:30 & 8:30 AM. Exams begin at 8:30. This VEC team does not charge for exams. All classes offered. For more info, contact Leo Patterson, KQ8E, [email: 6815484@mcimail.com] (304) 289-3576 or Gay Rembold, W3DFW (301 724-0674
For information, vendor registration and pre-reservations, contact Irv Barb, W4DHU (540) 955-1745, [email:ibarb@visuallink.com] Rt 3 Box 5385, Berryville, VA 22611. Download this flyer and vendors table forms from our Web site at: http://www.w3ic.com/inet/svarc/hamfest
The SVARC is a non-profit, non-commercial special service organization dedicated to the furtherment of Amateur Radio communications

Fig. 1-4 A flier from a very nice, midsized hamfest in northern Virginia.

The main disadvantage to these fests and shows are that people pull junk out from everywhere and sell it off. After you buy a unit and take it home, it's yours. There is no store or home address to take it back to—just an empty fairgrounds or convention center. Hence, the low prices.

But the equipment and the sellers vary widely. I have had everything from very honest and friendly sellers, who were not afraid to tell me anything that was wrong with a unit, to those who flat-out lied about their equipment. Once I bought a cassette deck for

$3. When the guy said that it worked fine, I thought "Yeah, right," but the price was excellent and the condition was good. I brought it home and it worked fine!

Strangely enough, out of all of the equipment that I have looked over during several years of hunting at hamfests, I have not seen any visible signs of stolen equipment. It seems as though the flea market section at these types of events would be a great location to sell hot equipment, but apparently they aren't. If anything, they are a great location to unload basement ballast.

Standard flea markets are not as good for finding stereo equipment. The prices and dealer honesty are about as variable as what you would find at a traditional hamfest. However, the dealers at hamfests are all interested in electronics, so there is a much better chance that you will find midgrade (or even high-end) consumer audio equipment. At the traditional flea market spot, you will only find low or very low-grade equipment: a $30 (list price) cassette deck in fair condition for $25, an 8-track player that would match the one that you saw in the Salvation Army last week, and a pullout AM radio from a '72 Pontiac.

EVALUATING YOUR NEEDS

In order to find the equipment that you want, you must first evaluate your needs and requirements so that you don't wind up with a bad-sounding system, a system that isn't useful to you, or a system that is overpriced.

Different people have different needs and preferences in sound. Personally, I am not terribly impressed with either very loud music or music with extremely good (audiophile quality) fidelity. Most of the music that I listen to is rock that is recorded with average or worse-than-average fidelity. Not only would I not need to spend $1000 for speakers that would accurately reproduce every high, but I also don't need a brigade of subwoofers to rock the neighborhood.

My lack of desire for super high-fidelity audio reduces my need for everything that is audiophile-quality, and my lack of desire to blast the bass reduces my need for equipment with massive power ratings. In general, although I do some experimenting and tweaking, my audio philosophy revolves around trying to assemble several decent, flexible systems for the bare minimum amount of cash. I've found cassette decks at hamfests and open-reel tape decks at yard sales, and have had friends give me old turntables, tube amplifiers, and preamplifiers that had fallen into disuse or disrepair.

Aside from knowing what type of sound you are interested in, you also need to determine how long you plan to be using the system. Do you only occasionally listen to music, and fidelity isn't a concern? Then a minicomponent system might be all that you need. However, if you have an appetite for finer sound or constantly listen to music, invest in better equipment. Not only will it sound more pleasing, but chances are that it will also last longer. If you are an audio head but don't have the money to buy an entire system at once, buy a system component by component. If you're in high school or college and can't afford the system, listen to a personal or portable stereo until you can save up some money for good equipment. If your equipment lasts a long time, it will save you money over the long run. You probably don't want to sink too much money into a system anyway until you land that all-important first "real" job and are furnishing your own digs.

When purchasing equipment, always check the specification sheets for information. Compare the fidelity ratings and the warranties. Excellent ratings for fidelity (such as signal-to-noise ratio, S/N, and total harmonic distortion, THD) and long warranties will almost certainly guarantee that the equipment is built well and will survive years of regular use.

CHOOSING A SYSTEM

One method of choosing a piece of equipment that is often effective, yet doesn't necessarily reflect quality, is merely to pick it up and feel it. In many cases, a heavier piece of equipment is built sturdier (both physically and electrically) than lighter equipment. Chances are that the five-pound cassette deck is sonically and physically inferior to the nine-pound model. This is because the best equipment uses metal cabinets and front panels for shielding, uses solid and cast mechanical sections for better strength and stability, and uses heavier-grade electrical components.

As mentioned in the previous paragraph, metal cabinets are important for electrical shielding and strength. Except for personal and portable stereo systems, where the emphasis is on cheap, portable audio, always try to avoid plastic. It is typically a sign of inferior audio quality and that the manufacturer skimped on the physical construction throughout the piece of equipment. Of course, not every piece of equipment in a metal cabinet will last as long as another encased in plastic, but it's a good general rule to follow.

TAPE DECKS

Cassette decks are still the favorite of the mass population yet are often scorned by audiophiles. Most people have cassette decks because they are capable of recording any type of audio: music copied from a commercial album, live music, lectures or interviews, etc. Audiophiles often scorn the cassette medium because the tape is so narrow and the sound is dependent on it moving at a precise speed across the pickup heads. With so much to go wrong, the sound is often much less than perfect.

Tape-based alternatives to the cassette are open-reel decks and digital tape (DAT and DCC). Open-reel tape decks were popular in stereo circles from the 1950s to the 1970s and in radio production up until the 1990s. For years, their audio quality far surpassed that of the cassette decks. But since the late 1970s, a huge number of vastly improved cassette decks have hit the market, and open-reel decks disappeared in the commercial markets. Open-reel decks were still the favorite in radio work—until the rise of computerized digital audio-editing broke through in the mid 1990s. Although open-reel decks might seem like audio dinosaurs, a good unit can offer surprisingly good performance.

The digital tape format experiments of the 1980s (DAT) and 1990s (DCC) have been met with varying degrees of success. Both formats feature the advantages of digital (CD quality) audio and cassette tape. With these formats, you can have clean sound, record digitally, and record multiple copies with no generation loss. The DAT (not compatible with cassettes) never made a dent on the commercial market yet is used in many recording studios and radio stations. The DCC tape (compatible with cassettes) was expected to displace cassettes from the consumer market, and thus also displace DAT from the professional audio market. Neither happened. For more information on tape decks, see Chapter 2.

CD PLAYERS

The CD is such a perfect format. How could anyone complain about it? Audiophiles find plenty of fault with CDs. Some of the claims include: the sound is sterile; the aluminum will deteriorate in 10 years; the audio should be sampled at a higher rate; the audio is damaged by artifacts, etc. Despite these minor complaints, it appears that the CD is destined to be with us well beyond the turn of the millennium—especially now that recordable CD discs (CD-R), recording CD players, and computer CD-ROM recorders are available (and dropping significantly in price).

TURNTABLES

The venerable old phonographic record, the audio champion of more than a half century, has faded dramatically from the scene. In the 1980s, the record was officially proclaimed to be dead and extinct, as hundreds of record stores dumped their last supplies in the bargain bins. Remarkably, the format hasn't died and it has mounted a comeback. It's no longer a part of mainstream music but is highly regarded by record collectors, audiophiles, and fans of independent music. Millions of inexpensive records are available at record swaps, record stores, flea markets, antique malls, etc. It's much cheaper to find an old record in good condition than to buy a new (or used) CD. Audiophiles love the record format because they say that the analog fidelity is better than that of the current generation of CD players. For more information, see Chapter 4.

RECEIVERS AND ANTENNAS

Do you listen to the radio? If so, your choice of a receiver could dramatically affect what you listen to and what equipment you choose. Few listeners (typical or audiophiles) really spend much time deciding which receiver would be best for their applications. More often than not, the decision is a matter of purchasing an amplifier with a built-in receiver or buying separate amplifier and receiver units. Another question is band coverage: AM, FM, TV, and shortwave (Chapter 13). There's a lot of radio out there, maybe more than you realized. For more information on receivers, see Chapter 5. Chapter 12 covers receiving antennas for all of the major broadcasting bands.

AMPLIFIERS

Power is one of the main factors in deciding the cost of the amplifier that is required for a system. Power has its price. A number of variables complicate the procedure.

Aside from the sheer power, a number of other features can be added to an amplifier. For example, many amplifiers also contain AM/FM receivers. A/V receivers are built for home theater systems, and accordingly, they have many inputs; a remote control; a built-in AM/FM receiver; and outputs to a main set of speakers, a back pair, and a subwoofer.

An amplifier should make the audio signal louder perfectly, without altering it in any way. Rather than adding as much gadgetry as possible, audiophiles strive for the simplest, most-perfect equipment that they can find. In many cases, they choose a dedicated tube or solid-state amplifier that might have no more controls than an on/off switch; some audio enthusiasts further simplify this method by using a separate mono amplifier for each audio channel. Which direction will best suit your needs? More information about amplifier power is covered in Chapter 5.

SOUND PROCESSING EQUIPMENT

One very basic piece of equipment is the crossover. Crossovers are built into speakers, so they are only worth mentioning if you are building speakers from scratch. Over the years, a number of people have been confused about what crossovers are and what they do. Crossovers are just a combination of a low-pass filter and a high-pass filter. The low-pass filter only allows low-frequency audio signals to pass through, and the highpass filter only allows high-frequency audio signals to pass through. With both filters working together, all of the high-frequency audio signals can be passed to the tweeters, and the low-frequency audio signals can be passed to the woofers or subwoofers. Without the crossovers, the sound system will sound mushy or distorted—especially if it has a few woofers or subwoofers. Also, without crossovers, the separate-speaker systems will have all the audio frequencies being played by all of the speakers. If much volume is used, it won't be long before the heavy bass movement blows out the tweeters. In these cases, crossovers are necessary as a safety precaution, as well as an improvement in sound quality. Crossovers are covered separately in Chapter 8 and speakers are covered in Chapter 6.

Another of the favorite pieces of sound processing equipment, the equalizer, actually changes the audio signal. An equalizer can boost or reduce the audio at a number of different frequency ranges. If an audio source is particularly muffled, you can raise the controls of some of the higher-frequency bands to "brighten" the sound. Or, if you want to perk up the bass on a certain track or album, you can boost the controls of the lower-frequency bands. With an equalizer, you can shape the audio to suit your tastes. They are especially useful if you listen to many different tape recordings that need to have the audio altered.

The last common component that you could add to a system is a digital sound processor (DSP), which is sometimes known as a sound processor. These systems can shape audio (music or talk) to sound as though it is a live performance in any number of different locations. Some of the different common sound-enhancement settings include "Jazz club," "Concert hall," etc. These settings allow you to adjust the sound. Some equipment reviewers have raved about their versatility, but are they worth the price to you? The units presently cost well into the hundreds of dollars, which could be quite a bit of money to you for an added bit of audio flexibility. Also, most purists, such as the people who engineered and produced the album that you are listening to, would say that the audio has been recorded in the way that it was intended to sound. Sound processors and equalizers are covered further in Chapter 8.

COMPUTER AUDIO

We're no longer living in 1980. We're at the turn of the century, and the hot topic is computers. Lately, the hot technological topics with the mass media have been the Internet and multimedia. With the advancements of multimedia home computers since the mid-1990s, the home computer can be used as the keystone of an audio system. More information concerning computers and audio is contained in Chapter 10.

WIRES, CABLES, AND CONNECTORS

For years, the key to great sound was to buy great equipment and speakers and listen to hi-fi recordings. By the 1980s, listeners began to question the connections and the cabling that delivered the sound from one component to another. Are the cables susceptible to interference from other components? Are poor connections inhibiting the sound that's reaching your speakers? To solve the problem, gold-plated terminals and connectors, and silver wiring was soon available for those who felt that good wires, cables, and connectors were worth the extra hundreds or thousands of dollars for their system. For more information on the controversy, see Chapter 11.

SIMPLIFIED EQUIPMENT SELECTION LISTING

The following list was constructed so that you could review it quickly and decide what system would be appropriate for your needs and your home. It is not intended to be a complete guide to comparing all of the many features that are available in stereo components. If each different feature, such as paper speaker cones vs. titanium speaker cones vs. polypropylene speaker cones vs. carbon speaker cones vs. resin speaker cones vs. neodymium speaker cones, etc., were covered, the list would be so long that it could not be of value to anyone but the audio expert, who already knows what he or she wants out of an audio system.

THE BARE MINIMUM

* Amplifier
* Cassette deck
* Bookshelf speakers
* Surge protector

Options: See other systems.

A/V SYSTEM

* A/V amplifier
* TV
* Stereo VCR
* Front speakers
* Rear fill speakers
* Subwoofer
* Surge protector

Options: Cassette deck, CD player, turntable, computer with audio/video editing capabilities, camcorder, and laser disk player.

COMPUTER-INTEGRATED

* Pentium computer with stereo sound card
* Amplifier
* Stereo speakers
* Surge protector

Options: Cassette deck, audio/video editing software, CD-ROM recorder, turntable, camcorder, and laser disk player.

THE AUDIOPHILE DELUXE

* Dedicated amplifier or two mono amplifiers operated in stereo
* Preamplifier or passive-control unit
* Receiver
* Open-reel tape deck or DAT deck
* CD transport
* D/A converter
* Turntable
* Speakers
* Specialty equipment racks and stands
* Specialty cables, cords, and connectors
* A power line conditioner
* An acoustically "perfect" room

Options: What else could you possibly want?

CONCLUSION

Thousands of different stereo components are available, and without keeping abreast of the recent information, you can easily get lost in the sheer numbers. The special 1997 directory edition of *Car Audio and Electronics* listed 1127 different models of dedicated amplifiers! Those are merely the models that were being sold by the manufacturers in 1997; Thousands of other models have been sold and discontinued in years past, and thousands more will be available in future years.

If you are interested in audio and plan to upgrade your system in the years to come, be sure to subscribe to one or more of the magazines on the topic and save all of the copies. If you are interested in purchasing used equipment from the 1980s, you can probably find the equipment covered in the back issues of the stereo magazines.

Remember, the keys to success in purchasing most anything are good information, level-headedness, and discernment. Don't be blinded by either amazing, expensive, brand-new technologies or by dirt-cheap prices. Buy the best-quality equipment that you can for the money that you are willing to spend.

2

TAPE DECKS

Cassettes are the modern-day people's choice in audio. Essentially everyone has a cassette player in their home. It is the least expensive, yet best-quality medium for recording. For years, the cassette has fought off and survived competition from open-reel tape, 8-tracks, DAT cartridges, and finally DCC. This chapter covers all of these tape formats and their advantages and disadvantages, but the focus is on the king of the pile, the cassette.

CASSETTE DECKS

Cassette players have been around for so long that most everyone seems to take them for granted. Most of the technological advances in cassette technology over the past 15 years have been in areas that aren't always noticeable. Clear plastic cassette shells are the most noticeable advancement of the lot. Most of the breakthroughs have involved adding more and denser ferromagnetic coatings, using coatings that are more permanent on the tape, developing tape that is more resistant to stretching, and creating plastics that do not shrink, warp, or melt in the presence of extreme heat. On the other hand, developments in the playback/recording technology have been remarkable over that same time period: higher-fidelity, harder playback and record heads; Dolby S and MPX noise-reduction systems; low-movement, low-vibration playback mechanisms; and much more. Cassette fidelity is still not competitive with that of CDs, but the improvement has been significant.

Cassette basics have been well covered in other books over the past few decades, but I've included a few here for general reference. This material is somewhat useful—certainly more useful than background information about the techniques of commercial broadcast transmitting and reception.

BASICS

The cassette is a miniature reel-to-reel tape that has been encased in a plastic shell to reduce the messiness and the potential for

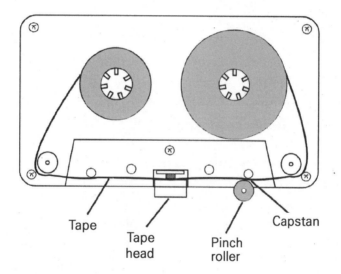

Tape   Tape head   Pinch roller   Capstan

Fig. 2-1 A look inside the case of a cassette: The tape reels and tape path, playback head, pinch roller, capstan, etc.

damage to the recording's sound quality (Fig. 2-1). This case contains two hubs, which are used as either takeup or supply reels, depending on which side the cassette is turned to. The cassette also contains a pressure pad where the tape contacts the heads of the player, and two guide rollers, which allow the tape to smoothly roll through the shell without wearing excessively. All of these parts are necessary for a cassette. However, one major record company produced cassettes for a while that were so cheaply made that no guide rollers were included. Instead of having the tape roll around the guide rollers, it rubbed its way around two plastic posts. Because of the poor design, the cassette squeaked as it played and started to wear out quickly. Upon discovering this, I cracked the cassette open and placed the reels in a much more solid, better-quality cassette shell.

Cassettes contain reels of plastic film that have been coated with ferromagnetic material. Technically, this material isn't all ferromagnetic (i.e., made with any compound or mixture of iron); some are made with chromium dioxide, other types are coated with a mixture of iron oxide and chromium dioxide, and still others use other elemental compounds, such as cobalt. This material can be magnetized or demagnetized with ease. The particles of the recording material are assembled in a particular manner on a blank tape. However, when you record something, these particles are magnetized so that they face in different directions, according to the sounds that are being recorded.

When this cassette recording is played, the tape passes over the magnetic heads of the deck. The heads consist of an electromagnetic coil (with a tiny open gap in the side that faces the tape) inside of a small metal enclosure. The particular formation of the magnetic particles on the tape induces a small signal voltage in the heads. These signals are then amplified and later turned back into audio by the speakers.

Cassettes were a real challenge for the manufacturers because the tape was reduced to about half of the width of that used for open-reel tape. As a result, they had to design much more efficient recording coatings. One cassette prototype from the early 1960s was huge— approximately the size of a videotape! For some time, the cassette was snubbed by audio experimenters because the medium simply could not compete with the record and open-reel formats. Later on, by the late 1970s and early 1980s, high-quality cassette technology was openly available and that helped trigger the boom in cassette decks, home recording, and car stereo systems.

The primary problem with the cassette medium is size. They are just too small for anyone to be able to easily produce a high-fidelity medium (not to say that it isn't possible, it just isn't easy). Cassette tape is narrow and it moves slowly across the heads. Thus, slight tape damage, such as a dropout, is very noticeable on cassettes. Also, because the tape is so narrow and divided into four separate tracks (Left A, Right A, Left B, and Right B). If the tape is just slightly off of its normal position on the heads, the sound will be garbled or muffled. This is the case if you have ever popped in the cassette and you could hear both the audio on the one side and the audio on the other side of the tape (backwards); then you took out the tape, popped it back it, and it sounds fine (Fig. 2-2).

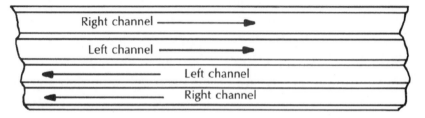

Fig. 2-2 The four different tracks of a standard analog cassette tape.

Another dilemma is that of tape speed. The cassette must be running at exactly the same, proper speed or flutter and wow will result. Flutter and wow are descriptive names of sounds that you hear when the tape speed varies. One of the best ways to check your system for tape-speed variations is to record an audio test record or CD onto cassette and play it back through your system. These test recordings typically feature plenty of constant-tone sounds. If the tone noticeably varies, then the cassette deck is probably noticeably altering the sound of everything that it is playing back. If you don't have a test record or CD, try listening to the system closely with music playing. Simple piano music, vocals with long-held notes, and stretches of guitar feedback are also good indications of how smoothly your system is playing. Because cheap cassettes and those that are miswound can also cause fluctuations in tape speed, be sure to try the test with several tapes before planning a cassette deck shopping spree.

Another factor that affects the sound and depends on the physical/mechanical aspects of how the tape passes over the heads is azimuth. *Azimuth* technically means "the horizontal direction expressed as the angular distance between the direction of a fixed point and the direction of the object." Head azimuth isn't nearly that complicated. It just means that the tape must be exactly perpendicular to the tiny gap in the tape head. If it isn't exactly perpendicular, the sound will be altered—typically the high frequencies aren't especially well reproduced and the recording sound muffled. The best cassette deck manufacturers take special precautions to ensure that the tape perfectly passes over the heads and that the heads can't become misaligned.

Incorrect azimuth adjustments aren't the only way that sound can be altered at the heads. Just by playing cassettes, the sound can be altered in two different ways. As the tape passes through the deck, deposits of dirt, dust, and especially oxide particles will form on the heads, pinch roller, and capstan. In order for the cassette audio to be at a maximum, these parts must be regularly cleaned (see Chapter 15). The other possibility is that the tape heads will be worn down from years of tape rubbing against them. You can see wornout heads; they will often make the head look buffed or even grooved (in the worst case).

The tape heads and tape transport are key factors in the quality of a cassette deck (Fig. 2-3). The following section covers many of the different features that you find in cassette decks. Modern decks can do almost anything (how long will it be until they can make a breakfast?), but these features are all garbage if the heads don't make the tape sound good, quickly wear out, or if the tape transport causes tape speed variations. Always invest your money in the best heads and tape transport system that you can afford. I have one cassette deck that I've used off and on for 12

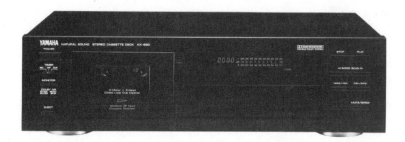

Fig. 2-3 Putting the quality into the components: The Yamaha KX-690 cassette deck with three heads, three motors, and two capstans. Yamaha

years and the heads still sound good; others have worn out in only a few short years of use. The bottom line is that a deck that performs well for 10 years is worth more than three times as much as a deck that dies after 3 years. Think about that when you are enticed to buy a deck with a few more features for $20 less.

As mentioned in Chapter 1, the best way to discover the quality of the cassette deck that you are interested in purchasing is to check the specifications. Most decks have specifications listings available—either from the manufacturer or from the sales catalogs at a stereo shop (Fig. 2-4). The most important ones to check are total harmonic distortion (also known as THD or harmonic distortion), frequency response, signal-to-noise ratio (S/N ratio), and wow and flutter. Signal-to-noise ratio and frequency response should both be as high as possible; THD and wow and flutter ratings should both be as low as possible. Wow and flutter is one of the most important specifications to determine the quality of the deck's physical construction because manufacturers must take extra precautions to make the tape transport and playback systems solid and stable.

Another sure way to pick a high-quality deck is to find one that contains a separate head for recording and for playback. Three heads are better than two because each is specially developed for its particular application: erasing, recording, and playing. Also, the heads would each take less wear than a record/play head.

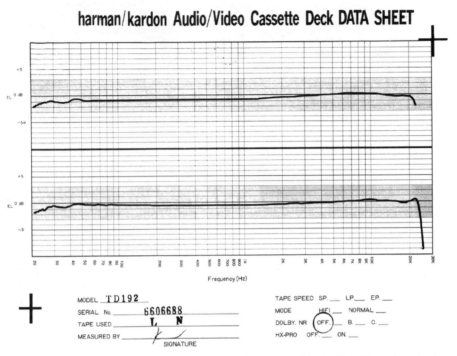

Fig. 2-4 Although most manufacturers supply general specifications for their equipment, only the best companies test each unit and send you the results.
Harman/Kardon

Unfortunately, heads are expensive, and only the best decks use three heads.

Aside from three-head decks, you can also purchase a deck with extra heads—a dual cassette deck. Dual cassette decks contain two separate cassette transports so that you can easily record from one cassette to another (Fig. 2-5). Typically, one cassette transport is only capable of playback and the other can playback or record (thus saving money on heads in the playback-only transport). I've always been suspect of dual cassette decks because the manufacturers often seem to skimp on the quality of the parts. Much of the expense of a cassette deck is contained in the heads and the cassette transport. Thus, a dual cassette deck should cost nearly twice as much as a single cassette deck of equal quality. Such is rarely the case.

Fig. 2-5 Double cassette decks: The Kenwood KX-W-6080 (top) and the Pioneer W616DR (bottom). Kenwood (top) and Pioneer (bottom)

My experience has been that dual cassette decks are a poor substitute for a good single cassette deck, and recordings—even on less-expensive single decks—sound better than those from dual decks. Fortunately, cassette technology is dramatically improving and some new dual decks boast good specifications, but they still aren't comparable to most single decks in the same price range. In most cases, it would be better to purchase a better single cassette deck and later purchase another single cassette deck of lesser quality. Most people record cassettes so that they have a rough-wear copy of one of their records or CDs. This being the case, it is sonically better to have one single cassette deck with excellent fidelity than a dual deck with less-than-desirable specifications.

PROFESSIONAL DECKS

In addition to the standard consumer single- and dual-cassette decks, many companies manufacture decks specifically for a variety of audio-related professions. Some of these decks are ruggedized (see *Ruggedized models* in the next section), some have unique timing features, and others are developed specifically for pro audio applications. The timing decks are used for logging telephone calls and conversations, and they often contain *vox* (voice-operated switch) functions and timers so that the cassette can be slowed down for hours of recording/playback per tape. The final pro-audio type of deck is typically called a *mini studio* because it contains multitrack line/microphone inputs, multi-band recording equalizers, and possibly some recording effects. These decks are especially useful for bands who want to record a quick demo or live recording (Fig. 2-6).

Fig. 2-6 A Fostex X-15 multitrack cassette recorder.

FEATURES

Like any audio component, the cassette deck can contain a number of different helpful functions that influence what you purchase (Fig. 2-7).

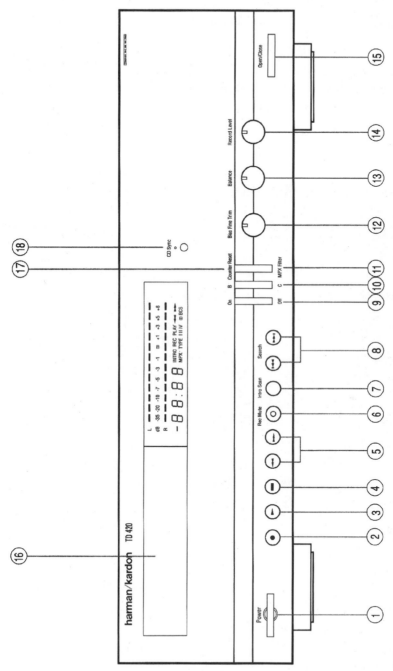

Fig. 2-7 Harman/Kardon TD 420 front-panel controls: (1). Power switch, (2) record/pause button, (3) play, (4) stop, (5) rewind/fast forward, (6) record mute, (7) intro scan, (8) search forward and reverse, (9) Dolby noise reduction, (10) Dolby B/C switch, (11) MPX filter, (12) bias adjustment, (13) balance control, (14) recording level, (15) open/close drawer, (16) cassette drawer, (17) counter reset, (18) CD synch.

Harman/Kardon

Noise suppression The most common noise-suppression techniques for recording are Dolby B and C, both of which were developed by Dolby Laboratories. The two Dolby systems are intended to remove the tape hiss that is evident when playing tapes—especially during quiet passages when high-frequency instruments are dominant. This tape hiss is picked up from various sources, but it primarily emanates from the tape head. Whenever Dolby noise reduction is used on a particular recording, the system suppresses some of the frequencies. When the correct Dolby setting is pressed during playback, the frequencies that were suppressed during the recording are now boosted by the same amount as they were suppressed. By using this method, hiss can effectively be reduced. I've never really liked using noise reduction, but I seem to be alone on this issue.

Dolby C is an improved version of Dolby B, but Dolby B is more common than Dolby C. Both are frequently used on the same units, however. If an album was recorded in Dolby B, it will sound better (or at least be more accurately represented) if it is played back in Dolby B—even if Dolby C is a feature of the head unit you're listening with.

Dolby S noise reduction is the highest-performance of the three systems. It is sometimes included with Dolby B and Dolby C in high-end decks. In the next decade, Dolby S will probably be much more common on cassette decks of all price ranges. For more information on the Dolby noise-suppression techniques, see the Web page at:

http://www.dolbylab.com

HX Pro Sometimes confused with Dolby noise reduction, Dolby HX Pro is a cassette recording technology that makes it possible to record loud musical passages with fewer high-frequency losses and less distortion. In addition to being available in many cassette decks, it is widely used by the recording industry to improve the quality of prerecorded cassettes.

Dolby HX Pro works by keeping the recorder's effective bias more constant with changing audio signals. This avoids the need to set bias as a compromise between low midrange distortion and good high frequency capability. Because Dolby HX Pro does not encode the signal like Dolby noise reduction, no decoding circuitry is required.

Autoreverse One of the first extra features to add to a cassette deck is autoreverse. Autoreverse is the function by which a cassette player will automatically move the heads over and begin playing the other side of a tape once it has hit the end. With this feature, a tape can play continuously for as long as you can stand it.

Blank skip With this function set, the tape player will automatically fast forward the tape (or at a speed that is slower than fast forward, but faster than play) when no audio is sensed. When audio is sensed on the tape, the player will stop at that point and resume playing. This feature is particularly useful if you have a narcoleptic friend who sends you audio letters.

Music sensor With this function set, you can press fast forward and the player will fast forward the tape until the song ends. Then, it will detect that the tape is blank and it will stop and resume playing. Likewise, the music sensor can also be used when rewinding. It will rewind until it detects the blank space at the beginning of the song. Then, it will stop and resume playing.

Automatic bias selector The setting of the playback mode, which is determined by the type of coating on the tape on the head unit, can negatively affect the sound of a cassette if the mode doesn't match the bias of the tape. The automatic bias control on a head unit senses what bias is being used on a given cassette and it automatically sets the proper playback mode.

Power load/power eject Power load and power eject both refer to the mechanism that installs or ejects a cassette into or from a head unit. In a unit with power load/power eject, you can enter the tape to a certain point, then the power mechanism will take over and slowly pull the tape into position. When you press eject, the motor will gradually push the cassette back out. With a standard unit, you must push the tape until it physically loads into place. When you want to remove the tape, you must press the eject button to physically eject the cassette from the inside.

Computerized calibration The values of just about any complicated piece of electronic equipment can gradually fall out of tolerance. Some expensive cassette decks feature computerized calibration that will automatically check the equipment and readjust it, according to its preprogrammed, ideal response.

High-speed editing High-speed editing is a feature often included in dual-cassette decks. The two decks are synchronized in speed. So, both cassette decks feed the tape through at faster-than-normal speed, and, in turn, the cassette that you are dubbing is finished in faster-than-normal speed (about 1.5 to 2 times normal speed is typical). High-speed editing is convenient, but often these copies are of a slightly lesser quality than those that would be made on the same deck at normal speed.

Simultaneous recording Nearly all dual cassette decks feature one side with a the option of recording and one side that can only play tapes. Dual cassette decks with simultaneous recording can record at the same time on both sides. If you don't have enough recordings and you can't acquire material fast enough, you might consider a dual deck with this feature.

Headphone jack Nearly every cassette deck has a headphone jack so that you can listen via headphones from the deck itself. A few of the high-end decks even feature an output level control so that you can adjust the volume on the headphones. This feature is only useful if you use a dedicated amplifier that contains no headphone jack.

Inputs Cassette decks have recording inputs for both microphone and line levels (which are different). So, the typical cassette deck is capable of recording from a microphone, if you want to capture a live performance, or from a CD player (for example), if you want to make a copy of a great CD to listen to in the car.

Mic mix One flashy feature that is rarely included in cassette decks is mic mix. It is a potentiometer level control that allows you to mix line-level and microphone audio. Mic mix is particularly useful if you want to save those evenings of karaoke on cassette for blackmailing purposes.

Level control The level controls affect the signal levels (volume) that are being recorded. Without the level control, some recordings could be weak (with a low signal-to-noise ratio) and others would be too high (producing distortion). Most decks have two level controls—one for the left channel and the other for the right channel. Other decks that only have one control also include a record balance control to properly adjust the left- and right-channel signals.

Expanders Radio stations often use compressors to make their audio sound tight and solid, punching right out of your speakers. Audioheads want their audio to sound the opposite, wide and expansive. Electronically, expanders are used to produce this effect. These effects alter the original sound of the music, so they are in the same category as DSPs and equalizers—a toy to play with, not equipment that will more accurately reproduce the sound.

Tape counter As any VCR owner knows, the tape counter is a numerical display that allows you to track the position of the tape in the cassette. The old VCR and cassette tape counters were relative only to themselves, and were not based on seconds, minutes, etc. Many modern cassette counters will display in minutes and seconds, which is certainly much handier. Some of the other counter-related features include repeat, tape length, and reset.

Timers Some high-tech cassette decks include timers so that the machine will turn of or on at a given time. This feature isn't terribly helpful, but it might provide you with a bit of extra flexibility when you record or play tapes.

Record return This is a great feature for those who frequently record cassettes and perform stop/start editing. With record return, you can press a button and it will search back to where the last bit of recorded material was, leave some blank space, and reset to the Record/Pause position.

LED level meters LEDs are light-emitting diodes. That might not mean much to you, but they are the little (often orange or red) lights that are used as indicators on electronic equipment or as the display on a clock radio. With LED level meters, the sound level is represented by two rows of LEDs that bounce in time with the music. This is passed off as a feature, but analog meters are much more accurate. Because of the higher cost of analog meters, they are typically only used in high-end amplifiers.

Ruggedized models Some cassette decks are ruggedized for particularly harsh environments. Many of these are professional decks for use in radio stations or recording studios. Often, these models are built with wide steel rack-mount front panels and extra-sturdy buttons (Fig. 2-8). Because most people have no need

Fig. 2-8 A ruggedized cassette deck for professional applications: The Teac C-3RX.

to drag their home stereos all over creation, ruggedized consumer-level decks are portable units, such as portable and personal stereos. Some personal stereos have even been designed in watertight cases for use while you're swimming. This is not only lighter, but much safer, than dragging your home stereo cassette deck into the pool.

OPEN-REEL TAPE DECKS

SOME LIGHT HISTORY

At one time not all that long ago, it was nearly impossible for most people to record and store any form of audio. You could do little more than listen to records or the radio. In the 1930s, some record-cutting equipment began to seep into the market. This wasn't record company equipment, but actually intended for consumers. It wasn't terribly popular because the technology was very new and the Depression was still depleting the spare cash of most people.

During World War I, several countries began using wire recorders, with the wire magnetized, instead of the coating on a plastic tape. Of course, tape was out of the question in the Teens because most forms of plastic didn't even exist then. Through the 1920s and 1930s, some forms of plastic were developed and widely used. One of the most common was bakelite, which was used as radio cabinets and for black telephones. Bakelite is hard and brittle; there's probably a better chance that you could make tape out of cheese than bakelite.

Everything changed during World War II. Vast amounts of money (spent by both the Axis and the Allies) were poured into research for all sorts of technological advancements. Naturally, plastics were extensively developed. During this time period, the open-reel tape deck was created and implemented. With the post-war economic boom, open-reel tape decks hit the consumer market and quickly replaced those old phonographic recorders. Time to pitch out those blank records! In the 1950s and 1960s, the open-reel tape deck reigned supreme, although its popularity was decimated by the cassette in the late 1960s and early 1970s.

THEORY AND USE

Open-reel (also known as reel-to-reel) tape decks use the same principles as cassette decks to produce sound. The sound is electromagnetically recorded onto the oxide coating of a plastic-based tape. This tape is fed from reels through a covered section that contains the tape heads, capstan, and pinch roller. The only physical difference between cassette and open-reel formats is that with the open-reel format, the take-up and supply reel are separate and loose—there is no plastic shell to protect the tape. The particular formation of the magnetic particles on the tape induces a small signal voltage in the heads. These signals are then amplified and later turned back into audio by the speakers.

The differences between the two analog tape formats are minor in theory, but major when you actually use them. "Popping" a tape in a cassette deck requires less than five seconds. With an open-reel deck, you must pull the tape reel out of its box, place it on the supply reel pin, pull the end of the loose tape around the capstan and the heads, and up around to the pickup reel. Then you have to stick the end of the tape into the pickup reel in the same manner that you would load film into a camera. If the tape isn't placed in well, it will pull off the reel and spill all over the table or floor. Also, you have to fix the tape reels in place with end caps. Without them, the tape will fall off the pins and roll across the floor!

As you can see, just preparing to use an open-reel tape deck is much more difficult than using a cassette deck. Besides the difficulty of operation, most people get timid when they handle recording tape.

Because consumer-model open-reel tape player/recorders virtually disappeared by the early 1980s, the format must be virtually useless, like a prehistoric version of the 8-track, right? Completely wrong. Open-reel decks are far superior to cassette decks of equal quality. The superiority is based on only one quality: size.

To fully understand why size is so important to tape recording, it's best to take a look at the history of the cassette. In the early 1960s, the mega Dutch electronics corporation, Philips, had a brilliant idea. Business people, secretaries, and reporters often needed to record letters and interviews. If a new system could be developed so that these people wouldn't have to lug around a big, "portable" open-reel deck and fumble with spools of tape, it would become a hit around the office. They miniaturized the open-reel tape, packed it into a plastic shell, slowed the speed down, and named it the compact cassette.

The cassette was never intended for music, it was supposed to be the ultimate dictation recorder. Open-reel tape decks use long, wide tape, typically 1/4" or 1/2" wide. This is important because if the tape is that wide, it can store that much more audio information per foot than a tape of a smaller width. Likewise, the speed is important because it affects how much information must be contained per foot of tape. For example, tape A might be capable of holding half as much information per foot as tape B. But, if you record and play tape A at twice the speed as tape B, the same amount of recorded information should pass over the heads per second, and both recordings should theoretically sound the same. On the other hand, if tape A is recorded/played at the same speed (or slower) as tape B, the audio won't be nearly as good.

If too little information can be stored on a tape, much of the fidelity will be lost. So, when Philips was designing the cassette, they reduced the tape down to a width and speed that would allow talk to be understandable, but nothing more. Unlike cassettes, which only have one slow speed of 1 7/8 inches per second (ips), open-reel decks could typically be operated at 15, 7 1/2, or 3 3/4 ips. For example, if a 1/4-inch open-reel tape was played back at 15 ips, 16 times more information would pass over the heads per second (assuming that the tape qualities of both are equal). Even if the open-reel tape was of much lower quality and could only hold 1/4 as much information as the cassette, it would still be capable of passing four times as much information over the heads per second.

As you can see, the speed and width of a tape makes a tremendous impact on the quality of a recording. For these reasons, it is nearly impossible for a cassette deck to beat the sound of a good open-reel deck. It is also why recording studios still use 1" and 2" wide open-reel decks to master albums.

ARE OPEN-REEL DECKS PRACTICAL?

I've given open-reel decks a glowing review in terms of audio quality. But even if you can tolerate their inconvenience, are they really practical as we cross into the 21st Century? It depends. For what reason do you want a 20- or 30-year-old piece of equipment in a format that's been extinct for well over a decade? Is it fidelity? Ease of editing? Home recording (such as for creating inexpensive demos for a band)? These are all good reasons, but chances are that you can find a modern format (such as CD-R) that will provide comparable quality for a comparable price.

The practicality of the open-reel deck today depends mostly on you. You must be willing to search hamfests, radio trade and audio classified ads, and the Internet for a machine that is worthy of your time (Fig. 2-9). Thereafter, you must also be willing to track down open-reel tapes from specialty recording distributors (often paying a much steeper price per tape) or from sources that sell used tapes, and you must have information ready so that you can find parts or specialty repair shops when the deck breaks down (this might not happen in your lifetime, but eventually it will require repair).

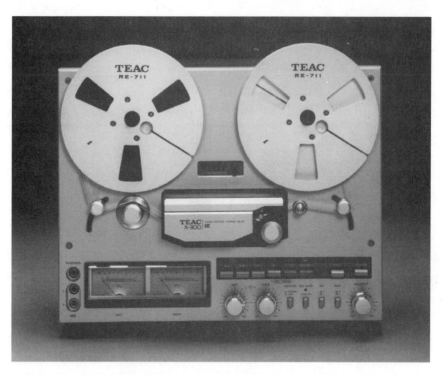

Fig. 2-9 In this digital age, it is much more difficult to find a good open-reel tape deck in excellent condition. If you can find a working Teac X-300 looking this nice, jump on it!

In most cases, unless you are hard core into radio or audio (as either a profession or a hobby), the open-reel tape format should be avoided. It's just not worth the trouble for a dabbler—especially with the advances in cassette deck and tape technology over the past 15 years. If cassette audio isn't up to your standards, and you have the money, try one of the other recording formats. Unless you're the type of audiophile that blanches just over the words "digital audio," you would be far better off with a CD recorder or a DAT deck. And if digital audio really bothers you, you probably already have an open-reel deck!

If you are looking for an open-reel deck or if you would just like to have one if one turned up at the right price, know what to look for. You can understand a lot about how an open-reel deck will perform, just by looking at it. First, eliminate all portable models.

TAPE DECKS

These usually have a case cover that snaps over the front, are smaller than most others, and has a handle or two. Some home-use decks also have a handle on top, but they do not feel portable! Another factor to eliminate lower-grade units is metal; if the case is not all or primarily all metal, don't get it.

One positive sign is if the unit contains four meters. That means the deck can record left and right on two different tracks. Because the manufacturer spent the extra money on such a high-quality feature, you can guess that the rest of the deck was constructed well, too.

Last, take a look at the brand name of that open-reel deck. This advice is also very helpful if you are checking classified ads in a newspaper, magazine, or on the Internet. The following companies manufactured high-end open-reel equipment for a number of years: Studer, Revox, Fostex, and Otari. Sony and Teac also manufactured some hi-fi decks, but they also made plenty of lower-end equipment, too.

As mentioned earlier, the heads of an open-reel deck are all-important and they can wear out. You might find a great price on a $3000 Studer deck, but if the heads are worn out, it will still sound bad. Be sure to check everything to be sure that it works, look for wear on the heads, and most importantly, listen to the sound of the deck. If you are ordering a piece of equipment, be sure that you can return the deck if you aren't satisfied with its condition. You will lose out on the postage if you send the deck back, but if the person or company is willing to take it back, chances are good that they are concerned about customer satisfaction.

For more information on vintage audio equipment, see Chapter 14.

DCC DECKS

In the mid-1990s, two new technologies were introduced with the intention of displacing the compact cassette as king of the audio mountain. The Digital Compact Cassette (DCC) was promoted as a digital alternative to the cassette. The MiniDisc was designed to be an easy-to-record, erasable digital disc (see Chapter 3 for more MiniDisc information). Both formats have failed commercially.

Physically, the DCC looks like a standard compact cassette that has reached another step in the evolutionary ladder . . . and in a sense, that's exactly what it is. Although the shape of the cassette is the same, it has changed considerably. The shell is a thick plastic that is tougher than the grade used for commercially recorded compact cassettes.

Unlike the completely bilateral nature of the compact cassette, the DCC is decidedly one-sided (Fig. 2-10). The top side consists of a flat

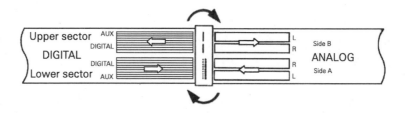

Fig. 2-10 Tracks on DCC tape (left) vs. analog cassette tape (right).

surface, where the album cover panel is set. Instead of just being a photographic label that is affixed to the surface, it is actually a sort of cassette card that is placed on the DCC tape. Then, a clear plastic panel is locked in place over the top of the card. The plastic panel adds to the overall strength of the DCC tape and it also protects the artwork so that the album covers won't look scuffed after a year of use, like an old 8-track cartridge.

The other side of the DCC tape is primarily a blank, flat, black piece of plastic, except for a piece of metal that is simply known as a slider. The slider is a protection device that covers all openings to the cassette to prevent dirt from entering the shell and to prevent other objects (such as fingers, pencils, etc.) from entering the bottom of the housing and damaging the tape. The metal slider is very similar to the spring-loaded metal guards that cover the openings in 3.5" computer floppy disks. In addition to protecting the tape, the slider also covers the two tape reel hubs that are only accessible from the underside of the DCC shell, like those on a VHS videotape.

Although practically everything about the DCC tape is like the cassette with a post-space-age twist, one thing that remains the same is the tape. Good 'ole plastic tape with a ferromagnetic coating. According to Philips, the tape was standard videotape with a coating of chromium dioxide or cobalt-doped ferroxide.

Although the recording tape is the same, even the manner in which it is picked up and decoded has changed. The tape no longer slides along over the top of the tape heads. Instead, the tape is pressed in against the tape heads, locked in at the top of the tape, and wrapped around at the bottom. This technique allows the tape to make more complete contact with the tape heads. Also, because the tape isn't just floating overtop of the heads, it will always be tracking perfectly, and not straying from side to side (azimuth error). In standard cassette recordings, the varying position of the tape can cause some variability in audio quality.

One of the most important physical and electronic aspects of the DCC system is that digital and analog playback heads are integrated into a single head. The DCC assembly for auto head units consists of two sets of head elements in a thin-film assembly: nine Magneto-Resistive Heads and two Magneto-Resistive Heads for analog playback. In the home DCC recorders, the heads also contain nine Integrated Recording Heads for digital recording. The digital pickup portion of the head is contained on one-half of the head surface and the analog pickup portion of the head is contained on the other side. As a result, both DCC and standard compact cassettes can be played on the DCC players without any adjustments or head shifting.

One really neat feature of the DCC is that it leaves a small digital track to carry information about the artist or about the tape you are listening to or playing back. This information appears on the LCD display of the head unit as a user reference and it can also be used to search for tracks. Some of this information includes the track number, the artist, and the title of the particular song. Other text, such as background information about the artist and the music's lyrics, can be displayed synchronously with the music. However, I'm not sure if the auto DCC players are capable of such complicated textual displays. The text mode also allows the system to reproduce simple graphics, several different type fonts, and 16 different colors. The DCC system is capable of placing all of this information on a tape in seven different languages so that the same DCC tape will be compatible with listeners around the world. In addition to this information, the beginning of each song is marked with start markers so that each song can be easily located by track number.

It seemed like DCC had everything needed to eventually displace cassettes: The format provided a smooth transition from format to format, the quality of the DCC tapes was much more solid than traditional cassettes, and the DCC audio was superior. The DCC didn't make a dent. I'm assuming that it just didn't have the marketing push behind it to become the overwhelming favorite. When the DCC was at its prime, I called or visited 14 different music stores in three states and four counties and none of the stores had them in stock. The responses ranged from "Are those the little, new things?" to "What's that?...I claim ignorance!" The attendant at one store even asked another worker for assistance, came back on the line and told me that they did in fact have DCC tapes for sale and she wanted to know what artists I was interested in. Instead of waiting on the phone for her to locate each recording, I just drove down. I was a bit perturbed when I found that after driving an hour to the store, it was totally devoid of DCC tapes and MiniDiscs.

Not long ago, new DCC decks were available from Damark for only $250 (list price of $750), but they probably won't last for long. Of course, used models will be floating around on the used hi-fi market for years.

DAT DECKS

In the late 1980s, several companies began to market DAT (digital audio tape) playback-only and recording decks. These decks were exactly what the name implies—a tape deck that could record audio digitally. For the first time, the consumer could record at approximately compact disc quality. As a result, many of the commercial labels were worried about the outcome of having a medium on the market that could readily duplicate albums so that each generation of recordings would be indistinguishable from the first. Because of these potential problems, the DAT recording decks were held at bay for some time before they reached North American consumers.

The DAT is entirely different from cassette and open-reel decks, in both theory and operation. The shells, tape, and heads are all different. Instead, the DAT is much more like a VCR. The heads of a DAT are not stationary, as in a cassette deck. Two playback/record heads are contained along opposite edges of a metal cylinder. This cylinder spins at a high rate of speed while tape passes across the heads. Even though the tape is moving across the heads at a much slower rate than with cassettes, the combination of moving tape and spinning tape heads results in an effective speed that is 16 times faster than that of a cassette.

Another similarity between the DAT and VHS tape is the way the tape functions when it is played back. Unlike the bottom of a cassette, where the tape is exposed, the bottom of DAT is covered with a thin plastic door. To play a DAT, the tape is placed into the sliding tray of the deck. When the tray slides back in, the DAT's door is opened and the tape is pulled out, against the heads. When it is played, the tape winds slowly across while the heads spin at 3000 rpm.

Although the DAT was revolutionary, the prices of the equipment remained very high. Few people were ready to shell out the money for an expensive deck. If they wanted less expensive digital sound, the compact disc was the way to go. The major benefit of DAT was that it could make "perfect" digital recordings. Unfortunately, however, the DAT tapes were not the same size as standard cassettes—the two are not compatible. Evidently, the manufacturers felt that they could create a new medium that would displace the cassette and cause millions of people to purchase new tape decks. If this was the plan, it backfired. The general public stayed with the standard cassette and accepted the compact disc. DAT decks only received widespread use in professional applications, such as in broadcasting, journalism, and studio recording, where near-perfect reproduction is essential.

Some audiophiles have stuck with the DAT format, in part because many audiophiles work in the audio industry, and they use the format professionally. Because of this little niche market, it appears that DAT tapes and decks will be used by a few people well into the future. Surprisingly, the popularity of the DAT will apparently outlive that of the DCC by a decade or possibly longer. Unlike the DCC, which hasn't become popular anywhere, the DAT's niche has prevented it from becoming a cheap, surplus format to play with. Instead, the DAT is too popular to hit the surplus market, yet not popular enough for the prices to drop from competition and mass marketing. If you are looking for the best combination of price, longevity, and compatibility, go for the CD-R. DAT is awfully pricey, considering that almost no one else has a compatible deck. Of course, the exception is if you are an audio engineer or work in a recording studio.

A VHS ALTERNATIVE?

The term *hi fi* hasn't been tossed around much since the 1950s and 1960s. It seemed to all but disappear by the time that the term began to be associated with middle-aged guys who listened to jazz in mono on a credenza. After a few decades erased this image, the term began to be used again—this time as a label for VCRs that are capable of audio playback in stereo.

The stereo VCR is a big deal in the home entertainment market (Fig. 2-11). Good stereo sound and crisp, large-screen video are

Fig. 2-11 Is it time for the hi-fi VCR to come out of the TV cabinet and find its place in the audio world?

the two essential components of a home theater system. Without the stereo audio, the home theater would lose much of its realism, and would generally fail in its attempts to draw you into the story of the movie. With this much faith placed on the audio quality of a VCR, would you trust it for just delivering audio for your stereo system?

The VHS tape format has some of the advantages of the cassette, open-reel, and DAT. It is packaged in a cartridge, so it is very convenient for playing, recording, and storing. Like the open-reel format, the tape is very wide, although much of this space would be wasted (used for video) when intended for audio only. Because the tape is wide and the heads are contained within a spinning cylinder, a single VHS tape can contain anywhere from two to eight hours of audio and video (depending on the type of tape and chosen speed); this is convenient and the cost per minute to record on VHS is less expensive than cassette recording. Finally, many hi-fi VCRs have better specifications for frequency response, wow and flutter, and signal-to-noise ratio than cassette decks.

So, could the hi-fi VCR be effectively used as an audio-storage medium? Absolutely. The problem with the format, however, is playback convenience. If you recorded a VHS tape in the four-hour format, you should have no problem fitting five albums on a single tape. If you want to listen to a specific song or album, you might have to rewind or fast-forward the tape for 10 minutes (or longer) until you find what you want to hear. Another problem is compatibility; you can't take it out and pop the tape in your car, and you probably can't take the tape to a friend's house to listen to on their stereo.

Currently, the only people that I know of who use VHS for audio recording are shortwave and scanner listeners (who like the long record times of the VCR and the ability to record via the timer) and hobby broadcasters (who also like the long record times, and who use the tapes as masters for their archives). VHS just hasn't been popular for home recording in the past. But with the increasing number of hi-fi VCRs on the market, and the suddenly dropping prices (it's now easy to get a good hi-fi VCR for less than $200), I think that more people will be recording audio on hi-fi VCRs in the next few years.

CONCLUSION

The tape deck might not be the highest-fidelity piece of equipment on the market, but it is the most popular for recording. For purchasing commercially recorded music, the overwhelming favorite is the compact disc (CD), the subject of Chapter 3.

3

DIGITAL DISCS

COMPACT DISC PLAYERS

Now that compact discs have been in common use for about a decade or so, the novelty is beginning to wear off and they are finally becoming a standard audio medium. No longer do you hear stories about how people have spent a few months of wages to gradually purchase 100 compact discs, only to lose them all to a collection agency after the frivolous spending spree. Now that I've seen new discs commonly available for $8 apiece and cutouts for less than $2, I know that the compact disc is truly the music medium for at least the first decade of the 21st century.

BASICS

The compact disc is simply a thin disc of aluminum that is encased in a plastic laminate to protect the recording (Fig. 3-1). The music that is to be recorded onto compact discs must be in a digital medium; that is, it must be converted into a massive amount of 0s and 1s. When the disc is recorded, a multitude of error-correcting data and system information (track information, markers, etc.) are also added to the disc along with the music. All of this data must be downloaded, so the aluminum disc is etched with minuscule pits. The pits and the unpitted areas translate as data that represents the 1s and 0s.

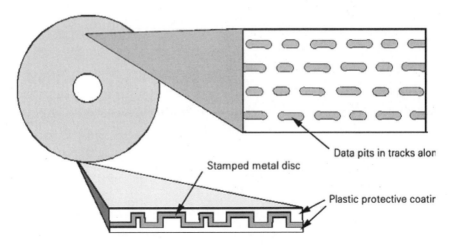

Fig. 3-1 Two super close-up views of the CD: the surface pits and the side of the disc.

One of the key components in a compact disc player is the laser optical assembly. When a compact disc is running inside of the head unit or changer, a low-powered laser is firing straight up through the player and at the tracks of the disc. The unpitted areas of the disc reflect the light back, but the pitted areas reflect almost nothing back. The result is a tremendously fast flickering of light—coded messages sent in the same manner, much faster than the boys could signal on "Hogan's Heroes." These coded reflections are received by a photodetector, which changes the light flickers into electrical impulses. These binary electrical impulses are then converted into analog impulses. Then, they are amplified and converted from electrical analog impulses into sound by the speakers.

Of course, this information about how a compact disc player operates is tremendously simplified. The analog-to-digital and digital-to-analog processes are extremely complicated—especially when you consider that such things as coding and sampling must also be configured into the system. *Sampling* is the process by which the compact disc player plays an analog sound, then checks the digital source, then plays another sound. This cycling occurs

44,100 times per second (44.1 kHz), although many players now sample several times more than that per second to make sure that the information being received/played is accurate and not error-ridden. Sampling at harmonic frequencies (as just described) is known as *oversampling*. Many of the high-cost compact disc players sample up to 8x the standard sample frequency. At this point, oversampling starts to become overkill and the law of diminishing returns kicks in.

Another factor, relative volume, also needs to be considered. Every audio waveform has a length (the frequency of the sound), which determines the pitch of the sound and a height (the amplitude of the sound), which determines the volume of the sound. In order for the compact disc player to accurately reproduce music and not wind up with all of the frequencies reproduced at the same volume, the samples are quantized to a 16-bit number between 0 and 65,535. Every tiny piece of audio that is reproduced by the compact disc can be reproduced at any one of 65,536 different volume levels (Fig. 3-2)!

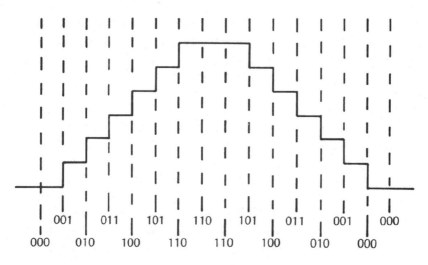

001   011   101   110   101   011   001   000
000   010   100   110   110   100   010   000

Fig. 3-2 A very rough representation of a digital audio wave.

These codes that determine various aspects of the compact disc's sound and technical operations all require a vast amount of information. A full compact disc (approximately 74 minutes) requires in the neighborhood of 34,000,000 bits of information to produce. If this information was all held on a standard computer floppy disc, the selection would have to be placed on 48 5.25" (13.34 cm) discs! The alternative to this is to determine some sort of compression code, which is how DAT and DCC tapes and MiniDiscs can be digital and hold as much music as they do.

Some of the high-end CD players are further broken into separate components. The standard is to divide them into two pieces: the CD transport and the digital-to-analog converter (also known as a *D/A converter* or *DAC*). The digital signal (0s and 1s) is sent from the transport through a cable to the D/A converter, where the signal is decoded and passed to the amplifier (Fig. 3-3).

The theory here is that the transport is mechanical and has already been ultimately refined. D/A converters, however, have been redeveloped over the years. Many high-end audio pundits believe that separates are best because you can choose a better D/A converter than is commonly sold; you can upgrade it with lower cost (because the transport doesn't need to be traded in, just the D/A converter); and that the separates are essential because they better shield the equipment from each other (which reduces noise).

Most of this reasoning is off base. You might very well find a better D/A converter than that which is currently in a particular CD deck. But with some searching, you should find a deck that you think sounds as good (or better) than that transport and D/A converter combination. It's all a matter of quality control and engineering. This is not to say that the separates aren't well built; many are fantastic machines, but just because most CD separates are excellent, that doesn't mean that it isn't possible to create an excellent-sounding CD player.

The second fallacy is that by purchasing separates, you will save money. The opposite is true. You might only have to buy a new DAC when you trade in, but that savings is quickly nullified by the other costs. The most significant cost is the price of high-end audio. Separates automatically mean high-end audio, which is often equated with higher expense. People will pay extra simply for the snob appeal of CD separates, thus the prices are higher. Also, each piece of equipment requires the company to manufacture separate metal cabinets and power supplies, further upping the costs. Finally, few people buy separates, so you won't save money as a result of mass production.

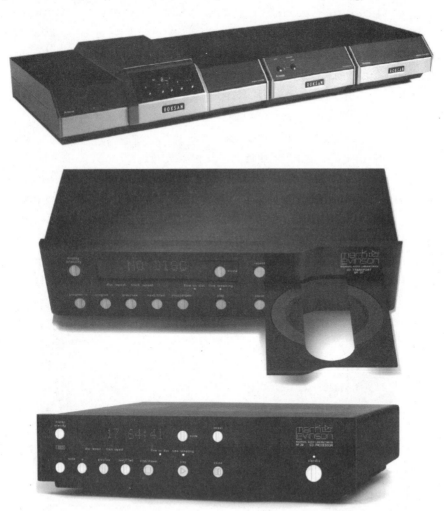

Fig. 3-3 Some of the best CD separates in the world: the Roksan Attessa CD/DAC/power supply combination (top), the Mark Levinson® №37 CD transport (middle), and the Mark Levinson® №39 CD processor (bottom). Roksan (top), Madrigal Audio Laboratories, Inc. (middle and bottom).

The last consideration, that placing the equipment in separate enclosures better shields the circuitry, is true. Of course, placing each section of a piece of audio equipment in a separate enclosure will reduce noise and crosstalk. However, with good engineering, equally good results can be obtained within a single enclosure. For that matter, I've never heard anyone complain that outboard D/A and A/D converters should be a separate option for DAT, MD, or DCCs.

The bottom line is that most CD separates are excellent machines that will operate reliably for decades. If you have the money, one of these "dream machines" might be a worthy investment. However, don't be conned into believing that you must have CD separates to achieve a sound that will suit your tastes.

CHOOSING A CD PLAYER

For well over a decade, CDs have been touted as a means of "perfectly" playing back music—no errors, everything sounds exactly as it was recorded. If you check out the manufacturer's specifications on CD players, you will notice that they do not perfectly reproduce sound. They have specifications for total harmonic distortion, wow and flutter, stereo separation, SNR, frequency response, and dynamic range, just like any other piece of audio equipment.

Except for the differences between bottom-of-the-barrel portable and personal CD players and high-end CD decks, you won't find massive differences between the CD deck specifications (Fig. 3-4). Likewise, it doesn't take much to figure out that better specifications will probably yield a better sound. However, beware of dome specifications. For example, frequency response is very misleading. Some pieces of audio equipment are rated for highs of up to 20 kHz, which is beyond the range of hearing for most people. And as you get older, your high-frequency hearing will continue to decline. So, you don't really need equipment with such high specifications—peaks around 18 kHz should do just fine. On the other end of the spectrum, many pieces of equipment are rated to emit sound at frequencies of 20

Fig. 3-4 Two feature-laden multi-CD decks (top and middle) and a high-end player (bottom): The Kenwood DP-J1070 (top), the Pioneer PD-F906 file-type CD player (bottom), and the Theta Digital Miles. Kenwood (top), Pioneer (middle), Theta Digital (bottom).

Hz (or lower). Few speakers are capable of outputting sound at such low frequencies; in addition, most rooms are too small to adequately reproduce the sound—even if the speakers are capable of pumping it out (see Chapter 9 for more information on system installation).

When comparing the specifications of different pieces of equipment, remember that although the ratings of some specs are better for one model, other specs are better for another model. So, if CD player A has a stereo channel separation of 80 dB and a dynamic range of 89 dB, and CD player B has a stereo channel separation of 90 dB and a dynamic range of 93 dB, which should you choose? Does it matter? Will you notice a difference? The only way to really know how important the specifications are to each model is to use your ears. Drop in at the local stereo store and either listen to different CD players with either the same good pair of headphones or via the same amplifier and speakers.

Listening is the key to everything in audio systems. You can get an idea of the quality of a piece of equipment from looking at the specs, or the reliability from seeing the cabinet and the construction of the equipment, but you won't know how it actually sounds until you listen to it.

CD vs. CD-R

Aside from the sound and the general features (see the next section), you will also need to consider the type of audio or audio/video system that you plan to install in your house before going out and purchasing a system. For the past decade and a half, your options have been to purchase either a CD player or maybe a CD transport and a D/A converter. Today's CD machines are more flexible, but can also be much more confusing when you need to make that final decision.

In the mid-1990s, several CD player/recorders were introduced to the high-end audio market. CD-ROM recorders have been available in the $1500+ range for a number of years. Although they can also record CD audio, they require the appropriate software. Like the DAT, the home audio CD recorder was held back from the market because of the major record companies, who were afraid that their albums would be perfectly recopied by bootleggers and individual music enthusiasts around the world. Their solution was to make the CD recording deck with limited recording capabilities. Although you can record from a CD, record, or cassette to a CD-R, you can't record from one CD-R to another CD-R. The theory is that although they can't prevent you from making copies of your CDs for yourself, they can make some of the mass recording more difficult.

The CD-R is different from a traditional prerecorded CD in many aspects, but the most noticeable difference is that it is pitless. Instead of pits, like a CD, a blank disc has guiding grooves called *pregrooves*, where the pits are to be recorded. The CD-R contains an additional layer of material, called the *dye layer*, where the pits will be formed. When recording, the source audio is fed to the CD-R recorder, where it is changed into digital information by the A/D converter. The pits are formed when a high-powered laser fires against the CD-R, according to the digital information received from the source. The laser burns the dye, making it opaque, to represent a pit. When you listen to the CD-R copy, the playback laser will read the surface, outputting 0s for each pit and 1s for the unblemished surface, just like a standard CD.

Some of the other differences that are not noticeable from just looking at a CD-R are located in the data-controlling sections of the disc. For example, the CD-Rs track information and antirecording information all must be added to tracks on the disc. It's not important that you know how these processes all work because the CD player/recorder will just do it as the disc is recorded.

As mentioned, the problem with recording onto CD-R discs is that they aren't erasable. If you record onto them once and make a mistake, that's too bad. It's got a mistake and, aside from throwing it away, there's nothing you can do. In this sense, DAT and DCC tapes, and MiniDiscs have a tremendous advantage over CD-R recording. The overpowering advantage of CD player/recorders is that they are compatible with equipment that nearly everyone else has—especially since the dawn of the multimedia computer age. Now, CD players are nearly as common as cassette decks. This situation alone will cause most people to risk recording on a CD-R.

Not long ago, CD player/recorders cost $2000, which placed them well beyond the means of the typical consumer. Considering the universal nature of the CD and that the technology has just been introduced to the market, it seems certain that the CD player/recorder will survive for many years to come, with steadily dropping prices. As it is, computer CD-ROM recorders are presently available new for as little as $400, and blank 74-minute CD-Rs presently cost $7. In a few years, CD player/recorders should reach this price range. Until then, it's best to stick to the older forms of recording while the prices drop and the technology is revised.

CD vs. CD/CD-V/LD

CD recorders aren't the only option on the digital disc market. You might opt for a CD/CD-V/LD (laser disc) player. In addition to playing standard CDs, these decks are also capable of playing CD-V and laser discs (Fig. 3-5).

Fig. 3-5 Is DVD/LD in your future? The Pioneer Elite DVL-90. Pioneer

CD-V discs are CDs that contain both audio and video; the audio can be played on a standard CD player, but the video can only be viewed via a laser disc player or CD-ROM drive. CD-V discs are commonly used for rock album/video combinations. If you play it on a CD player, you can listen to the music. If you try it in a laser disc player or CD-ROM drive, you can also watch the videos.

DIGITAL DISCS

Laser discs are a video-oriented storage medium. Unlike CD-V discs, which can also play back audio on CD players, laser discs can only be played back via a machine that has been specially manufactured to handle this format. Unlike the big, record-sized silver discs of the early 1980s, modern laser discs are the same size as standard CDs. Today's laser discs are so small because the system uses much more efficient compression algorithms than the system from nearly two decades ago.

A CD/CD-V/LD player is especially flexible, but is it the piece of equipment that you want as the keystone of your playback system? Probably not. These laser disc players cost much more than a CD player with comparable audio specifications. Also, you can't record video with a laser disc player, so if you have any interest in video, you will still need to purchase a VCR. Although more than 8000 movies are advertised to be available on laser disc, they are much more expensive than videocassettes. In the long run, you will pay more for the equipment, more to watch the movies, and you will still need to buy the same amount of equipment. And because North America is still making the most of the low-resolution NTSC standard (the 525- X 425-dot standard that has been in effect since just after World War II), you probably won't discover any noticeable gains in picture quality with the laser disc.

The bottom line is, unless cost is of little or no concern, hold out for HDTV with recordable laser discs before jumping after a laser disc player.

FEATURES

Because of the more accurate music reproduction from compact discs, fewer extra features are necessary in order for them to play well. Most of the features are computerized and relate to the manner in which the discs are sorted and searched.

Number of discs The parallel to the cassette players' autoreverse function for CD players, including compact disc changers, is the number of discs that can be stored in a unit. Some changers can handle as many as 200 discs at the same time. Even computer CD drives are now able to handle up to three discs at a time. The prime consideration here is the length of time that you can listen to the music without having to pop out the discs. With the 200-disc changers, you could potentially listen to continuous music for 246 hours (10+ days). This system isn't terribly practical in your home, but it would be great for playing background music in a restaurant.

Disc access time Disc access time refers to the amount of time between a disc being inserted or changed and when it begins to play. This figure seems to vary quite a bit in meaning from manufacturer to manufacturer. Even so, the times would only vary by a few seconds. If you need to brag to your friends about how your changer can access discs 1.26 seconds faster than theirs, then you really need to get out more often.

Random access When you pile a boatload of discs into a changer, it is interesting to hit the random access function. This feature will pick out tracks at random from any of the discs. Random access isn't quite as exciting when used on a 1-disc head unit, but perhaps it will spice up an old favorite a bit. In the case of a store using a 200-disc changer, the random-access function is a perfect way to seamlessly diversify the music.

Intro scan The intro scan executes similarly to the radio scanning features. Press the button and it plays the first few seconds of each song. After it moves through the entire disc, you can choose what songs you want to listen to. Or you might just choose another disc.

Repeat The repeat function allows you to repeat the track or the compact disc that you just listened to.

Changer·remote control Some compact disc changers have their own remote controls so that it is possible to have some of the useful programmable features that are otherwise only found on head units. Most of the features that are on the remote controls relate to the playback of the discs, but this is still a handy feature.

Disc-management screens Some Pioneer CD players have the option of computer organizing the CDs via a control pad and your TV screen. With this system, you can assign titles to your discs and even search for songs by title. This is the near-ultimate refinement for the gadgeteer or the restauranteer, who occasionally takes requests.

MiniDisc players

The MiniDisc is somewhat like a quarter-scale CD, locked inside of a floppy disc case. In this sense, the relationship between the compact disc and the MiniDisc is the same as that between open reel tape player and the cassette tape player. The protective cartridge is an important advancement. This means that an entire commercial recording from an artist will fit onto a 2.7" x 2.7" (6.86 cm x 6.86 cm) disc. Unlike the CD (or the record, which the CD replaced), the disc doesn't need to be pulled out of its case and placed into the playing device; just pop the whole package into the player and that's it.

But the smaller size and the computer disc-style case are not the only positive physical differences between the MiniDisc and the compact disc. The major difference is that the MiniDiscs can be recorded upon—over and over and over again. Sony's laboratories say that a MiniDisc can be recorded on over one million times and not show any degradation in quality. This reliability is based on the fact that the disc is digitally encoded and optically read by a laser. No parts or heads wear against the recorded material and eventually ruin the surface. In fact, MiniDiscs are claimed to be virtually indestructible. The manufacturer says that only a combination of laser and electromagnetic signals can erase the tracks, so you won't have to worry about the discs being erased while sitting in the sun or on top of a set of speakers.

One problem with the MiniDisc format is the flip side of the question "how do they fit all of that music onto such a small space?" In order to fit in the recording time, the manufacturers were forced to compress all of that digital information into a 2 1/2" (6.35 cm) diameter disc. Using a special digital compression technique, the system purges the audio frequencies that are above and below the human hearing range. By reducing the overall width of the audio, less space is required to copy that information, and more music can be recorded in the same amount of space. In the case of the MiniDisc, more information can be recorded in much less space.

There is a problem, though, with removing those frequencies when the disc is recorded. Considering that the frequencies are out of the human hearing range, theoretically, there should be no decline in audio quality. But this is the real world, and what might appear to work on paper, sometimes doesn't in real life. The general consensus has been that MiniDiscs don't sound quite as good as compact discs, but that they sound much better than the average cassette. That being the case, an audiophile would be bothered by this slight difference in audio quality, but you might not even notice.

This same technology produces some amazing results when coupled with the flexibility of digital disc recording. Tracks from any part of the MiniDisc can be erased. Then, any tracks that follow the one that was deleted, move up in order. For example, maybe you recorded 32 songs on a MiniDisc and you decide that you don't like the nose flute song that was recorded on track 8. You can delete track 8 and track 9 becomes track 8, track 10 becomes track 9, etc. If the nose flute song (formerly track 8)

lasted 2:33, then you have an extra 2:33 of space left on the disc.
Maybe you then want to round off the disc with a song by
One*21, just to scare your friends. You have 2:33, plus whatever
space was left over on the disc from before. This new song becomes track 32.

Along with these wonders of digital recording come other little
touches that add to the convenience of MiniDiscs. For example,
the fixed-position (car and home decks) feature an electronic
display that shows the song title and track number of the song
that is being played. This information is all stored in a disc table
of contents, along with the the title of the disc. The recording
MiniDisc decks have a keyboard so that you can enter pertinent disc
and song information onto the disc that you are recording. With this
system, you could record a copy of an album onto a MiniDisc, type all
of the song titles, and they will appear on the readout of the deck
every time that you listen to the album. This information can be
changed, so if you misspelled a song title or decide to eliminate a
song, all of the information will update correctly.

Obviously, the MiniDisc has some real advantages—especially when
used for mobile or portable applications. For people with large collections of compact discs or even records, it would be much less risky to
record these albums onto MiniDiscs and keep these copies in the car.
That way, even if your car was robbed or if it fell into some other
disastrous situation, your masters of the music would still be safe at
home. Also, the MiniDiscs are smaller and much more convenient to
pop in and out of a deck than a compact disc.

The MiniDisc was developed by Sony to drive the cassette off the
market. Like its competition from Philips, the DCC, it failed miser-
ably. The DCC, which was reported to lose less audio information
than the MiniDisc, and yet still be compatible with the standard
cassette, was virtually driven from the market. The MiniDisc fared
better, but not by much. Instead of being snapped up by the buying
public, the format was virtually ignored. Like the DCC, many people

in North America have never heard of, let alone seen, a MiniDisc. However, just like the DAT, the MiniDisc found a niche that will probably keep the format on the market for years. The ease of tracking, the speed at which tracks can be accessed, and the fact that the MiniDisc can record makes it perfect for radio applications. For years, radio stations used endless loop tape cartridges that looked something like 8-track tapes. To play the tapes, special (expensive!) "cart machines" were used. Overall, carts worked well, but they are much more expensive, more difficult to record, and more difficult to use than MiniDiscs. In the course of a few years, MiniDiscs replaced carts at many of the radio stations in North America—just as the CD-R was beginning to emerge.

If you are interested in using MiniDisc systems, it's mostly a waste of time and money, unless you are involved in radio. Then, you can use MiniDiscs at home and work, which could be handy in some instances. Otherwise, just wait for some good prices from CD player/recorders.

CONCLUSION

After surviving many marketing wars, the CD is the king of digital audio, digital recording, multimedia (CD-ROM), and digital video (laser disc and CD-V). It appears that the CD and its many derivations will dominate media storage for decades. Despite this overwhelming trend, audiophiles and some other die-hards still vote thumbs down on the CD, opting instead for the sound of a format that's nearly a century old. The turntable (phonographic record) is covered in Chapter 4.

4

TURNTABLES

After nearly two decades of the CD, it's about time for teenagers to start saying, "What is that round, black piece of plastic?" It's the teenager who wondered what band Paul McCartney was in before Wings. That round, black piece of plastic is, of course, a phonographic record, usually just called a *record*. The record is one of the oldest pieces of high-technology mass media still in existence, dating back to the early twentieth century when the early audio manufacturers voted for the flat piece of plastic over the original Edison cylinder. In the near-century since the record was created, it has changed very little, except for one speed change (78 rpm to 45 and 33 rpm), and some slight changes in record thicknesses and the types of plastics used.

When the CD hit the market in 1983, millions of consumers howled with relief that they could finally dump their archaic records. Now they finally had a medium that was convenient, indestructible, and that finally was up-to-date with the modern, technologically advanced music that they were listening to. By the end of the 1980s, most people had pitched their records—sold them at yard sales or via classified ads, traded in a big stack of them at a store for a CD or two, or simply threw them away. They had finally unburdened themselves of these technological also-rans.

Those people were duped by a massive advertising campaign.

Despite the fact that records were created before television and FM radio, they are generally considered by audiophiles to be sonically superior to CDs. Also, CDs are far from indestructible; you still must treat the pit side of a CD with the same care that you must treat a record. And CDs have only been in existence for about a decade and a half; we really have no idea if CDs will last for hundreds (or even dozens) of years without sound degradation.

I'm not an audiophile, so I can understand why some people might trade a slight difference in audio fidelity for the convenience and small size of a CD. However, one of my more ingrained qualities is that I'm cheap. When the records were flushed out of the market by "perfect sound" and "technological advancements" of the CD in the late 1980s, records were selling in mall music stores for $8 to $10 for new releases. The CDs that replaced records were selling in the same stores for $14 to $16. These prices, coupled with the lower fidelity of CDs and the fact that CDs cost less to manufacture than records, made the deal no sweeter. The result was that many consumers (in the true sense of the word) dumped all of their records, only to pay twice as much to replace them. While this was happening, the independent record labels, who had not yet acquired the technology or available cash to rerelease all of their recordings on CD, were squeezed from the market.

But that was the 1980s, and the market has begun to change. Although the price of new CDs in such places as mall music stores has not dropped, many independent companies sell their offerings for $8 to $10. Some new sampler CDs are even available new for $4. In addition, clean, used CDs will offer the same sound performance as new CDs for much less money—typically, $4 to $10 apiece. On the other hand, all but the rarest records are nearly worthless. A few years ago at a used record store, I picked up clean copies of records by Pink Floyd and The Police for 9 cents apiece. In the CD format, these albums would probably cost about

$12 to $16 new or $6 to $10 used. With prices like this, why would you not consider records?

FINDING A TURNTABLE

Finding a turntable can be easier than you might think in some respects, and more difficult in other ways. I have heard a number of people say things like "Hey, look. A record player. I didn't know that they made these things anymore." Most major music companies never stopped manufacturing turntables, and you can find one or two different models in most every stereo shop or manufacturer's catalog. It is no problem to find one, and cost is not really a problem either; the most common turntables cost about $80 to $120.

The difficulty in locating a turntable is finding a good model at a price that you can afford. If you pick up one of the $80 to $120 models at your local stereo and appliance store, chances are that it will not be capable of making your records sound better than CDs. This might not be a concern; you might only be interested in playing old records that you have in your collection or finding loads of cheap records and being able to listen to music for a fraction of the cost of CDs or even recording onto cassettes. If this is your motivation, go for the less-expensive turntable. You will be glad that you tracked down all of those records. If your motivation is price or old records, not fidelity, then skip to the end of this chapter, unless you are interested in some of the light basics of turntables and why high-end turntables are better.

That advice is helpful if you just want the music, but what if you want the full analog fidelity? Then, the search is more difficult because turntables are the ultimate component for physical tweaking. Instead of letting the manufacturer alter an algorithm (as in the case of a CD player), the turntable manufacturer must change countless aspects of the turntable and use heavier-grade components. Using a "heavier-duty" algorithm does not alter the physical aspects of a CD player, but heavy-duty parts add plenty to the cost of a turntable.

THE RECORD

The phonographic record is an incredibly simple device that is somewhat similar in theory to the CD. In both systems, the platter spins the disc around, and the data is read at one point from the disc. But that's where the similarities end.

When the record is made, a blank disc must first be cut. The audio from the recorded tape is amplified, then passed to a record-cutting lathe—a large piece of equipment that looks like a cross between a turntable and something from a chemistry lab. The electrical impulses from the amplifier are translated into physical movements by the cutting lathe. The head of the record cutting lathe moves up and down, in near-perfect accordance with the music. On the turntable of the cutting lathe is a blank lacquer disc. As the head moves in time with the music, it cuts a tiny groove in the lacquer, and the tailings are quickly sucked away (to prevent scratching the disc).

After the lacquer has been cut, the disc is thoroughly cleaned, then sprayed with a silver compound. The silvered lacquer disc is then placed in a plating bath, where, through the wonders of electrochemistry, the disc actually grows a metal master—a negative of the sides of the record. The metal master is then used to produce a mother—a positive copy of the original silvered lacquer disc. Then, negative stamping plates are produced so that the final product can be stamped out. The extra steps, with the metal master and the mother disc, are used to protect the silvered lacquer disc from damage. This way, the original-cut disc and the metal master will not be degraded or ruined, and future records could be repressed—even if the mother or the stamping plates are damaged.

When one of these freshly stamped records is plopped down on the turntable, you swing the tone arm over and place the cartridge needle in the groove. The tone arm is held firmly in place, but the needle moves up and down as it tracks through the groove. The needle is just the tip of the iceberg, or in this case, the tip of the cartridge. The cartridge contains a set of coils and magnets. As the needle bounces up and down with the music, the needle is causing the coils to move inside of the magnets, making the electrical fields change. These alterations in the electrical fields produce tiny electrical signals that are passed on through the system and amplified thousands of times (Fig. 4-1).

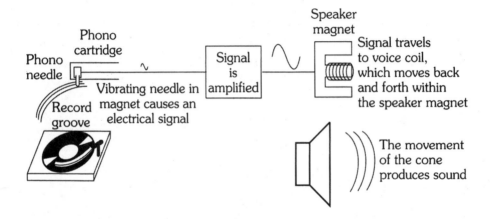

Fig. 4-1 The process by which the grooves on a record are changed into sound.

The most complicated theory behind records is how those grooves can produce two channels of stereo sound, differences in loudness (amplitude), and the differences in frequency. The volume of the signal is produced from the depth of the groove. The width of the cut produces the range in frequencies. The outside of the groove is dedicated to the right channel of the recording, and the inside of the groove is the left channel (Fig. 4-2). A record, like the entire phonographic playback system, is extremely simple. The difficulty lies in the execution of that simple idea.

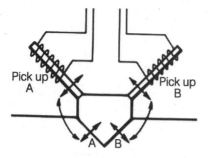

Fig. 4-2 The stereo stylus receives information independently from the inside and outside of the record grooves.

ELEMENTS OF THE TURNTABLE

The turntable, also known as a *record player*, *phonograph*, or *record changer*, is simply a piece of equipment that enables you to play back records. It is a very uncomplicated piece of equipment, with very few parts, and virtually no high-tech electronics (Fig. 4-3).

Fig. 4-3 A fairly typical modern belt-drive turntable, the Dual 506.

The only pieces of equipment in a turntable that must move are the platter and the needle in the cartridge. The platter must only spin at a constant speed. The needle is spring-loaded in the cartridge, and it requires no extra assistance. So, it seems to make sense that most every turntable, except for the Strawberry Shortcake Sing-Along model, would sound pretty much the same.

It would be great if all turntables fantastically reproduced the sounds of the record, but many don't. The problem isn't the electronics, but the physical aspects of the turntable. Now back up and take a look at the theory behind turntable operation. The needle is moving through a tiny groove and fluctuating an even tinier amount. As a result, nearly anything (either external to the turntable or a part of the assembly) can alter the speed and sonics of a turntable.

VIBRATIONS

Some examples of external vibrations would include someone walking in the room where the turntable is located, rumbles from passing traffic, the movement of the platter, and even vibrations from the sound waves of your speakers. The results of these noises can cause rumble, a low-frequency distortion that sounds like its name. Rumble is bad because it alters the sound of what you hear. Even worse is skip, which occurs when the needle jumps off the groove to a different groove.

To reduce the effects of external vibrations on the turntable, manufacturers go to great lengths to provide a solid piece of equipment (Fig. 4-4). It is common for manufacturers to mount the turntable on large rubber feet to absorb vibrations that travel upward from its mounting location. Also, the base of the turntable is typically heavy, and it might be manufactured from metal, wood, a wood composite (flakeboard), or even a hollow assembly that has been filled with lead shot. (Because the lead shot is loose, it will absorb even more energy.)

Two opposite approaches are sometimes taken for turntable placement. The best approach is for the turntable to be located on a

Fig. 4-4 Solid foundation: a heavy-based JVC turntable on a three-posted metal stand

heavy, solid floor, such as a concrete basement floor. Such a floor is essentially dead to external noise and vibration (except speaker noise). Not everyone can have their stereo on a solid concrete floor. In these cases, vibrations will travel through the floor. The most common theory in audio circles is to deaden the vibration with mass. Most advocates of this system place the turntable on a heavy rack, with legs filled with lead shot or sand. I've even heard of enthusiasts who have mounted the turntable on large slabs of marble to deaden vibrations. The opposite approach is to isolate the vibrations. The college radio station where I used to work had flimsy floors under the on-air studio and the main production room. Rather than install a marble slab, which might have resulted in a spacious two-story-high studio, the station engineer chose to isolate the turntables with foam. First, a solid wooden table was constructed and nailed to the floor and a 2-inch-thick piece of foam rubber was glued on top. Then, a large laminated flakeboard top was glued on top of the foam rubber, and the turntables were placed on the top. It was a cheap fix, but it worked.

The platters in turntables are isolated from vibration in a variety of ways. Many platters are spring-loaded, but the best will have a nice, cushy feel to them. Some really cheap spring-loaded turntables from decades past had bouncy platters, like bobble-head dolls. Platters with poorly spring-loaded platters like these will cause vibrations to be amplified—a virtual noise fest. Even good turntables that have solid spring-suspended platters are susceptible to slight ringing. Because of the problems with ringing, some turntable manufacturers have resorted to suspending the platter over the frame, and balancing it on rubber or foam.

MOTOR

Although the most high-tech electronics component of the turntable is the cartridge assembly, the other components can also be problematic. For example, the motor can cause slight variations in platter speed, depending on its construction. Some motors contain only two magnetic poles, inside which the armature spins. Because the armature is only being pulled from two different directions, the motor is likely to cause vibrations. For smoother operation, other motors are constructed with four separate magnetic poles, located at even points around the armature. Yet another potential vibration-causing problem at the motor is the ball bearings. If they are not carefully engineered, they will also cause noise.

DRIVE SYSTEM

The last major noise source related to the motor is the drive system that lies between the motor and the platter. If the type of drive system used is not properly engineered, the motor will transmit vibrations through the drive to the platter. However, the motor must also be connected to the platter in a manner so that it will spin smoothly, without variation. Although it might be relatively easy to design a drive system to run at a set speed or to run the turntable so that little vibration is transmitted to the platter, it is very difficult to do both.

One of the most problematic drive systems over the years is the belt-drive turntable. In this system, the belt is wrapped around both the motor shaft and the inner wheel of the platter. When the motor turns, it turns the belt and causes the platter to spin. The main problem with belt-drive turntables is the belt; it can become slippery, stretch, crack, or break. If the belt begins to slip, the records will suddenly slow down or speed up, seemingly at random. If it stretches, cracks, or breaks, the platter will typically just stop—even though you can hear the motor still turning. You can expect that rubber belts will eventually require replacement, and most Americans seem to equate maintenance with nonworking junk. Tearing apart that piece of audio equipment is just unappealing.

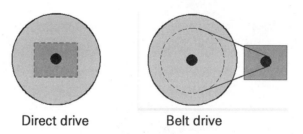

Direct drive   Belt drive

Fig. 4-5 Direct-drive vs. belt drive.

To avoid the problems with consumers and turntable maintenance, the popular consumer turntable manufacturers switched to direct-drive units (Fig. 4-5). Direct-drive turntables contain no belts. Instead, the motor is geared directly to the platter, which it spins. The problem with the direct-drive system is that all noise and vibration from the motor is transmitted directly to the turntable, rather than being absorbed, in part, by the rubber belts. The end result is that nearly all direct-drive turntables require little maintenance but offer mediocre performance.

TONE ARM

The last major part of the turntable that is prone to vibration problems is the tone arm. The tone arm is a long arm that must reach from the edge of the record back to the base of the turntable. Because the tone arm is thin, must be capable of turning, and is nearly a foot long, it is a prime vibration transmitter. The problem is to dampen the vibration and accurately reproduce the sound. To see just how shaky 10" of tone arm can be, try holding on to the very top of a pencil while writing on paper in a moving car (of course, only try this test as the passenger of the car). You will have less control of the pencil, and those tiny vibrations will cause the pencil to bounce all over the page (unless you are riding in Pennsylvania, where the potholes would cause the pencil to bounce across the seats and doors, too). As you can see, the tone arm is one of the most important pieces of technology in a turntable; without a good tone arm, the needle will not be able to smoothly and accurately track through a record.

Once again, designing the perfect tone arm is an exercise in trade-offs. A very light tone arm will smoothly track through the grooves of a record. The problem is that if the tone arm is too light, it will be susceptible to vibrations from the turntable and even from the grooves of the record. The vibrations will distort the great sound that has been picked up by the needle. But if the tone arm is too heavy, the needle will be so weighted down that it cannot respond to all of the intricacies of the record grooves. Unlike the too-light tone arm, the too-heavy tone arm will produce an incomplete representation of the music. As in party politics, the only solution is compromise. Engineers strive for a perfect tone arm—one that will be light enough to reproduce the music accurately, yet heavy enough to prevent the tone arm from vibrating.

An entirely different sound consideration with the physics of the tone arm is the angle by which the needle passes through the record grooves. When the record grooves are cut, the cutting head is always perpendicular to the position of the record. It makes sense that the best sound would be reproduced if the tone arm could always be parallel to the groove. This system is called linear tracking. In this system, the one end of the tone arm slides across a bar while the stylus is running in the record grooves. This is how cutting heads make records, so you would think that this method is far superior to any other. It's not. Instead, it's so complex that it is susceptible to vibrations and rough tracking across the record. Some linear tracking systems (Fig. 4-6) are on the market, but because of the complexity and the required engineering precision, most of these are nearly all very expensive (ranging from several thousand to tens of thousands of dollars).

Fig. 4-6 A rare relatively inexpensive linear-tracking turntable, manufactured by Realistic (Radio Shack) in the 1980s.

Instead, most tone arms pivot onto the record from a point near the end of the tone arm, where it is attached to the table. The problem with this system is that the stylus will not track linearly across the record; it will start off tracking linearly and finish in a completely wrong angle. So, decades ago, audio engineers countered this problem by angling the head of the tone arm in toward the record at an angle of about 25 degrees. This quick-and-dirty fix didn't exactly solve the problem, but it reduced it to a tolerable level. With the angled head, the stylus is only off linear by a few degrees (at most).

The tone arm is available in a few different shapes, including straight, curved, and S-curved. These shapes have nothing to do with the angle the tone arm has, in relation to the grooves of the record. Instead, the shape of the tone arm is used to improve its balance as the stylus plays through the record grooves, and also to dampen the vibrations that pass up through the tone arm.

THE CARTRIDGE

Considering that the cartridge is equivalent to the heads on a tape deck, the cartridge has the most important electronics job of any part of the turntable (Fig. 4-7). As mentioned earlier in the chapter, the stylus moves through the record groove. It is directly connected to a coil of wire that lies between magnets. (In some systems, the stylus is connected to a magnet that lies between coils of wire.)

Fig. 4-7 A classic: the V15 phono cartridge has been manufactured for more than 30 years for audio professionals. Shure

Like the other aspects of the turntable, the cartridge is very simple in theory but requires plenty of precise physical engineering to ensure that everything works properly. The stylus must be of a perfect shape and not so hard that it will cut the record grooves, yet not so soft that it will quickly wear out (Fig. 4-8). It

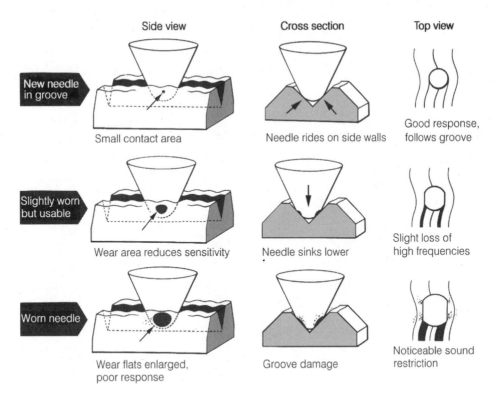

Side view   Cross section   Top view

New needle in groove — Small contact area — Needle rides on side walls — Good response, follows groove

Slightly worn but usable — Wear area reduces sensitivity — Needle sinks lower — Slight loss of high frequencies

Worn needle — Wear flats enlarged, poor response — Groove damage — Noticeable sound restriction

Fig. 4-8 Unless the stylus is replaced, it will wear and eventually cut into the grooves of the record.

must be suspended perfectly so that the coil (or magnet, depending on the type of cartridge) bounces along simultaneously to the music. Of course, the coil must also be wound precisely, and the entire assembly must be resistant to vibration. See Chapter 15 for more information on cartridge and stylus replacement.

Despite the fact that it is the only component of electronic significance in the entire turntable, the cartridge is the least important. It's better to spend your money on a turntable with a solid, relatively vibration-resistant base, an excellent tone arm, and an inexpensive cartridge, than to buy a cheap turntable and load it with an expensive cartridge. In the latter case, the vibrations and speed variations would cause the expensive cartridge to be incapable of picking up that exquisite sound. Besides, some good, inexpensive cartridges are available. And wouldn't you rather purchase a Grado ZTE+1 cartridge (which received a good rating from *Stereophile*) for $30, rather than a $5,000 Symphonic Line RG-8 gold?

SOMETHING COMPLETELY DIFFERENT

For the most part, every turntable is based on the principles that have already been covered in the preceding sections. To the best of my knowledge, the only other entirely different working turntable system is used by the ELP LT-1XA and LT1LA (Fig. 4-9). Unlike standard types, these turntables have no stylus or any other physical material to ride in the record grooves. Instead, laser beams scan the inside of the groove and "read" the depth and fluctuations in it. According to the manufacturer, the laser reads at a point in the groove higher than where the stylus tracked—thus, the playback of a worn record will sound better than if it were played with a standard turntable. Because a laser tracks the groove, the ELP turntables will even play broken and

Fig. 4-9 The ultimate in care for record playback: the ELP LT-1XA laser turntable. ELP

cracked records, as long as they are neatly glued or taped (with clear tape) back together.

Because the technology is so unique, you might guess that it is also expensive. At about $20,000 for one of these ELP turntables, you guessed right! The price is tremendously high for an individual. But considering the technology, the turntables could be well worth the money for rare record libraries, professional recording studios, and even some private record collectors.

ELECTRICAL SEPARATION

You might have spent thousands of dollars on a turntable with a totally "dead" base and tone arm, the motor is of the highest precision, the cartridge is the best you can find, and everything is sunk in concrete. Still, the sound is a bit off, but you can't locate the problem; you have covered everything. What's wrong? Aside from wasting too much money, the problem might be the power that the turntable is receiving from the outlet.

Although the ac power that passes through your house is typically rated at either 110 volts ac or 115 volts ac, the actual voltage in your house is probably different from that figure. When the power station is manufacturing electricity, it is passed to the power line at a very high voltage. It is then dropped to house voltage (240 and 115 volts ac) by very large step-down transformers. Depending on a number of circumstances, including the amount of power that is being drawn by a particular appliance, the line voltage in your house will vary. A good example of this is a number of years ago when an underground radio station from the Netherlands was operating with 10,000 watts of output power. The transmitter placed such a drain on the power grid that the lights of the apartment building where the station was located actually flickered in time with the music!

In this case, the line voltage in the building was greatly variable. Although the voltage in my house doesn't vary that much, it does vary significantly; the lights often dim, usually quickly, but sometimes for a few minutes. If the house voltage is so variable, what can be done to save the sound quality? Two solutions are available: Purchase a power-line conditioner or operate your entire stereo system from batteries and a power inverter.

The power-line conditioner filters the noise from the ac voltage and also regulates it. With a power-line conditioner, you can expect a steady voltage, not a hashy, variable mess. Audiophiles believe that the music "sounds better, more alive" with a good power-line conditioner. But beware; a typical model runs from $150 to more than $2,000.

ALIGNMENT

For optimum performance, turntables must be meticulously installed and aligned. This typically isn't too difficult. Just follow some common-sense laws of physics:

   * *Set the turntable in a low-vibration location.* This was covered earlier in the chapter.
   * *Set the turntable so that it is perfectly level.* Measure the table with a carpenter's level. Keep working until you get it exact.
   * *Use a cartridge-alignment tool whenever replacing the cartridge or purchasing a new turntable.* Incorrect cartridge alignment can cause the audio to be negatively altered, or it can even cause record damage.
   * *Use a test record to adjust the tone arm.* For example, some test records have a blank section so that you can adjust the antiskating control of the tone arm. If this control is not set properly, the stylus could ride hard against one side of the groove, altering the sound and damaging the record.

★ *Regularly change your cartridge.* If you regularly listen to records (nearly every day), replace the cartridge about every two years. A worn stylus can damage records.

THE BOTTOM LINE

This chapter has covered a number of different features in turntable construction. If you chose the best elements of a turntable described throughout the chapter, you would wind up with a system that cost thousands of dollars. Chances are that you either don't possess such money for a turntable or you are unwilling to spend it on just one piece of stereo equipment.

If you want to listen to cheap records or if superb audio quality isn't that important, just purchase a direct-drive turntable from one of the big names in home audio (such as Technics, Pioneer, Kenwood, Sanyo, etc.). They can't compete with the typical $2,000 turntable, but they are inexpensive and require little extra maintenance. Better yet, you might find one of these models used at a yard sale, in a classified ad, or free from a friend or relative. Just be sure that you pick a decent turntable—that AM/FM/phono/8-track stereo from 1977 is basically a piece of junk. Don't put your records on it! With a turntable like this, don't worry about purchasing a power-line conditioner, but it is worth your time to level and test the system for optimum output.

If you have your sights set a bit higher, shop around and read the magazines. Just beyond the direct-drive turntables manufactured by the major consumer electronics companies is a huge world of equipment that receives very little exposure. With a little research, you can discover some turntables that sound as good as other models that cost much more. For example, one turntable that cost $450 was rated much higher by *Stereophile* than another with a $1,000+ price tag. Companies such as Rotel, Thorens, and Rega all specialize in equipment that fills the gap between the consumer-special and megabuck turntables. Of course, be sure to research all of the models from a given company; very few companies sell 100% highly rated equipment. Most hatch a few dogs here and there. This grade of turntable is also common in the used high-end audio market because many audiophiles eventually move up to more expensive units. See Chapter 1 for more information on purchasing used equipment.

If you don't mind spending $10,000 or more for your audio system (and you are an audio fanatic), get the best-sounding system that you can afford. If you only notice a very slight difference in sound quality between a $1,500 turntable and a $3,200 turntable (and the sound damping, etc., features are similar), get the $1,500 model. Otherwise, you will just be tossing your money away. With this kind of money invested in a turntable, you should also purchase a power-line conditioner to optimize the record playback performance. (It is useful, but not essential, for the low high-end equipment.) If you are interested in a high-end audio system only because you always insist on the best for everything or because you want to impress people, then take a vacation and think about your goals and priorities in life.

CONCLUSION

Of all the pieces of audio equipment, the phonographic turntable is the most enigmatic. A spinning paradox, the machine is sonically superior, yet technologically inferior; it is electronic (by nature), yet it is sonically dependent on physics. Like the turntable, another piece of outdated but popular electronics is the electron tube. Amplifiers, including many electron tube models, are covered in Chapter 5.

5

AMPLIFIERS

Amplification might not appear to be a very exciting topic. After all, amplifiers are just "bigger components that make the sound louder," right? It's a bit more complicated than that, and precision is of key importance. Except for the stronger output, the signal exiting the amplifier should be as close as possible to the same as that which entered it.

If the previous "bigger components that make the sound louder" statement was entirely true, the issue of exact signal reproduction/amplification should not be difficult. However, as any signal is amplified and/or passes through more electrical stages, it is subject to being corrupted by various noise sources. For example, an electrically "dirty" amplifier power supply can add a hum to the audio; an inferior grade of components can alter the audio; or low-values of capacitors can cause distortion—especially at low frequencies. There are also several different ways in which a stereo signal can be powered, divided, and amplified. In addition, several different classes of amplification prove to be more useful for various applications.

PRINCIPLES OF AMPLIFICATION

This section is only intended to provide some basic background information behind how amplifiers work and nothing more. A number of books were written on the theories and design examples of amplifier and high-fidelity circuits several decades ago. These days, however, few people ever consider picking up a book and experimenting with building their own stereo equipment. So, rather than being a guide to the theory that could enable you to build an amplifier for your home, this section is intended to provide you with a few of the interesting theories that could help you to purchase an amplifier to suit your requirements and budget.

Years ago the key to amplification was the electron tube (also known as an audion or valve), which has since been virtually replaced by the transistor and the integrated circuit. Typical electron tubes are glass envelopes with anywhere from four to eight steel pins at the bottom. Early receiving tubes were approximately 8" (20.32 cm) high and 2" (5.08 cm) to 3" (7.62 cm) wide, but as the industry miniaturized, receiving tubes were reduced to about 1.5" (3.81 cm) high and 0.75" (1.9 cm) wide. The very early tubes looked something like a lightbulb, but later on, the appearance changed considerably (Fig. 5-1).

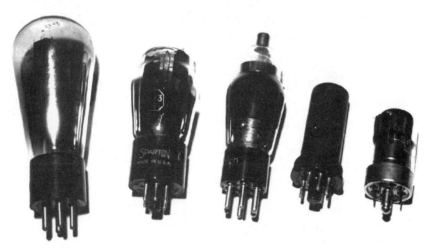

Fig. 5-1 A few electron tubes, from as early as the 1930s for the tube at the left.

The first real tube, the diode, was invented by Lee DeForest in the early 1900s. It was a breakthrough that helped propel radio into the beginning of its glory in the next decade. As radio technology progressed, other more complicated tubes, such as the triode, tetrode, and pentode were invented. These tubes were used for a variety of applications, such as regulating voltages and controlling the direction of signal flow, but they were essential as the key element in amplifiers.

Amplifier tubes could raise the input signal level many times. To generate the power to amplify the signal, the tube required high voltages at various pins. As a result, it could, in effect, change electricity into audio impulses.

Several decades ago, it was discovered that some elements with a high resistance to electricity could be used in applications to regulate and amplify signals. These elements, such as silicon, germanium, selenium, arsenic, etc., were known as semiconductors and were later used to make diodes and transistors. By the mid-1950s, these devices started to appear in consumer products instead of tubes. This sort of hybrid tube/ transistor equipment was often of strange design. The relatively tiny transistors were used to save space wherever possible, but transistors had not yet replaced tubes in every function. Also, transistors did not "behave" like tubes; they had different requirements, were sometimes less stable, and required different types of biasing. The end result was something like a patchwork quilt of new and old technologies.

By the early 1960s, not only were transistors becoming widespread, but transistors were being built into packages with several other parts like diodes, capacitors, resistors, etc. Before long, small circuits were being integrated into a small semiconductor chip, hence the name *integrated circuit (IC)*. Today, technology has miniaturized to the point where large circuits and even some power amplifier stages can be built into a single, small IC chip. Because of this miniaturization, a very powerful high-fidelity audio amplifier can be built into a very small case.

For that matter, because audio amplifiers can now be built into an integrated circuit, these circuits can be assimilated into small, light amplifiers or portable stereos.

One misconception is that tubes are a technological joke. This is not the case. Transistors replaced tubes, not so much because of superior performance, but rather because of the tiny amount of space and energy that transistors require. One difference in performance is that tubes slowly degrade with use; they gradually become weak. Transistors, on the other hand, either work or they don't. In optimum conditions, transistors will last forever. The problem is that semiconductors can easily be destroyed by such conditions as overvoltage. This is a severe dilemma, considering that a very small amount of electricity can cause catastrophic damage. Even the static electricity on your hands that is generated from walking across a carpeted room is powerful enough to destroy most modern semiconductors. (To combat these problems, people who work with semiconductors wear a grounded wrist strap, which will funnel all of the static electricity to ground.)

Because of the miniaturization and problems of catastrophic destruction, electronic equipment is increasingly looked upon as a "throwaway" commodity. When one tiny part is destroyed, a number of parts are likely to have been damaged or destroyed, as well. This is compounded by the fact that so many of the surface-mounted parts are tightly squeezed together that many electronics service centers simply replace the entire circuit board, rather than repair the equipment.

In years past, radios and audio equipment were built to withstand most any kind of physical or electrical abuse. Even after they were severely damaged, they could be repaired. This is not to say that older electronic equipment was better than that of today, just that some of it was more useful in different applications. And, yes, one of these applications is often in tube amplifiers. The different types of amplifiers are covered further toward the end of this chapter. For information on maintaining tube equipment, and finding and purchasing tubes, see Chapter 15.

CLASSES OF AUDIO AMPLIFICATION

The different classes of amplification are based on how much of the input signal cycle (to the amplifier) the output current passes through the amplifying device. This is an extremely complicated theoretical process. For the most part, you can assume that if the output current flows over a longer amount of the cycle (in degrees), the amplifier will be correspondingly less efficient, but it will be capable of producing low-distortion audio. Likewise, you can also assume that if the output current flows over a shorter amount of the cycle (in degrees), the amplifier will be correspondingly more efficient, but it will not be as capable of producing low-distortion audio.

Class A Class-A amplifiers operate in a manner that is similar to the first assumption in the previous paragraph; the class-A ampli-

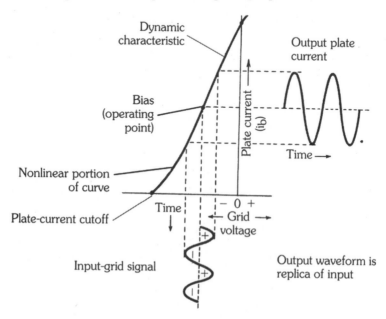

Fig. 5-2 The amplification waves for a class-A amplifier.

fier has a very clean output, (Fig. 5-2) but the efficiency is poor. In fact, most class-A amplifiers only operate at about 20% to 30% efficiency. That is, if the amplifier requires about 100 watts of input power from the line, it will only output about 20 to 30 watts of audio signal to the speakers. Because class-A amplifiers output such low powers, they can't compete, in terms of power, with other classes of amplifiers. But, because they have such a clean output, many of the class-A specialized tube amplifiers appeal to audiophiles. Because of the precision and quality materials, class-A amplifiers are often very expensive. For example, the Audio Note Ongaku amplifier is handmade (many of the components are even handmade!) and it contains 21 lbs. of silver; the final cost is $89,200!

Class B In class-B amplifiers, the output current of the amplifier only flows through 180 degrees of the input signal cycle (instead of the full 360 degrees, as in the case of class-A amplifiers). Theoretically, this class of amplifier is two times more efficient than a class-A amplifier, although in practice, those figures aren't

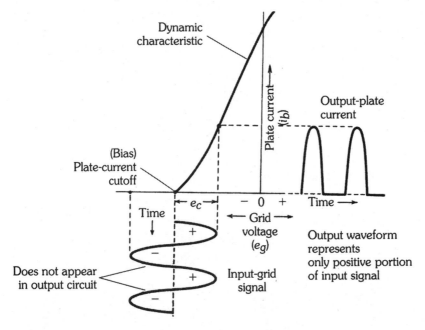

Fig. 5-3 The amplification waves for a class-B amplifier.

quite met (Fig. 5-3). With the great increase in efficiency, it appears that class-B amplification would be the ideal choice for audio amplifiers. But the problem is that class-B amplifiers take the other extreme and cause audio distortion. One attempt to avoid this problem is to run two output transistors in a push-pull configuration: each one applies current for an opposite half cycle. Operated in this manner, the push-pull class-B amplifier can be effective for power amplifier applications, but distortion still exists at the points where the transistors turn on and off. As a result, the amp designer will more than likely use a different class of modulation.

Class C In class-C amplifiers (Fig. 5-4), the output current of the amplifier only flows through approximately 120 degrees of the input signal cycle. As you can imagine, the class-C amplifier is even more efficient than the class-B amp, but it also adds that much more distortion to the audio. Class-C amplifiers can reach an efficiency level of up to about 75%, so they do have some obvious advantages, but they still aren't particularly useful in applications where high fidelity is a requirement.

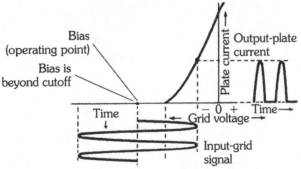

Fig. 5-4 The amplification waves for a class-C amplifier.

These are the three groupings of audio classifications. So, if class-A operations are too inefficient and class-B and C are too distorted, what is the alternative? Modify the existing classes.

Class AB Class-AB amplification is the last of the four original classifications, and it is considered to be a separate class, rather than merely a subset of a class. By developing the amplifier so that it is between the A and B classifications, it will be more efficient than a class-A amplifier yet will have better fidelity than a class-B amplifier (Fig. 5-5). Most high-fidelity audio power amplifiers use class-AB amplification.

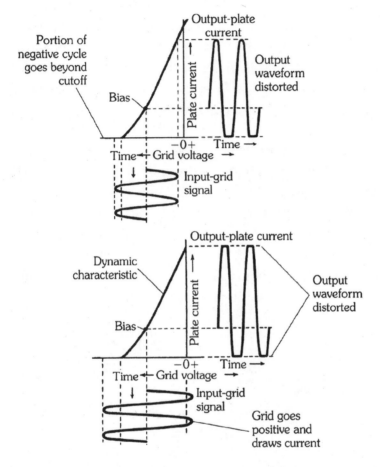

Fig. 5-5 The amplification waves for a class-AB amplifier.

Class D Class-D amplification is a new finding in the amplification frontier, which was thought to already have been thoroughly scouted. Instead of a traditionally designed analog amplifier, the class-D amplifier is digital. Instead of developing output current during the complete input wave or part of it, the class-D amplifier switches on and off—hundreds of thousands of times per second—in keeping with the digital data that is being output from a compact disc player. These amplifiers are amazing because the amplifier turns on and off so quickly that it is very efficient. As a result, the class-D amplifiers are much smaller than most other amplifiers that are in a comparable power class.

These classes of amplifiers are used for many different applications: Classes AB, B, and C are used frequently for a variety of transmitter circuits. Class AB is typically used for high-fidelity audio amplification, and class A is used for voltage amplification. Of course, these are only a few of the different applications for amplifier circuits.

As far as car stereo is concerned, class AB seems to be the most frequently used class of amplification. Class A is much more often used in home stereo systems—especially in costly high-end tube amplifiers (Fig. 5-6). Several of the MARS car stereo amplifiers can even be switched between class-A and class-AB amplification for precise sound control.

Fig. 5-6 A Luxman M-05 dual-mono class-A amplifier.

Interestingly enough, according to Joseph Carr (from his book *Mastering Solid-State Amplifiers*), nearly all of the lo-fi car radios in the 1950s and 1960s used class-A amplification. They were not built to handle large amounts of power, so efficiency was not a problem, and the alternators developed so much power that plenty was available. It's funny how the features and techniques used in supposedly antiquated equipment sometimes become sought after!

Once again, like the tube amplifiers, class-A amplifier operation is not going to rule the world. The creation of after-market class-D amplifiers could revolutionize the market with smaller, lower-cost, high-quality amplifiers. Because digital audio is prevalent, the market will likely turn in that direction. Even so, for decades into the future, a handful of audiophiles will choose class-A operation and be able to afford these amplifiers. Chances are that most of the other amplifiers will operate in class D, and the rest will be class AB.

FEEDBACK

Feedback occurs whenever a signal is fed from the output of a circuit back into the input of the same circuit. The most common type of feedback (or at least the type that most people immediately think of) is when the sound of an electric guitar returns (feeds back) through the pickups of the guitar. If the feedback is strong enough, the guitar will oscillate and a high-pitched sound will squeal through the speakers. This sort of feedback distorts the audio, and it can be either desirable or undesirable, depending on the situation. Now, however, most rock musicians seem to avoid feedback (by using amplifiers with built-in antifeedback circuits) because it is much harder to control than other types of distorting effects. Of course, the musicians who aren't afraid to lose control have more fun!

One of the important terms in the principles of amplifier operation is that of loop gain. Any amplifier has a particular amount of gain; that is, it will amplify a signal by any given factor. Unfortunately, every amplifier also has a certain amount of distortion and noise. These audio impurities are quite disruptive in the basic building-block amplifier. In order for any amplifier to be useful, the designer must implement any of several different distortion-reducing methods.

The most common method is to use feedback. However, the signal doesn't feed back through pickups to the point of oscillation (obviously). Instead, the signal is directed through the power stage, where it is amplified. Then, part of this signal is then fed back around the power amplifier stage and into the line. Instead of causing any feedback squeals, the two signals are combined and, for the most part, the noise and distortion are canceled out of the signal.

The catch when using feedback in amplifiers is that the desired audio signals are also canceled out to some extent (i.e., the final output of the amplifier is lower than original loop gain). And amplifier designers are stuck with the dilemma of choosing between more power or increased clarity. Of course, it isn't that easy, either. The designer must choose between different circuits and feedback situations to obtain an optimum power versus clarity ratio.

In the example from the previous paragraph, feedback was used to help eliminate the noise and distortion. This circuit didn't oscillate because it was using negative feedback. Positive feedback, on the other hand when used in this example, would have caused the traditional squeal over the speakers. The difference is that although negative feedback reduces the final output signal, positive feedback actually increases it. Positive feedback is more limited in its uses for hi-fi audio amplifiers.

Various amplifier ratings and specifications

Because you can't test every amplifier, you must rely, in part, on manufacturers' specifications when selecting equipment.

Power ratings

Power ratings for dedicated power amplifiers are the one piece of technical information that consumers base most of their purchases on. And, it makes sense. Sound quality is subjective. You just want to fill your home with good-quality sound (or perhaps blast music through the neighborhood). Either way, the major concern is the sound level from your speakers. You shouldn't have to worry about the sound quality because the amplifier merely boosts the sound level, right? Yes and no.

As covered earlier in this chapter, power amplifiers do color the sound that passes through them. Because most amplifiers are designed fairly well, choosing a fair-quality amplifier won't make your system sound bad, but it could make an otherwise great-sounding system merely sound good.

Most people think of amplifier wattages as being linear. When they buy, they get a 100-W amplifier because it is twice as loud as a 50-W amp, and so on. The problem is that sound levels are not based on a linear system of measurement. Instead, sound levels double, based on orders of magnitude. For example, if your amplifier is rated to output 100 W, adding another 100-W amplifier will not double the sound pressure level, which is normally measured in decibels (dB). Instead, to double the loudness of the system, you would need to replace the 100-W amplifier with a 1,000-W system of amplifiers!

As you can see by the difference between wattage and actual sound levels, you will not normally notice the difference between a few watts here or there if the systems are rated for over 25 watts per channel. More than likely, you will notice more of a difference in loudness just from the different means that manufacturers use to determine the amplifier power ratings. To inject some advice at this point, it is better to purchase a high-quality medium-power amplifier than it is to buy a cheaply built high-powered amplifier. Chances are that the audio will be a bit better on the better amplifier, it will have more features, and it might be rated for less power than it is actually capable of (although the "high-powered" amp might actually be capable of less power than it is rated for).

Depending on how the equipment is rated, the amplifier could sound differently than you would expect for the level at which it is rated. For example, most audio amplification stages will distort at an increasingly higher level if they are driven beyond a certain point. For the 2 ×100-watt amplifier that you just picked up, do you know what the percentage of distortion was when those 100 watts per channel were measured? Perhaps it was 0.01% or perhaps it was 10%. The difference is incredible. If the distortion was only 0.01%, it should still sound good above 100 watts per channel. But if the distortion was 10% at 100 watts out, the actual usable power might be more like 50 watts per channel, but considering the level, it would probably be useless at any output power. That amount of distortion is just too great, even for listening by people who aren't interested in good audio.

Thus, the rated amount of power in an amplifier depends, in part, on how much distortion the designers believe is allowable. Not only is the maximum amount of allowable signal distortion subjective, but it is not based on a standard amount. As a result, some amplifiers perform as the examples in the previous paragraph: one 2 x 100-W amplifier might be capable of well over 100 watts per channel, although another 2 x 100-W amplifier might actually only be capable of 50 "clean" watts per channel. The first time I noted this difference was when I went shopping for a stereo tuner/amplifier when I was in high school. I had to choose from some major brands with many extra features and basic offerings from a higher-end brand. The salesman showed me how the 50-W per channel amplifier actually didn't sound as loud as the conservatively rated 35-W per channel amplifier, in part because the former was much noisier and it began to distort after a certain volume. Incidentally, this story isn't just based on good salesmanship; the amplifier that he was pushing was a cheaper model than the one that he was telling me to avoid.

SHOPPING FOR AMPLIFIER SPECIFICATIONS

So, how do you know what to expect from an amplifier? The last thing you want to do is search for an amplifier that fits your needs for power, only to find that it can't deliver the power that you purchased it for. As you might suspect, these power ratings can be used to deceive consumers, and unfortunately, some companies seem to purposefully mislead their customers. Very few people have the resources to be able to test and rate the amplifiers on the market for power ratings and sound quality.

Average output power is only one way that amplifier power can be rated. The ratings covered so far have generally been for average output power. Amplifiers, as well as most other electronic devices, can also be rated in average input power, peak input power, peak output power, and several other means. Input power is the amount of power that is consumed by an amplifier. Depending on the class of amplifier that is used, the amount of output will vary considerably from the amount of power that is input to an amplifier. As a result, *input power* is a nebulous term. *Input power* is not frequently used to describe audio amplifiers, but it is a common manufacturers' specification for amateur radio transmitters and amplifiers. Breaking this term down further, *peak input power* is the maximum input power that the amplifier can safely handle, and a*verage input power* is the average amount of power that is used by an amplifier during its operation. Likewise, *average output power* is the average amount of power that an amplifier outputs to the speakers during its operation and the *peak output power* is the maximum power that the amplifier can safely deliver to the speakers. Because the only rating that matters is one based on what you hear, only average output power is useful for determining how much power you need for your system. Peak and average input power are both important for determining whether your electrical system can tolerate the requirements of your amplifier.. *Peak output power* is used to determine what power ratings your speakers must have so that they won't blow on a peak.

NOISE

One problem that occurs during the process of amplification is *noise*. This term can easily be confused with *distortion*, which occurs because the amplifier alters the signal as it amplifies it. Noise is sometimes called *line noise* because it is a low-level sound, usually a hiss or maybe a hum, that is present in the source and is amplified by the amplifier. Also, some line noise develops in the amplifier because no electronic circuits are perfect, although digital audio certainly improves upon this problem. You can check various amplifiers in this regard. Just find the rated specifications for the signal-to-noise (S/N) ratio of the particular amp.

You should look for the highest S/N ratio possible because that is the ratio of actual amplified signal to the amount of noise that is developed in the amplifier. The signal-to-noise ratio is rated in decibels (dB), so it is quite easy to determine which amplifier has the best ratio; just look for the highest numbers!

The only problem with this rating is that the rating must have a specific reference or the figure is worthless. The typical reference signal for amplifiers is one watt. If any figure above one watt is used, the number of dB above one watt must be subtracted from the listed S/N figure to find the standard S/N ratio. If you are worried about signal-to-noise ratios, check the equipment box for the manufacturer's information, look for reviews in the audio magazines, or call the manufacturer.

DISTORTION

One of the figures that you will commonly see listed in the amplifier specifications is *THD (total harmonic distortion)*. Any amplifier will cause some distortion to the audio signal. In the case of THD, the amplifier distorts the audio by producing harmonics of the input signal. These harmonics are not "clean" representations of the audio; rather, they make it sound more ragged.

Like the signal-to-noise ratio, the THD depends upon a reference (in this case, a reference power and a reference bandwidth) or the figure is virtually useless. The standard range that THD is measured in stretches across the entire audio frequency from 20 Hz to 20 kHz. Most amplifiers will have a higher or lower THD at different frequencies, so if the THD is only rated for one particular frequency or for one portion of the entire audio frequency range, beware. The THD will most certainly be higher for other frequencies inside of the audio range because any manufacturer who lists in this manner would pick a low THD in order to get a better figure.

AMPLIFIER DESIGN CONFIGURATIONS

Well-designed system configurations can make a difference in the sound quality and the size or the number of the required amplifiers.

MONO OR STEREO

You might be surprised that anyone would consider using a mono (single channel) amplifier. In this day and age, the only people who listen to music in mono are still singing along with Mitch Miller. But alas, mono amplifiers are yet another one of those technological throwbacks to an age where the boys wore coonskin hats and the girls thought that poodle skirts were all the rage.

However, unlike like those days long past, mono amplifiers are not normally used alone. For that matter, the only time a mono amplifier will be useful is when it is used in conjunction with other amplifiers.

LEFT OR RIGHT

The one popular use for mono amplifiers is a crossover method from audiophiles who have used it in their home systems for decades. One option when picking out an audio system is to buy a single stereo amplifier that might have trouble keeping the left and right audio channels separate. Although some people might not notice the separation of left and right channels, the audiophile will notice the difference (for example, if the cello is coming from 30 degrees to the right instead of from 45 degrees). This difference in stereo separation is disconcerting to someone who expects to hear everything exactly as it was recorded.

The audiophilic option to tolerating less-than-precise stereo separation is to use one mono amplifier to boost all signals from the left channel and another mono amplifier to boost all signals from the left channel (Figs. 5-7 and 5-8). In this configuration, the

Fig. 5-7 A pair of Mark Levinson® №33H power amplifiers. Madrigal Audio Laboratories, Inc.

signals will probably be cleaner than with one stereo amplifier. Also, with the separate power supplies, PC boards, and enclosures, the system would be operating well below its rated limits.

Center channel

The other use of a mono amplifier is to provide a center audio channel to "beef up" the sound. The center channel is generally a nonphysical entity—an image that is created by having audio reproduced in both the right and left channels. Important infor-

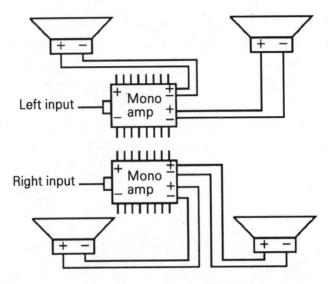

Fig. 5-8 Exacting stereo audio from two mono amplifiers.

mation, such as the vocals, are contained on the imaginary center channel. In some cases, the stereo effect of a system will be so prominent that the center channel image will be weak. In order to develop a strong center, where one previously was not present, some people install a physical center channel (Fig. 5-9). This

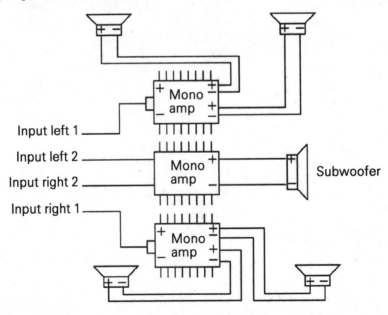

Fig. 5-9 Using an extra mono amplifier to power a subwoofer.

technique can be effective to boost a weak center channel, but if it is not tweaked properly, it could cause some of the stereo effect to disappear. So, if installed improperly, the center-channel technique can degrade the audio quality more than it would boost it. Center-channel amplifiers are rarely used because, instead, the speakers can just be moved to improve the stereo imaging. Unfortunately, using center-channel amplifiers and speakers will ruin the channel separation and imaging. Avoid it.

MONO SUBWOOFERS

Mono amplifiers are especially effective when they drive woofer or subwoofer systems. The wavelength of low frequencies is longer than the entire length of a typical room (e.g., the wavelength of a sound wave at 50 Hz is 22' or 6.7 m). As a result, the sound pressure wave is virtually the same at all distances, compared to the wavelength (22' or 6.7 m, as was given in the previous example). For that reason, stereo subwoofers within most rooms are virtually useless. The benefit of the "directionless" bass is that you can install a subwoofer most anywhere in the room and not have to worry about the sound noticeably emanating from one particular location. Considering the size of most subwoofers and their enclosures, this is a great relief!

For lower-powered systems, you can often bridge a subwoofer across the negative side of one of the stereo output channels to the positive side of the other output channel. Check your amplifier or the one that you are considering purchasing to see if it is possible to bridge it in this manner. If you can't do it, then a dedicated subwoofer amplifier might be in order. Even so, the high-powered systems require separate subwoofer amplifiers because bridging the subwoofers across the outputs of the other amplifiers probably won't drive the subwoofers properly. Another downside to bridging subwoofers across the outputs of the stereo amplifier is that you lose the volume control on the bass. With a dedicated woofer or subwoofer amplifier, you can tweak the low frequencies to the levels that sound great to you.

AMPLIFIERS

Some dedicated mono amplifiers on the market are made specifically for subwoofers, so they are more efficient at amplifying the low (and not the other) frequencies. If you need more power for your woofer or subwoofer, then a step into the post-Mickey Mantle days of mono amps might be right for you.

POWER SUPPLIES

The words "power supply" can mean several different things to different people. For home power, the supply would be related to the wall sockets, the power lines, or the power generators that are operated by the local utility company. A parallel to this would be the alternator and the battery in a vehicle.

The power supply of any piece of electronic equipment is a device that regulates and supplies the proper voltages to the various circuits that are contained within. This definition of a power supply is often contrary to what the average nonelectronics-minded person thinks of. Before you start thinking of whoever came up with this term as being a clueless dweeb, think of the power supply for any given piece of electronic equipment as being the input stage or the stage that supplies power to the rest of the amplifier.

The power supply is very important because if it is built to provide less power than the amplifier is capable of producing, it will be easy to overdrive it. When an amplifier is clipping (the top of the power waveforms are snipped off), it is being overdriven, whether it has reached its specified output or not. Clipping is not just a problem because the condition distorts the audio, but because it can easily blow out the speakers. The chopped-off waveforms can cause the voice coils in the speakers to overheat and subsequently be destroyed. The only solutions to the problem are to either listen to music well within the means of the amplifier (which might mean listening at lower volumes than you would like) or buying another amplifier that you could use in conjunction with the first one.

STEREO SEPARATION

Another problem than can occur with the power supplies in amplifiers is interaction between the power and audio stages. Sometimes the audio will draw power from the power supply, but instead of supplying a steady energy source, the voltage will fluctuate. The voltage fluctuates along with the audio signal, and it makes a sort of duplicate of the audio signal. This duplicate voltage signal can interfere with the two real audio signals. Of course, there is only one source of power; so, when the audio signal modulates the voltage, and it in turn interferes with the audio, the stereo separation will become less prominent. In one magazine article that I read a few years ago (I haven't been able to locate it since first reading it), the audio experts involved isolated the dc power in an amplifier (that was in operation), and they were actually able to demodulate it to the point where the songs were recognizable!

The standard for rating stereo separation is in dB at 1,000 Hz, which is within the midrange and where the difference is most important. In some of the recently rated amplifiers, the stereo separation has ranged from 33 to 78 dB—quite a difference. Even so, stereo separation, although helpful in establishing a great sound, is not nearly as important as some figures (such as THD) and some of the features (such as built-in receiver, A/ V inputs, etc.).

Still, stereo separation is a factor for audiophiles to consider. One of the best ways to clean up the problems with separation between the left and right channels is to use two (or more) mono amplifiers—one (or more) for each channel. Another solution is to purchase one of the high-end amplifiers that solved the problem by building in either a separate power supply for each channel or building two separate mono amplifiers into the same cabinet to achieve virtually the same results.

AMPLIFIERS ON THE MARKET

The most commonly purchased type of stereo amplifier on the market is the receiver/amplifier, often just called a *receiver*. The receiver/amplifier is a stereo amplifier that also contains an AM/FM receiver, amplifier controls, limited equalization (bass and treble), and inputs for many other pieces of audio equipment (Fig. 5-10). A maxi version of the receiver/amplifier is the A/V receiver (Fig. 5-11).

Fig. 5-10 The receiver/amplifier is the keystone of most stereo systems: The Kenwood KR-V990D. Kenwood

The power amplifier does nothing but amplify signals. It has no controls, except an on/off switch and, in some cases, a volume knob. Because it has no controls or inputs for all sorts of other audio equipment, you need to use a preamplifier or passive control to use the system. And you still need an AM/FM receiver (unless you purchase one that's built into the preamp).

The last variation is somewhere between the previous two categories. It contains all of the advantages of the receiver/amplifier, without the receiver. Essentially, these are a combination of a power amplifier and preamplifier. This piece of equipment is typically called an amplifier, which can be confused with the other types of amplifiers.

116

Fig. 5-11 The Kenwood Stage 3 A/V amplifier system: The KC-Z1 controller with visual touch panel (left) and the KM-Z1 six-channel amplifier. Kenwood

AMPLIFIERS

As mentioned in the previous paragraph, the piece of equipment that is typically called "an amplifier" is essentially a combination of a power amplifier and a preamplifier. Of course, the power amplifier aspect of the equipment means that it will increase the amplitude of a signal (make it louder). As mentioned earlier in this chapter, a good amplifier will do no more than very slightly alter the information of the incoming signal.

Aside from the amplifying job that amplifiers perform, they also act as a control center for the entire stereo system. They contain a number of jacks so that different audio sources can be fed in, and you can push a button to choose which will be pumped out through your speakers. In this way, the amplifier acts like a preamplifier, which is used as a control center in conjunction with power amplifiers. The typical amplifier contains inputs for a cassette deck, VCR or CD player, and turntable. The turntable inputs are interesting because they must be preamplified so that you can hear them. The signal level is so tiny that the turntable output must be connected to a special "Phono" input on an amplifier or receiver; if you are an audiophile using a power amplifier and a passive control box, the turntable must also have a special preamplifier.

Some amplifiers feature a few more inputs, such as two or three marked "AUX." The AUX inputs are typical line-level inputs that will work fine for amplifying signals from receivers, open-reel tape decks, additional cassette decks, etc. Most amplifiers aren't loaded down with inputs because they are typically more directed toward the audiophile, who is looking for simplicity, not a billion features and buttons (Fig. 5-12). These days, the feature-laden amplifiers are all A/V receivers, which contain audio inputs for VCRs, DVDs, and all of your audio equipment.

FEATURES

Aside from the typical amplifying and switch box features of amplifiers, they also contain a few features that are common to preamplifiers and receiver/amplifiers as well.

Volume The volume controls the amplitude (how loud or quiet the sound is) of the signals being output from your amplifier. The volume control is a potentiometer (variable resistor) that is typically a rotary unit (knob), although some amplifiers use slider controls or pushbuttons (on remote-control A/V receivers).

Bass The bass control is a simple equalization knob or switch. It can boost or weaken the bass frequencies that are being amplified by the amplifier.

Treble The treble control is a simple equalization knob or switch. It can boost or weaken the treble frequencies that are being amplified by the amplifier.

Balance The balance control is a knob or slider control that allows you to shift the sound to different speakers (left or right). Typically, the balance is a linear control, so that you can shift the appropriate amount of sound to the left speakers and right speakers. In a perfect system, a balance knob would be unnecessary, but it is required because speakers cannot always be placed so that each will perfectly output sound to where you are sitting.

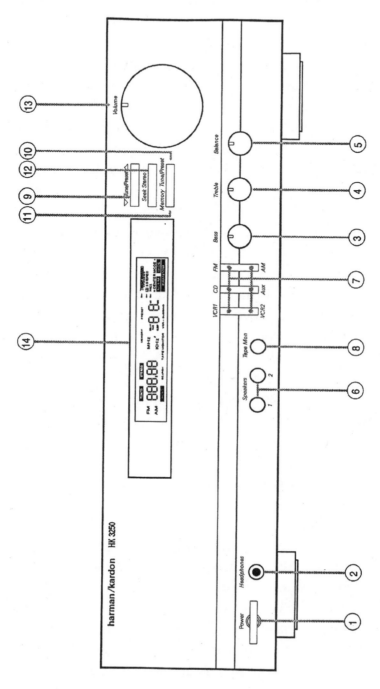

Fig. 5-12 Front-panel controls for the Harman/Kardon HK3250 receiver: (1) power button, (2) headphone jack, (3) bass control, (4) treble control, (5) balance control, (6) speaker switches, (7) input function buttons, (8) tape monitor button, (9) tune/preset button, (10) tune/preset scan buttons, (11) station memory button, (12) seek stereo button, (13) volume control, (14) display window. Harman/Kardon

Loud function The loud (or loudness) function is fairly typical on home and mobile audio systems. The loud button functions as a bass and midrange booster; press it and the music punches through with a much thicker sound. Human hearing has a much higher threshold for audibility at the lower frequencies. As a result, if you normally listen to music at low volumes, it will sound thinner than if you rocked the neighborhood. To compensate, manufacturers added this circuit so that music could be faithfully reproduced, whether or not the volume was high or low. Because of its purpose, the loud function should not be used if the volume is already cranked up.

Stereo/mono The stereo/mono switch controls whether the system output is the same or different between the left and right channels. The major typical application for this function is when listening to radio stations. If the signal is fairly strong, but not solid, it will sound very hissy, occasionally breaking up. To remedy the situation, just switch over to mono and the signal will be much clearer, although not as realistic.

Speakers The "speaker" controls on an amplifier are typically a pair of pushbuttons or switches that allow you to use two different speakers, independently or simultaneously. Either you can use two different speakers in tandem for each channel, use different speakers when listening to different types of music, or place a pair of speakers in front and behind you for a pseudosurround sound.

GUI Over the past decade, computer technology has emerged in many different products. As the lines between some audio components have melted into those of the video sector, the use of computer technology in audio components has risen. The most common is a *GUI (graphical user interface),* which is also known by some other names, such as *on-screen control,* etc. With many of these systems, the user-control menus are displayed on the TV and you can input commands via the remote control. In the case of the Kenwood Stage 3 controller, the display is an LCD screen that is located in the remote control (Fig. 5-13).

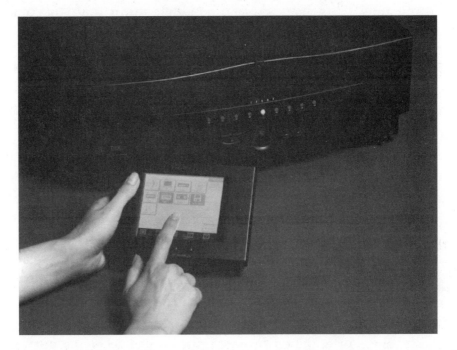

Fig. 5-13 A bit different than standard GUI, the Kenwood Stage 3 controller uses a touch screen built into the remote control, as opposed to control via an on-screen menu. Kenwood

RECEIVERS

In the topsy-turvy world of audio terminology, a receiver typically means two different things. The most common piece of stereo equipment that is called a receiver is actually an AM/FM receiver/amplifier combination that is contained in a single box. A typical receiver tunes the entire AM (medium wave) band from 530 to 1710 kHz and the FM (VHF) band from 88 to 108 MHz. It will also contain typical amplifying circuitry (see the following sections for a list of some of the more-common features and their functions) that will output anywhere from 25 to 100 watts.

I don't really know how the trend to combine amplifiers and receivers started. However, I would assume that it began because in the 1930s and 1940s, most people only had one piece of audio equipment: a tabletop or console radio. Most of the console radios featured a big 12-inch speaker and enough power that you could crank it up. Some of the deluxe consoles even contained pull-out or slide-out turntables. Those that didn't often contained phono jacks so that you could patch in your turntable, if you had one. By the 1950s, some of the radios also included an AUX jack so that you could play audio from your open-reel tape deck. This tradition has been passed down to the present age of digital audio. And why change it? Receivers and amplifiers (using solid-state components, not tubes) are less likely to break down than any other parts of the stereo system, so they make a perfect match. Combining an amplifier with a relatively high-maintenance piece of equipment, such as a cassette deck, would only make for higher repair bills.

Dedicated receivers are available. They run the gamut from low-cost models that seem to be tossed in a component system as an afterthought to systems for the professional listener. For most radio listeners or audio enthusiasts, the typical receiving portion of a receiver/amplifier is just fine. If audiophiles want to enjoy high-fidelity music, they will listen to records or CDs. People who just want to listen to the radio typically don't mind if the signal-to-noise ratio is a bit lower than it could be.

However, for a minority of listeners who typically live in rural areas and desperately try to hear stations with different formats, the receiving portion of the system is important. As is the case when choosing any other piece of stereo equipment, it's a great idea to check out the equipment specifications. Unfortunately, the specification types vary significantly from receiver to receiver. For example, "Spurious Response Ratio," "Image Response Ratio," "IF Response Ratio," "AM Suppression Ratio," "IF Rejection," "Image Rejection," and "AM Rejection" all relate to how the receiver responds to signals.

Image rejection is the signal strength in dB of a signal on a different frequency that will be rejected. For example, you might have a powerful local broadcaster on 1010 kHz; a receiver with great image rejection will prevent false signals from this station (images) from appearing all over the radio dial. These terms are all very important (although they mean slightly different things) because nearly everyone has a local station, and you don't want to have that one signal appearing all over the band. Although all of these figures aren't equivalent, they all have one thing in common: the higher the number (in dB), the better.

Sensitivity is the capability of a receiver to pull in weak signals. If the receiver has poor sensitivity, weak stations would not be audible on this receiver (strong signals will still be audible on a set with poor sensitivity). Sensitivity is a very important specification for those who live in rural areas and are desperately trying to hear stations from far away. Sensitivity is measured in microvolts, which might seem like a complicated measurement. But there's an easy way to check the sensitivity; the lower the number, the better.

Selectivity is the capability of a receiver to choose between different radio signals. For example, a very strong local station might be on 1,010 kHz, and a weak signal might be on 1,020 kHz. On a receiver with poor selectivity, the station on 1010 kHz would interfere with the station on 1,020 kHz. A receiver with excellent selectivity will have no problem separating the signals.

The specification list for a receiver will also typically list a few specs common to other pieces of audio equipment. Signal-to-noise ratio, distortion, and stereo separation are listed for nearly all receivers. As is always the case, be sure that the specifications are based on the same operating conditions (for example, distortion and stereo separation are both typically rated at 1 kHz; if they were rated at 500 Hz or 3 kHz, the difference could be significant).

RADIO AND AUDIO TECHNOLOGY

Although many people don't understand all of the basic theories behind AM (MW) and FM (VHF) broadcast radio, that's okay for these purposes. Understanding the differences in modulation techniques between these two mediums won't do you a bit of good when tuning in a station on your stereo system. Although the broadcast basics are not covered within this book, some of the other, newer technologies and options are included. A million and one different stereo features are currently available, in part because a few of the high-end components overlap their features into other types of audio components, such as signal processors, equalizers, and amplifiers. Most of these functions are not listed here because they are not common in most receivers and because they are covered in other areas of this book.

RDS

RDS (Radio Display System) is a system where radio data can be received on a standard radio. Instead of merely transmitting music and talk, some FM radio stations are beginning to broadcast data as well. Even though this signal is being transmitted along with the broadcast material, you can't hear it. Instead, this data can be received by your radio and the computer technology inside is capable of deciphering and displaying this information. None of this information is very complicated (they aren't transmitting books, line by line), but it could be extremely useful. The various RDS modes, as configured by Denon, are as follows.

This amazing technology is more than just glimmering on the edge of the horizon; it's here right now. RDS has been especially popular in car head units, where it is especially handy to see what station you've tuned in. Eventually, the plan is that stations will send traffic and other information. Unfortunately, many of the home stereo components do not contain RDS displays because, I suppose, the extra cost hasn't yet justified the demand. Still, some manufacturers are including RDS in their receivers, but it hasn't been the runaway hit that was expected.

Program Service Name (PS) The call sign or slogan of the station that the radio is currently receiving is displayed.

Program Type (PT) The different radio formats are broken down into 31 different categories. The broadcasting station will broadcast its format, which is then displayed on the RDS head unit. This is useful because you can pick a format and the receiver will automatically tune a station that is broadcasting that particular format.

Alternative Frequencies (AF) If the station that you are listening to becomes weak and the receiver is set in the AF mode, it will automatically tune the radio to another station with the same format that has a stronger signal.

Program Identification (PI) Members of various radio networks have a PI code, which identifies them as being a part of that particular network. If you store several radio stations in the memories, you can use the PI mode to automatically tune to another station from the same network. This is especially useful in car head units, where stations fade out as you drive out of their coverage area.

Traffic Program Identification (TP) If the TP symbol appears on the display, then that particular radio station also provides RDS traffic data.

Traffic Announcement Identification (TA) With the receiver set to the TA mode, the radio will automatically tune to a station that is about to broadcast traffic information. If you are listening to a cassette or a compact disc, the receiver will automatically preempt it to play the traffic update.

Clock Time (CT) Rather than set your own clock, the clock can be controlled by the time that is transmitted by the radio stations, for more precision.

With most high technologies, few people consider the potential damage that it could cause. Although RDS systems are both amazing and handy, I reserve a few fears about some of the side effects that might occur as a result of their use. For example, if someone wants to hear jazz, the AF function of RDS will allow them to listen to a jazz radio station without touching the radio, no matter where they go in the United States, and at least a few other parts of the world. That's convenient, but not particularly enlightening. I'm no country music fan to say the least, but most of what I know about the genre has been from tuning through the radio and from being forced to listen to it for hours at a time while working a construction job. Listening to other styles is interesting and enlightening. Other fears that I have with this system are that radio stations will feel forced to adhere to a specific popular format, and in turn, further homogenize the overall sound of American broadcasting, which is already quite bland. And what if radio stations start programming the names of their advertisers to appear on your display, along with their callsign or slogan? We've stomached so much commercialization already.

But, despite the growing number of stations airing RDS information, the question seems to be not whether it will further damage radio, but whether it will survive.

Automatic radio muting and control circuits Some companies have added various automatic radio muting and control circuits to alter the reception quality of broadcast stations. With some radios, if you tune off of a station or if two stations are overlapping each other, the radio will play static or interference. In other cases, receivers have extra circuitry so that if a weak signal or no signal is detected, this circuitry will automatically reduce the volume of the radio so that you aren't blasted with static. A more basic feature is the automatic stereo/mono switch, which some receivers have. When a stereo signal is received that is above a certain level, it is put out in stereo; if it is below that predetermined level, it will be heard in mono so that the extra noise will not be heard. In another system, the higher frequencies are gradually rolled off as the radio signal strength decreases so that the interference will be less noticeable.

LCD display Although it isn't a function in and of itself, the LCD (Liquid Crystal Display) is necessary for all of the feature-laden receivers and receiver/amplifiers. The LCD can be built for much more specific and complicated applications than LED (Light-Emitting Diode) displays can. As a result, for complicated head units such as those with RDS and DCC capabilities, LCD displays are necessary.

Preset memories One of the most convenient applications of computer technology that has been applied to radio is preset memories. In the analog era, radios had several pushbuttons. With some work, you could program each one to move the dial to a certain point whenever you pushed the button. Now, you can quickly program a number of different buttons, and each will immediately put you on the exact frequency. (The old mechanical pushbuttons often varied in frequency each time you pressed the button.)

Scanning With the scanning function, the head unit will tune through the radio band that you have selected and it will allow you to hear the different strong radio stations. Like many of the features here, the scanning function varies a bit among different manufacturers. In some cases, it finds a strong station, stops for a brief amount of time to allow you to hear what's on, and then it moves on. When it hits the end of that particular broadcast band, it stops. In other cases, the scanning function will stop every time that it finds a strong station. It will only be reactivated if you press the button again.

Remote control Remote control is one of the highlights of A/V receivers. With it, you can control nearly all aspects of your audio system without even having to get out of your chair. Of course, for the terminally lethargic, remote control can be more damaging than healthful.

Local/DX control The local/DX control can attenuate the radio signals that are received. If you want to hear local stations without the problem of overloading the front end of the radio and having some radio stations splatter across the band, then you should set the control to the local position for attenuation. If the signal is weak, then switch it to the DX position and the signals will no longer be attenuated.

Tuner call With tuner call, the radio will automatically begin playing on the radio frequency that you were last tuned to. This feature is handy if you enjoy listening to cassettes and flipping back to hear what is on the radio.

POWER AMPLIFIERS

If you read the stereo magazines, you will notice that a currently large number of small American companies build high-end home-stereo tube amplifiers. Transistors and integrated circuits were all the rage throughout the 1960s and 1970s. But by the 1980s, some people became vocal about how the old tube amplifiers sounded better than the solid-state ones. And some musicians prefer the sound of tube guitar amplifiers, too. As a result of this publicity and some comparisons, audio enthusiasts began to pull out their old audiophile amplifiers manufactured by companies such as McIntosh, Leak, Marantz, Western Electric, etc. And dozens of tiny companies began producing handmade audiophile-quality tube amplifiers. Many people seem to think that tube equipment sounds "warmer." Whether it does or not, it certainly does feel warmer!

Although many tube amplifiers have appeared in the marketplace, I do not believe that they will displace the many different popular-selling models of amplifiers that use semiconductors. Nearly all of these power amplifiers are now using metal-oxide-semiconductor field-effect transistors (MOSFETs) to amplify the input signals. MOSFETs have been an amazing electronics breakthrough because they are inexpensive, can be used in high-power applications, and are well known for their ability to amplify a signal to a much higher level. Also, some professionals and hobbyists say that MOSFETs are much more stable than transistors and that their behavior in circuits is much closer to that of tubes.

But even though the tube amplifiers might not displace the popular receiver/amplifiers and A/V receivers, they certainly have made an impact on the high-end amplifier market. These days, nearly all of the large audio companies only manufacture solid-state receiver/amplifiers and A/V receivers, not power amplifiers. However, most modern power amplifiers are vacuum tube models that are manufactured by relatively small companies. Except for Luxman, none of the larger companies produces tube amplifiers. For that matter, Harman/Kardon is one of the only consumer-oriented companies that even produces solid-state power amplifiers. As a result, audio entrepreneurs have flowed en masse to the high-end power amplifier market. Now, hundreds of different companies are making high-end tube power amplifiers (Fig. 5-14)

Tube power amplifiers have a real advantage for the small companies and audiophiles over receiver/amplifiers. Audiophiles want the best in sound and they want to finely control each aspect of the process. Most people would rather not pay extra for the inconvenience of having both a power amplifier and a preamplifier. The major companies would have a tough time turning a profit on such a low-production area, so the companies that fill the void are able to concentrate on quality.

PREAMPLIFIERS

Preamplifiers, as mentioned in the Amplifiers section in this chapter, are control boxes that boost the signal levels so that the power amplifiers can appropriately amplify them (Fig. 5-15). All amplifiers require a signal of a particular strength to be able to amplify them to the peak output level. If the signals are too

Fig. 5-14 Big, black, and beautiful: A high-end tube power amplifier (top) and separate power supply (bottom) from VTL. VTL

strong, such as if you ran the output from one amplifier into the input of another, chances are that you will damage it. If the level is too weak, such as if you ran a turntable output into the line input of an amplifier, the audio would be weak and hissy (the background noise would be highly amplified). Power amplifiers require a higher signal level to drive them than the standard amplifiers do (because the preamplifier stages are already integrated into this equipment).

Fig. 5-15 A combination preamplifier and amplifier: the Yamaha CX-2 preamplifier (top) and the MX-2 power amplifier (bottom). Yamaha

Like the other amplifiers, an ideal preamplifier should have no net effect on the sound of the music. It should come out sounding exactly like the tape, record, or CD recording. Unfortunately, every amplifier at least lightly alters the signal as it amplifies and passes it to the amplifier.

SHOPPING

With three different general types of amplifying systems and literally hundreds of different amplifiers on the market, the question is not so much what to choose, but where to start narrowing down your choices. Fortunately, amplifiers don't perform too many different tasks, and their primary function is to not be noticed, not to do anything spectacular. This makes a formidable task much easier.

The easiest way to start narrowing your options is to look at the three different groups of amplifiers. Now, determine what you want the amplifier to accomplish and take a look at your budget. If convenience and integration with your audio and video system are most important to you, then you're best off buying an A/V receiver. If the budget is a concern, go for a receiver/amplifier or perhaps an A/V receiver. If high fidelity is most important, opt for the preamplifier and power amplifier combination.

The best way to find the amplifier of your dreams should be to go visit the local stereo shop. Unfortunately, most stereo dealers sell only a few different brands of mass-produced and marketed equipment. As mentioned earlier in this chapter, expensive amplifiers produced by niche manufacturers are only available via high-end shops and mail-order companies. So, if you visit the typical stereo and appliance shop, it probably won't carry any power amplifiers, just receiver/amplifiers and A/V amplifiers. If this is the type of equipment you're looking for, you're in luck. These stores often sell at heavy discounts, and floor and discontinued models can regularly be found at great prices.

If the amplifier of your dreams is a power amplifier not manufactured by one of the 5 or 10 companies represented at your local stereo shop, then you might be in for some researching. The best places to find power amplifiers and preamplifiers are in specialty high-end audio shops and via mail-order companies on the Internet or in ads in *Stereophile*. If you are serious about such a system, then you should definitely go visit a high-end audio store. You just can't expect to purchase equipment for thousands of dollars, sight unseen.

No matter if you are searching for an A/V receiver, a receiver/amplifier, or a power amplifier, you should always test each piece of equipment that you are interested in. Most stereo shops are organized so that you can not only listen to all of the equipment, but you can quickly test different amplifiers in the same system. All you need to do is switch or patch in amplifier #1, then switch or patch in amplifier #2. Of course, be sure that the source and speakers are the same during the tests or your results will be worthless. Even if you aren't an audio fanatic, you will notice differences in sound between amplifiers. At this point, pick whatever sounds the best and has the features that you need at a price that you can afford.

You might decide that you want an audiophile-grade amplifier, yet you can't afford one. You have two options: buy a used model or improvise until you can afford what you want. Notice that today's high-end amplifiers are simple tube designs. Many of these designs are simple derivatives of tube amplifiers from 40 years ago. Although some of this equipment has been rounded up by antique audio collectors, a number of high-end amplifiers still turn up at hamfests, yard sales, auctions, and in classified ads. These classic pieces are typically sold for much less than an equivalent modern tube amplifier. However, unless the amplifier is being sold by a dealer, who has tweaked it back up to specs, only buy an old tube amplifier if you are good with electronics and the price is great.

The other solution is to improvise until you can afford the amplifier of your dreams. Amplifiers rarely break down, yet are sold frequently. So, a glut of amplifiers, many old and poorly built, are available for little or no cost. Look around and you might find something for free (or almost nothing)— maybe an AM/FM/cassette/phono system from the early 1980s or possibly even a Pioneer or Marantz receiver/amplifier from the 1970s (Fig. 5-16). With an amp like this, you can spend your money on good source equipment, such as a turntable, tape deck, or CD player.

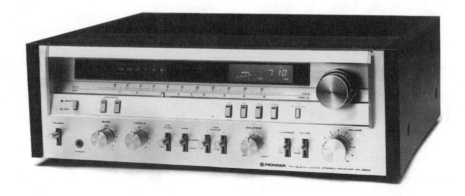

Fig. 5-16 If your budget is preventing you from purchasing a good stereo system, don't give up. You might even find a good second-hand receiver, such as this Pioneer SX-3800, for little or no cost.

You can listen to the music on headphones or through the cheapo amplifier. When you've nearly completed the system and you have enough money for the amplifier, you can finally replace it. It sure beats paying 14% interest on a credit card balance that carries over from month to month.

CONCLUSION

The amplifier in an audio system is like the catcher on a baseball team. It is often forgotten, yet it controls the entire system. Every bit of audio passes through it, so it could conceivably negatively alter every signal from your stereo system. Another part of the system, the speakers, also have a direct impact on every sound emanating from your system. Speakers are covered in Chapter 6

6

SPEAKERS

Although some elements of home audio and its components might be foreign to you, speakers should be familiar turf. Probably over half the pieces of electronic equipment on the market are equipped with a speaker of some sort. As common as speakers are, there is still a huge difference between the various grades of quality that are available. Some speakers cost as little as 99¢, yet others cost into the hundreds of dollars. What is the difference? Before throwing out some numbers (but not too many), here are a few basics behind speaker theory.

SOME SIMPLIFIED SOUND BASICS

A speaker is just one part of a broad category of components that are known as *transducers*. Transducers change one form of energy into another. One of the other very common types of audio transducers is the microphone. Understanding what a transducer does is a very important part of understanding how high-fidelity audio systems work and can be improved upon.

Whenever a microphone picks up a sound, it changes sound vibrations into electrical impulses (Fig. 6-1). The sound waves strike a thin element that is called a *diaphragm*, *ribbon*, etc. There are a number of methods by which the sound waves are converted, but in one of the common techniques, the diaphragm is held within a magnetic field. Whenever the diaphragm vibrates, it moves within

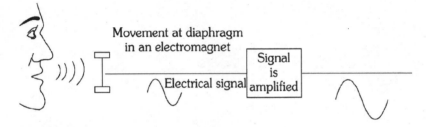

Fig. 6-1 The traditional analog process by which sound is changed into electrical impulses.

the magnetic field. These movements create an electromagnetic signal that will travel through the line cord. In some cases, the microphones contain preamplifiers to boost the signals up to a more usable level.

With the phonographic record (which is used here because it illustrates the point more clearly than the other methods), the same vibrational pattern that the diaphragm made is translated back from an electromagnetic pulse into physical vibrations. These vibrations are cut into a wax disc, and they exactly match the vibrations that the diaphragm made (with the time factor added). After the records have been pressed, the sound process takes an opposite route. The record needle bounces up and down within the grooves. The depth of the groove controls the volume of the recording and the width controls the frequencies (wide grooves for low frequencies and narrower for higher frequencies). Like a microphone, the phono cartridge contains an element that vibrates within an electromagnetic field when the needle bounces along in the grooves. These electrical impulses travel to an amplifier, where they are considerably boosted in strength. These signals travel through the speaker wire to the speaker inputs. There, a coil of wire that is known as the *voice coil* is suspended between a powerful permanent magnet and an iron core. The voice coil is directly connected to the speaker cone (often made from paper), which is what most people assume the actual speaker to be. The electrical impulses cause the voice coil to pump in and out within the magnet and the iron core. Because the voice coil is connected to the speaker cone, the cone vibrates in and out from the center of the speaker, sort of like the action that a piston makes.

As peculiar as it might seem, the audio from a radio, stereo, television, etc. is entirely produced because the thin paper cones are being pushed in and out. Even after years of using speakers and understanding the basic concepts behind how they work, it still amazes me that the thin pulsating paper cone can sound as clear and loud it does. These vibrations from the speaker cones are, in turn, transmitted through the air.

Sound waves, like any form of energy, will dissipate slowly. Fortunately, because of the enormous wavelengths across the voice frequency range, sound has a very limited range. If it didn't, you would constantly be hearing noise from all around the world. Instead, most sounds are restricted to a range of a few hundred feet or less, and only extremely loud sounds (such as explosions) will travel for longer than one mile. Chances are that the room in which you will be installing an audio system will be of an "average" size: anywhere from 10 feet x 10 feet up to about 15 feet x 20 feet. In these cases, you shouldn't require a more-powerful amplifier and higher-power (rated) speakers. If you have a contemporary home with a large, open floor plan, then you might consider purchasing a higher-power system so that you can adequately cover the house.

SPEAKER ACTION AND COMPONENTS

Any speaker consists of a number of components that must work together as a team (Fig. 6-2).

MAGNETS

As stated in the previous section, the voice coil is a coil of wire that moves within the speaker magnet and an iron core in the

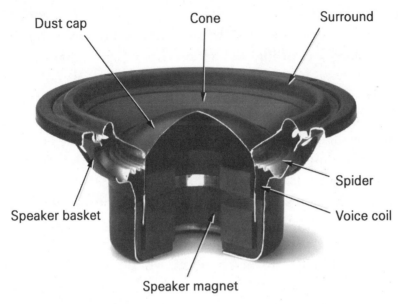

Fig. 6-2 A cutaway view of a speaker that exposes its individual parts.
Morel Acoustics

center. Because the magnet (Fig. 6-2) is the key to the magnetic field that the voice coil moves in, a stronger magnetic field is necessary for the speaker to be able to handle greater amounts of power. Generally, with the speakers from one particular manufacturer (or from a particular product line), you can go by the rule that the larger and heavier that the magnets are, the better the speakers are. This isn't always the case though, because some magnets have a stronger pull per pound than others. Most speaker magnets are made from ferrite (a form of powdered iron), and ceramic, although some of the speakers that can handle high power have strontium magnets.

Although most people can deduce whether or not they would be satisfied with a particular speaker system just from the catalog specifications, it is always best to preview any potential purchases beforehand—especially if you are an audiophile. Some speakers are not designed as well or use materials of lower quality, but still have heavy magnets. This difference will generally occur in the higher-end speaker class; large speaker magnets are expensive and few manufacturers will blow their profits on overstocking a speaker with extra magnet material.

Another problem with judging speaker quality by sheer magnet weight alone is damping. *Damping* is the reduction in the speaker cone's ability to move properly. The problem is that a large magnet with a strong pull is necessary to handle large amounts of power, yet too much magnet strength will restrict the movement of the speaker cone and will in turn reduce its low-frequency response. The engineering trade-off is to design a heavy-duty speaker that can handle the power output of a small nuclear reactor and yet still be able to produce thundering low frequencies that could crack the former presidents' ears on Mt. Rushmore.

So, you can deduce quite a bit from the magnet size and composition, but not everything. That is part of the difficulty with choosing speakers; you can choose by price, by manufacturer, by advice, or by the features in the catalog descriptions, but you won't know what any given speaker sounds like until you listen to it.

VOICE COILS

The speaker voice coil (Fig. 6-2) generally consists of a very fine gauge of enameled copper wire wound around a bobbin, which fits in between the permanent magnet and the iron core in the center (Fig. 6-2). The bobbin must slide straight back and forth within this space without grinding against the magnet and the iron core or it will hang up and fail. For this reason, you should be very careful to clean up any wood chips and sawdust if you decide to build your own speaker enclosures (more on that in Chapter 7). If you leave them behind, they could work their way into the voice coil of the speaker and destroy it.

The most common cause of speaker damage results from voice coil failure. When a speaker is driven by more power than it can safely handle, the voice coil will overheat and finally short together. Some high-powered speakers use air-ventilated or liquid-cooling methods to prevent the voice coil from becoming too hot and opening. This is an excellent method to prevent speaker damage. Tweeters are the most fragile of all speakers. The voice coils in woofers and subwoofers must move across large distances, and they are often pumped with huge amounts of power. If possible, purchase tweeters, coaxial speakers, woofers, and subwoofers with liquid-cooled voice coils if you plan to install a high-power system. But the liquid-cooled speakers are more expensive than speakers without additional cooling, so they might be out of your budget.

DUAL VOICE COILS

A handful of the more-expensive car audio speakers on the market contain dual voice coils (nearly always in woofers and subwoofers). Each speaker coil is an equal length of coiled wire of the same gauge and wire-loop spacing. Then, one coil is placed inside of the other. Rather than being entirely independent, both voice coils are connected to the same speaker cone and they both pump it in and out. Also, these speakers have two sets of connections, one for each voice coil. Otherwise, the performance is similar to a standard single voice coil speaker.

The peculiar aspect of the dual-voice coil speaker is that the performance is not really affected by having the extra coil. In fact, if the two voice coil connections are hooked up to a stereo amplifier, the one voice coil will be operating from the right channel and the other will be operating from the left. Because they are both operating the same speaker cone, the voice coils will push and pull out of synch with each other and cancel out. The cancellation is on par with standing waves in speaker boxes or weak, flexible walls in a speaker enclosure, where the some of the frequencies are canceled out and the response is uneven. In other words, they are not meant to be hooked up in stereo.

The usefulness of dual voice coil speakers lies in the flexible ways to install and connect the speakers because of the impedance and the extra speaker terminals. For the most part, dual voice-coil speakers are most useful in car stereo systems, when trying to manipulate impedances.

SPEAKER CONES

Although the voice coils do most of the actual work in a speaker, the speaker cones (Fig. 6-2) account for the sound that you hear.

CONE MATERIALS

For years, speaker cones have been made from paper or cloth. The improvements in speaker cone materials are one of the great advances in speaker design over the past decade. Presently, a number of different materials are used to make speaker cones, including: polypropylene, polymerized paper, corrugated fiber, Kevlar-reinforced paper, titanium, titanium/polymer composite, Mylar film, etc.

Any particular cone material is chosen over another type for reasons of cost, speaker type, sound quality, sound environment, and durability. For example, paper speaker cones are commonly used in home audio systems. However, if speakers with paper cones are used in car stereo applications, they could easily warp from dampness or degrade in the sun's ultraviolet light. Instead, many of the speakers for the car use polypropylene or other resistant material cones (Fig. 6-3) because they will not warp as a result of dampness in the car. On the downside, polypropylene is not touted at the world's best-sounding speaker material, but it lasts longer. So, although speakers with polypropylene cones might be fantastic in your car, you wouldn't choose them for your home.

The materials for speaker cones are also chosen for the frequency range of the speaker that they will be used in. Heavier cone mate-

Fig. 6-3 This speaker cone consists of woven fiberglass. Polydax

rials are used in the low-frequency speakers and thinner, stiffer cone materials are used in the high-frequency speakers. For example, thick, polymerized paper cones are often used in woofers and subwoofers because the thick material is strong and flexible. Its representation of high-frequency signals is poor, but that's fine because it is only intended to radiate the low end of the audio spectrum. Titanium and other very stiff materials are used in tweeters because they are strong and reproduce shrill sounds very well. These materials cannot tolerate the low-frequency sounds because they would be quickly destroyed by the long, deep movements that are required to reproduce sound at these wavelengths. Because of the medium range of the mid-range drivers, they are often a compromise in materials between the woofer and the tweeter.

You can't effectively choose your speakers based on materials alone. So many different factors are involved in the final sound (everything from the magnet, enclosure type, and cone materials to the engineering design of the system) that the only way to choose a speaker system is to (once again) just listen to it.

Dust caps

Dust caps are merely dome-shaped caps that are sealed around the center of the speaker cone over the area of the voice coil

(Fig. 6-2). The dust cap is primarily intended to prevent dust, dirt, and debris from entering the small space around the voice coil, and consequently, destroying it.

Dust caps can have an impact on the sound and they do push in and out along with the speaker cones. As a result, they are also often made of the same material that the speaker cone was constructed from, although some other materials are sometimes used. In auto woofers and subwoofers, one of the prime applications of dust caps is as a bright "billboard advertisement" for the speakers.

SUSPENSIONS

The following sections cover the components that form the suspension of a loudspeaker.

SURROUNDS

As the speaker cones are pumping like pistons in a car engine, the surround is flexing and holding the cone to the speaker's frame (Fig. 6-2). The surround consists of a thin ring of polyester foam, polyether foam, butyl rubber, paper, or cloth that attaches the outer edge of the speaker cone to the top outer edge of the metal basket. The surround helps to control the speaker movement and it also absorbs energy from the speaker cone. This combination is flexible enough to allow the speaker cone to move and produce high-quality sound, yet it is tough enough to keep the cone in place without tearing away.

The surrounds take the worst physical beating in the speaker and they are also one of the few weak links in speakers over the course of years. The problem is that the material must be flexible enough to bounce in and out smoothly. This requirement alone generally reduces the possible materials down to some synthetic foams (although, as mentioned, cloth and paper surrounds are sometimes used). The problem is that these materials have not been able to withstand damage from ultraviolet light in the past. After a few years of sitting in strong sunlight, they have broken down and cracked. Then, they are usually thrown out or replaced. Recently, some companies and small speaker repair shops have begun to replace speaker surrounds, and Parts Express offers do-it-yourself surround replacement kits.

SPIDER

Contrary to unpopular beliefs, the speaker spider was neither named after a Fiat or because this form of suspension is made out of ground spiders. Frankly, I have no idea why this ribbed, circular, resinous piece of cloth mesh is so named (Fig. 6-2). My wife believes that it's because spiders were often found in hardened resin and were fashioned into jewelry. Either way, the spider of a speaker is a piece of cloth that has been soaked in resin, so it is still and it holds its shape, yet it is still flexible. Like the surround, the spider is connected to the speaker cone and the speaker basket. Likewise, the spider also helps to control the speaker cone and prevents it from distorting in shape (and, in turn, in sound quality). In spite of its colorful name, the spider is a mostly ignored part of the speaker.

SPEAKER BASKET

The speaker basket looks and functions like the name implies—it is a metal basket that holds the speaker components (Fig. 6-2). If the speaker was an animal, the basket would be the exoskeleton; it provides the necessary strength and rigidity to hold the entire unit together (and it is all on the exterior). It is important for the speaker baskets to be constructed out of one piece of metal to prevent any rattling at high volumes. Many of the high-end speaker baskets are even cast out of aluminum for extra strength with less weight.

SPEAKER CONNECTIONS

Most speakers have a pair of lugs that are mounted on a small piece of circuit board material. This board is then mounted on the side of the speaker basket. Nearly all speaker companies use standard lugs that mate with slide-on connectors. However, a few of the high-end companies, such as Hart Professional and AVI, use gold-plated screw terminals. Considering that few speaker companies use gold-plated terminals, it is difficult to recommend that your speakers have them. However, it does make sense that if you are going to spend the extra money on gold-plated amplifier terminals and RCA plugs, that the final interconnections (the speaker terminals) would be gold plated as well. Gold is resistant to corrosion, but of course it is also quite expensive.

SPEAKER CLASSIFICATIONS (BY FREQUENCY)

This section covers the actual speakers that are used inside of an enclosure. It is important to know the function of speakers if you are building your own speaker enclosures and need to purchase your speakers separately. Or you might be nosy and want to know exactly what's behind the grille cloth of that great-sounding walnut cabinet.

To some extent, speakers (themselves) can be classified by size or maybe even by the materials that they are built with. But, a more-accurate method of classification is to sort the speakers out by the frequencies that each model is most capable of reproducing accurately.

Other than woofers and subwoofers, no speakers can fit into more than one classification. It just wouldn't be accurate for a speaker to be listed as a "tweeter/midrange/woofer." In that case, it would simply be a midrange. Most speakers in stock car audio systems simply use one inexpensive, all-purpose midrange speaker. These speakers will reproduce audio frequencies across much of the hearing range, but they are deficient in several ways.

Frequency-wise, these stock midranges are most lacking in their response at the lower frequencies. Because of the small wavelength of the much higher frequencies, they can be reproduced via small speakers that require fewer materials and are much less expensive to build. However, to reproduce the bass and low bass frequencies, a much larger speaker is necessary.

TWEETER

A tweeter is a speaker that is designed to reproduce high-frequency audio (Fig. 6-4). The general frequency-reproducing specifications of tweeters are from 4 to over 20 kHz. One of the most important actions of a tweeter's speaker cone is to move very quickly—otherwise, it will not be capable of reproducing the high frequencies. Because of this need, tweeter cones are often made of stiffer materials than those that are intended for lower frequencies. Some of the speaker cone materials used in tweeters are paper, aluminum, titanium, polymer, ceramics, silk, polymide, cloth, and graphite. Tweeters are much smaller (often as small as 2" in diameter) and more fragile than the other speaker types. Tweeters must be used in conjunction with other speakers.

Fig. 6-4 A speaker with a textile dome. Polydax

Fig. 6-5 A midrange loudspeaker. Polydax

MIDRANGE

Midrange speakers are designed to reproduce audio in the middle frequencies (Fig. 6-5). Midranges are a bit less interesting because the woofers and tweeters operate in a specialized manner, but the midranges are much more of a compromise between the two designs. To classify as a midrange, the speaker should produce audio frequencies in the range from about 400 Hz to 5 kHz. These frequencies overlap a bit with the tweeters and woofers because every speaker varies a bit in the styling and the frequency range that it is intended for. Most midrange speakers are approximately 4 to 6" (10.16 cm to 15.24 cm) wide, so they are somewhat convenient for mounting, unlike woofers.

For many years, audio enthusiasts concentrated on the bass and treble frequencies because they were at the edge of the hearing range and were more difficult to reproduce than those in the middle. Times have changed and people are realizing the importance of the once-forgotten midranges. Most of the human hearing lies within the midrange frequencies. If you concentrate on the high and low frequencies, you will be emphasizing frequencies that humans don't hear as well and also ones that aren't as critical musically. As a result, if you are working from a separate speaker standpoint, it is best to first buy a good set of midrange speakers, and then build the system from there. After all, if you have great speakers, it's best to use those that operate in a frequency range where you can best hear them.

MIDBASS

Midbass speakers aren't especially common, but they are designed to reproduce audio in the upper end of the woofer region/lower end of the midrange region. Most midbass speakers will cover anywhere from approximately 200 Hz to 3 kHz, which is anywhere from the bass region up through the midrange. Most midbass speakers are approximately 6" (15.24 cm) in diameter, which could be a prohibitive size, depending on where you plan to mount them. Overall, most midbass speakers are designed in the same style as woofers, except smaller. The midrange speaker in Fig. 6-5 is called a "bass-midrange" speaker in the Audax catalog, so it would also work here.

For your system, midbass speakers might be handy. They should work best in systems where separate speakers (not multiple-drive speakers) are used. Midbass speakers work well without any woofers, but they work better in conjunction with subwoofers or crossovers. That way, you can prevent the subwoofer and the midbass speakers from reproducing the same sounds, which will probably make the bass sound boomy and less crisp. Otherwise, you could use a crossover (either a separate unit or one that is built into the amplifier) to make sure that the frequencies that are intended for each speaker don't overlap.

WOOFER

Woofers reproduce bass frequencies, generally in the range from approximately 30 Hz to 2 kHz (however, they do much better in the lower end of their collective range). Woofers are characterized by their large sizes and heavy-duty construction. Most woofers range in size from about 8 to 18", although the most favored woofer sizes are 10" (20.54 cm), 12" (30.48 cm), and 15" (38.1 cm)(in diameter) for full-sized three-way speakers. As was mentioned previously, the speaker cone materials are often (but not always) thicker and tougher than those for high-frequency applications. Some of the woofer speaker cone materials include: paper, polypropylene, "organic" fiber, glass fiber, Kevlar, graphite, carbon, etc. The overall favorite for woofers and subwoofers seems to be paper or some combination of paper and another material.

SUBWOOFER

A microcosm of woofers, subwoofers reproduce the low bass frequencies, generally in the range from approximately 20 Hz to 1 kHz. In many cases, subwoofers are not considered to be a separate grouping, but are instead considered to be a subset or just lower-range woofers. There is some basis for this lack of a separate grouping because the frequency specifications for subwoofers are not significantly different from those of woofers, and also because the size and construction of the two types are very similar.

The general division between woofers and subwoofers in home audio systems are that woofers are included in an enclosure with the midrange and tweeters. Subwoofers are like your weird Uncle Fred—they're a part of the speaker family, but they're always stuck off in their own enclosures, by themselves. In many cases, subwoofers are large, and their enclosures require a sizeable chunk of space, too. Often, subwoofer boxes are designed as a big, stylish wood box or sometimes as an ottoman—anything to take your eyes off the huge "thing" in your living room.

MULTIPLE-DRIVER SPEAKERS

Multiple-driver speakers are typically used in car audio applications, where space and mounting locations are minimal (like trying to buy real estate in Manhattan). Because a house should have plenty of available space (like trying to buy real estate in rural Nebraska), the manufacturers don't bother with combining several speakers into one unit.

Multiple-driver speakers have several speakers that are built into one basket. The most common type of multiple-driver speaker is the three-way arrangement, which has one midrange and two different frequencies of tweeters built onto the frame above the midrange cone. Other possibilities are the standard two-way (coaxial) speaker and even the four-way speaker.

Multiple-driver speakers are designed with the tweeter (or tweeters) mounted in the center of the midrange speaker cone. This is tough because the tweeters must be mounted to something solid, yet if they extend out into the edges of the midrange speaker, its sound will be muffled. To solve this dilemma, the tweeters are bonded together on a plastic "shelf" and they are in turn mounted on a post that runs to the center of the midrange speaker. This creates further problems because the post runs straight through the area where the dust cap should be. Instead, the dust cap is not used and the post is connected to the area in the center of the voice coil. The fit around the center post must be close to prevent dirt and dust from getting in the space between the voice coil and the magnet. Some multiple-driver speakers even attach a piece of felt to the middle of the midrange cone or a piece of foam wrapped around the center post to prevent this from occurring.

Otherwise, most multiple-driver speakers operate as autonomous speakers. In these cases, each of the tweeters have their own magnets, etc. They are merely three speakers that have their input leads connected together—usually in parallel, but possibly in other configurations, depending on the whims of the engineers.

Some multiple-driver speakers include a parasitic passive "speaker." In this case, the parasitic speaker is a small tweeter that is mounted above the midrange, usually beside a real tweeter, to make a sort of three-way speaker. The parasitic tweeter is merely the cone of a tweeter. The sound waves from the midrange are caught by the tweeter cone, and it, in turn, vibrates at a higher frequency. These parasitic speakers have the advantage of being a bit cheaper to build than traditional three-way speakers, but the sound quality generally isn't quite as good as with "real" speakers.

Typically, speakers sound a bit better when they are separated. So, the auto multiple-driver speakers don't sound quite as good (as good separate speakers), but they are built to be physically and electronically rugged. Although parasitic tweeters are occasionally used in home audio applications, multiple-driver speakers are almost never designed for home use.

In theory, there is no reason to consider multiple-driver speakers for use in your home because their benefits are mostly lost. However, like anything, there are a few exceptions. The major benefits of using old car speakers is size and cost. I know I just said that size wasn't relevant, but hang with me for a minute. Because cars are wrecked from time to time and audioheads constantly upgrade their systems, some good car audio box speakers (don't just buy the speakers unless you plan to also build the enclosures) are often available in classified ads for a nice price—often less than half of the original.

If you are on a tight budget and live in an apartment, a good, used set of car box speakers is the way to go. The sound will be pretty good, the price is great (probably $25 to $50 used, unless you happen to have your own set around), and the speakers are small and easy to move. A better choice would be a set of Baby Advent or bookshelf Bose home audio speakers, but the only way that you will find them in this price range is if you get lucky at a pawn shop or find someone who is bankrupt and needs money FAST (more on buying speakers in the next section).

The second application for multiple-driver speakers in the home is when attempting to provide surround sound on a budget. You might already have a decent component stereo system that cost about $700 to $1200. If you have the money to add a surround-sound kit to your system (typically about $200 to $500), then go for it. But, you might consider using used car box speakers because the price is great and these speakers will typically do a fine job of filling background audio. But, beware of car audio speakers if you have a light-duty amplifier or if you often blast the volume, pushing the amp to its limits. Home audio speakers were designed to operate at 8 ohms of impedance and car speakers run at 4 ohms. The end result is that car speakers will make the amplifier work harder (at the same turn of the volume knob) as 8-ohm speakers.

HIGH-END SPEAKER ALTERNATIVES

Not all stereo speakers are of the standard cone/voice coil variety. A few speakers have been successfully designed and manufactured in alternative means to produce a thin wall of sound. The two major varieties are electrostatic and ribbon speakers. These types of speakers are both uncommon and extremely expensive, so this section only very lightly covers each type.

Electrostatic speakers are completely different in theory and construction from typical loudspeakers (Fig. 6-6). The primary components of the speaker are two large, flat, parallel pieces of metal, called *stators*, and a piece of mylar stretched between, called a *diaphragm*. The diaphragm is the equivalent of the speaker cone and the stators fill the function of the magnet and voice coil. A very high voltage is applied to the diaphragm and the amplifier audio output is applied to the stators. The changes in the audio signal alter the electrostatic field, pushing and pulling the diaphragm, as a speaker cone would pulsate.

Fig. 6-6 An old electrostatic, ribbon speaker from the late 1950s.

Ribbon speakers are very similar in theory, but much different in construction from typical loudspeakers. They are similar in the sense that they both contain magnets—on one side is a north pole, on the other is the south pole. But instead of having a voice coil, the amplifier output signal is applied directly to each end of a thin, long piece of metal. The audio signal interacts with the magnetic field from the magnets and the ribbon fluctuates, producing sound.

The primary reason why more people don't purchase electrostatic or ribbon speakers is simply the cost. Who really wants to spend into the five figures for speakers, no matter how good they sound? For example, the MAS triple set Emperor with cherry wood frames costs $100,000 (however, the standard Emperor model costs "only" $32,000). Some other lesser factors are that both types recreate higher-frequency audio better than low, unless a huge adult-sized (or bigger) system is used.

BUYING SPEAKERS

Buying speakers can be a big problem because, as far as sound quality is concerned, speakers are the most important components in your system. Yet, you can't necessarily rate speaker quality by looks, size, size of the magnet, speaker cone materials, or price (Fig. 6-7). Because of the variables in speaker construction and design, it is somewhat common for most people to give a better rating to a speaker that costs half as much as another. Notice that I said "most." Beyond a point, good-quality audio is completely subjective. Although the ultimate goal of most people is to have a system that exactly reproduces the music that was produced as it was being recorded, some actually would rather have a system that is inaccurate. One example of this are the "bassheads," who would rather boost the bass higher than the proportion at which it was recorded. When it gets down to intricacies such as these, it's your system and you have to buy it. Pick the sound that you like.

Fig. 6-7 These speakers, the Thiel CS3, are graced with both good looks and great quality.

Similar to the situation with amplifiers, one of the worst problems with picking out speakers is the sheer number on the market. Literally hundreds, if not thousands, of different enclosed and separate (raw) speakers are on the market from year to year. Which ones will you pick?

When it comes right down to it, the main factors that will affect your choice of speakers are cost and availability. With so many different speaker varieties available, chances are that you will not be able to find some of the brands and models. No stereo stores have the facilities to buy every model that's on the market; very few would even have 1/20 of those in stock. Pricewise, chances are that you will get the most for your money from the large companies that sell in such volume that they can afford to offer lower prices or to offer special discounts to the distributors who buy many of their units. Of course, many audio enthusiasts will also note that some of the larger companies use their big name to sell substandard equipment. So, where do you turn?

If you don't really care about audiophile-quality sound, you might just plan to purchase a system from one of the major names in consumer stereo equipment (such as Technics, Sony, Kenwood, etc.), and use the speakers that come along with the system (Fig. 6-8). Taking this route will typically provide you with a decent system for the price. But, chances are that you would have been happier with the final result by assembling the system yourself. If price is a factor, shopping around for closeouts, floor models, and used equipment is definitely a help.

On the other hand, if you are concerned about the sound of your system, research anywhere you can and gather as much information as possible. Read the magazine reviews and tests for all of the speakers that might catch your interest. Unfortunately, many of the audio magazines on the market specialize in expensive, high-end equipment. *Stereophile*, for example, rarely reviews speakers that cost less than $1000 per pair. It can be difficult to even find a pair of speakers for less than $1000 in *Stereophile*

Fig. 6-8 A nice audio/home theater system. Pioneer

classified ads! For more-affordable audio systems, check the prices in *Stereo Review*.

Next, go to audio stores and listen to as many different speakers as you can. These shops have their own sound rooms so that you can test out the various speakers on your own (Fig. 6-9). Of course, the speakers will all sound different when they are mounted in your own house, as opposed to being mounted in the wall of a big show room. Still, they will give you an idea of what you can expect from a set of speakers. Be sure that you go to each testing session adequately prepared. Take a few examples of music that has excellent audio/recording quality and that you know very well. Listen closely to the various parts of the songs and see how well the speakers reproduce the sound. Listen to the tracks at home in tandem to your listening test trips as possible. Unless you have been tweaking audio systems for a few years, you will probably not have the experience to automatically know what a system is lacking.

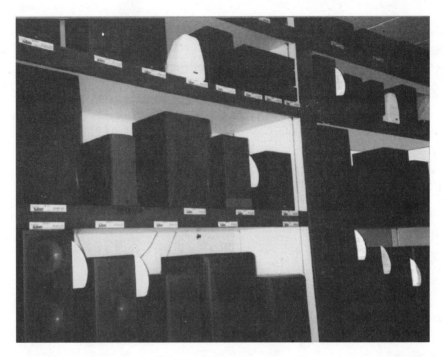

Fig. 6-9 The well-stocked speaker shelves at a local stereo shop. Wee Bee Audio

While you are at the audio stores, ask the salespeople as many questions as possible. Ask questions about system designing, repairs, warranty information, and anything else that might come to mind. Also ask for opinions because chances are that the salesperson knows these speakers far better than you do. Remember that anything that the salesperson says is going to be colored by the fact that they will be getting a commission off of their sales (possibly from you). They will be biased toward any product that their store carries, and they will generally lean toward the more expensive products that they sell. It is very rare, but if the salesperson recommends equipment that is sold elsewhere, be sure to take the advice; the salesperson is going against store policy and personal interests to give you honest advice.

If you have a computer, be sure to check into the computer bulletin boards and networks for some of the best and timeliest audio information available. The computer bulletin boards that specialize in home audio are operated by people who are dedicated to the hobby on a noncommercial basis. In most cases, they are participating because they love the hobby and not because they will benefit financially from any transactions in cyberspace.

The computer BBSes are starting to disappear around the country as more people go onto the Internet (and avoid the long-distance telephone bills of dialing an out-of-town BBS). It's sad to see these long-established BBSs disappearing, but many are reappearing as Web sites on the Internet. The first sites to visit when researching your next purchase are:

http://home1.swipnet.se/~w-10118/hifi

This site is an enormous, comprehensive listing of other audio-related sites on the Internet. The sheer volume of audio sites is amazing!

rec.audio.high-end Get ready to shell out the big bucks! If you want to get some information on those hand-built custom speakers from the tiny village in Denmark, visit this.

rec.audio.opinion More opinions on audio systems. But this group is touted as an opinion group, not a simple newsgroup.

Like any of the Usenet groups on the Internet, expect plenty of arguing. Part of the problem is that audio is a subjective hobby and people have different standards to follow. This alone causes plenty of arguments and disagreements. Also, people generally are not very nice. Some people are just bent on arguing, no matter what the topic. The following advice is common sense: If a subject line contains expletives, don't bother to read the message. It's not worth your time. I wouldn't even mention it, but I've been enticed by some subject lines that read something to the effect of "Brand X speakers are &%$@ed up!!!!!!!!!!!!!!!!!!" I check it out, and the message is probably either wrong or misleading. Worse yet, you might catch a response to this sort of message and discover that the 47 different messages on the same subject are actually an argument about the possibilities of a Communist takeover in the United States or about the musical integrity of Janet Jackson.

The bottom line is that although the Internet is a fantastic wealth of information, in the worst case, it can be a misleading waste of time. When you investigate on the Internet, have a game plan of what you want to learn, be very perceptive, and keep an eye on the clock.

OTHER SPEAKER SPECIFICATIONS

In addition to the frequency ratings, several other ratings are important when you are considering a group of speakers to purchase for your system. The power specifications can be even more critical than the frequency ratings, so read and choose carefully.

INPUT SENSITIVITY

The input sensitivity is the sound pressure level in dB that is output when 1 W is delivered to the speaker. This measurement is taken at a range of 1 meter from the front of the speaker, at a given frequency (usually 1 kHz). The input sensitivity rating is only important if you are building your own speaker system. If you are just buying commercial speakers, skip the rest of this section.

The input sensitivity is important because if you have mixed and matched your speakers, some might have a much higher sensitivity than others. This being the case, some of your speakers might overpower others in the system, and you might need to attenuate each of the more sensitive speakers with a resistor. Typical input sensitivity ratings for speakers are generally all between 87 and 101 dB. Woofers, tweeters, midranges, etc., are found throughout the range, although the woofers and subwoofers are, on average, a bit higher.

A higher input sensitivity rating does not necessarily mean that the speaker is better than another; it only means that it is more efficient with its output power. The input sensitivity rating might be a factor in determining the best speaker for your system after you have compared speakers and they sound just as good to your ears. Otherwise, a solid, clean-sounding speaker with a flat response is much more important than a loud speaker.

To confuse matters further, not all speakers are measured by the manufacturers at a frequency of 1 kHz. Some of the cheaper speakers do not have a flat response and the level will vary across the frequency spectrum. Some of the less-honest manufacturers have been known to rate their speakers' input sensitivity at one of the spikes in the response, which obviously is not accurate.

RESPONSE

The response of a speaker is a graph of its output across the entire frequency range. To understand speaker response, imagine if the input sensitivity measurements for a speaker were taken across the entire frequency range, then all of those measurements were listed on a graph. That's it. The best speakers will have a plateau-shaped response with a fairly sharp roll-off on either end. Most speakers have somewhat sloping responses, etc., but as long as they are relatively flat, they should do fairly well. Beware of speakers with many spikes and valleys throughout their response graphs; they will not accurately represent the sound of your recordings. Unlike the sensitivity rating, the response graph is very important when determining whether the sound of a particular speaker will be worthy of finding a place in your home.

The frequency response of a speaker is also known as the range within which the speaker will output within a certain power rating. The high and low points, where the response drops below the predetermined level (usually $+/- 3$ dB), determine the specified frequency response for a given speaker.

NOMINAL POWER HANDLING

The nominal power handling rating of speakers is the amount of power that a speaker can handle continuously. The nominal power handling rating is the practical power limit that you should ever consider inputting from your amplifier. For that matter, if the amplifier is driven at high levels, a system is much better off with speakers that are rated approximately 10% higher (in watts) than the power output of the amplifier, just to be safe (e.g., if you have a 100-watt amplifier, your speakers should be rated to handle at least 110 watts).

PEAK POWER HANDLING

Not to be confused with nominal power handling, the peak power handling rating is the instantaneous amount of power that a speaker can safely tolerate. The peak power handling rating is more of an academic figure than one that you could use to design a system. In many cases, you will not know the output levels of your amplifier on peaks while you use it, unless you have electronic measuring equipment. Rating a system by the peak power and not the nominal power would be pushing the system for a little more. It's much safer just to use the nominal figure and play it safe.

SPEAKER POLARITY

If you look closely, you will notice that every set of speaker terminals has a + sign on one side and a – sign on the other side. Likewise, the amplifier will also either have these same markings or a red terminal (positive) and a black terminal (negative). These markings are to enable you to match the polarity of the speakers to the amplifier and to the other speakers, if they are connected in series or in parallel.

However, the speaker polarity is nothing like the polarity of capacitors; they won't be destroyed or explode in your face if you connect the speakers to the wrong polarity. In fact, if you connect the speakers to the wrong polarity from the amplifier, you might not even notice a difference in sound quality. The speaker polarity actually is the phase in which the audio signals arrive at the speakers. The speaker polarity is marked on the speakers and the amplifiers because if the two signals arrive at the speakers out of phase, some of the audio frequencies will cancel and will thus reduce the frequency response. But the phase of the signals might have even been altered by an amplifier, an equalizer, or by some other piece of equipment before this point. As a result, the signal could already be out of phase (i.e., the polarity would be the opposite from what is shown at the speaker terminals) and following the directions for connecting them would be incorrect.

Speaker polarity is one of those "if it sounds good, do it" subjects. Connect your speakers, and if you think that they don't sound quite as good as they should, try reversing the connections and listen for a difference. Chances are, you will notice only a slight difference, at best.

SPEAKER PLACEMENT AND ROOM ACOUSTICS

The placement of your speakers, the size and shape of your listening room, the surface materials used to build the room, and the objects in the room all affect the final sound of your stereo system. For more information on speaker placement, and system design and installation, see Chapter 9.

CONCLUSION

Speakers are the most important component, as far as sound is concerned, in any audio system. They are also very complicated and potentially expensive, so it is a must to choose your speakers carefully so that you can get the best sound for the money.

7

SPEAKER ENCLOSURES

The all-encompassing topic of speakers is one of the most important factors in any type of audio system. You can spend half of your stereo budget on purchasing a stereo system and half on the speakers; chances are that you will have a better-sounding system than someone who spent a great deal of cash on the stereo equipment and little on the speakers. Most of the difference in price is because of the extra equipment features: skipless CDs, memory presets, RDS systems, remote control, etc. You might find these features to be very desirable, but the fact is that they don't positively alter the sound quality under normal listening conditions. The same argument holds true for speaker wiring, amplifiers, equalizers, signal processors, etc.

Although good-quality speakers are very important, they still must be properly installed and positioned. In fact, expensive speakers can still sound lousy if they are not installed properly. For more information on installation and systems, see Chapter 9.

The standard speaker enclosure consists of a solid rectangular box with the speakers mounted in the front of one of the two long, wide sides. A good speaker cabinet is not just intended to look nice or to be portable—the cabinet is intended to improve the actual frequency response from the speakers. Thus, the purpose of a speaker cabinet is to isolate the air mass that is in front of the speaker from that which is behind it. Without the cabinet, the lower-frequency waves will cancel out and the audio will be much weaker, with a tinny, thin sound.

In addition to shielding the front air mass from the back, the walls of the enclosure should also be solid. If they aren't, the walls will vibrate and these waves will, in turn, cancel out more audible frequencies. The best speaker enclosure should be "dead": the walls should be solid and virtually flawless, the enclosure should be physically strong, and the joints should be sealed.

ENCLOSURE MATERIALS

A number of materials can be used to make speaker enclosures, but some work much better than others. If you go to a stereo shop, you will notice that the more expensive home audio speakers often use expensive wood, such as oak, to build the enclosures, yet commercial auto audio enclosures are usually covered with carpeting. This difference is merely cosmetic: fine wood is used in home systems to fit in with the decor of a house, not because of any desirable acoustic qualities. Likewise, carpet is used to cover auto audio enclosures because it matches the car's interior and because its finish won't scratch like a stained or painted surface, not because of any beneficial sound-damping qualities.

Although wood covers nearly all of the home speaker enclosures, the wood is not a part of the actual box. Instead, the wood is veneered or a board is glued to the enclosure. Wood is not normally used for enclosures because the grain and knots provide an uneven surface density. The grain lines and knots are much denser than the wood that is in between. As a result, the surface of the wood won't be "dead;" it will vary, depending on the grain. Strangely enough, for a good-sounding, "dead" box enclosure, you'll get the best results from getting one of the cheapest, least-expensive materials that's available from hardware stores and

Fig. 7-1 A speaker kit that includes seven ready-to-assemble pieces of particle board (also known as MDF).

lumber yards: particle board (Fig. 7-1). It's ugly and cheap to make, but a length of particle board is also evenly dense and about as heavy as a refrigerator. All of these qualities make it a great pick for speaker enclosures. Don't confuse particle board with flake board, which is a cheap grade of plywood-type material that consists of big chunks of wood. Sometimes other materials, such as thick plywood, are used, but plywood is much more expensive than particle board and only the best grades of it are somewhat evenly dense. Cheap grades of plywood will often contain gaps in the layers that can buzz and absorb sound energy. Multiply subflooring is another option that would work well, but it is also very expensive.

ALTERNATIVE ENCLOSURE MATERIALS

As you might guess, many other materials have been used to build speaker enclosures. Some of these have been peculiar, but if you have a taste for experimentation, they might provide some interesting tests. Because one of the most important qualities for speaker enclosures is sound deadness, very dense materials that are not easily vibrated by sound are desirable. Metals are normally out of the question, unless you can cast a 1" or 2" (2.54 cm or 5.08 cm) thick aluminum box (that would cost more time and

effort than it would be worth). Also, such a cabinet would resonate, producing a ringing sound (like putting a speaker in a bell).
Stone or brick enclosures would also normally be out of the
question, unless you commute to Bedrock everyday to work. But,
the Flintstones-style enclosure is along the line of three of the
more interesting enclosure experiments that I have seen.

The first is a very feasible project that is included in *Great Sound
Stereo Speaker Manual with Projects* by David B. Weems. In this
case, the author made a diagonal cut through one piece of ceramic flue tile to produce two potential enclosures with sloping
front sides (Fig. 7-2). The insides of the tiles were carpeted,
special crossovers were built, the boxes were braced on the inside
with pieces of wood, and pieces of special heavy-duty 13-ply plywood were cut for the front and back of each speaker. Then, the
speakers were installed and wired, and the front and back plywood sides were glued to the flue tiles and sealed with silicone
caulking. The author said that the sound is very natural, which is
good and bad. The bass is a bit lighter than that from most larger

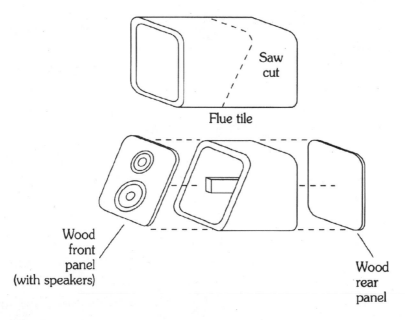

Fig. 7-2 A ceramic flue tile speaker enclosure.

speaker enclosures, but they do well whenever the recordings have deep bass. Otherwise, they will not compensate and beef up the bass.

The Weems ceramic tile enclosures are at the opposite end of the practicality/usefulness chart from a pair of concrete subwoofer enclosures that were used in a 1986 Mercury Cougar that was featured in *Car Audio and Electronics* (see "Heavy Weight Mercury Cougar," February 1994, p. 36–44). The subwoofer boxes weigh 260 lbs and were set into the trunk just behind the back seats. Because of the extra weight, the owner had to replace the rear suspension with one from a Ford F-150 pickup truck. The owner said that the concrete has tightened the sound of the bass. If you're a stone mason and you think that cementing a subwoofer in an unused chimney sounds like a cool idea, you might consider trying it (of course, if it doesn't perform up to your standards, you'll have to rip it back out!). Otherwise, drop the idea like a ton of bricks.

SPEAKER ENCLOSURE SHAPES

The shape of the speaker enclosure does not make as much difference in the sound quality as the materials that the box is made from, but it is still very important. Because speaker enclosure shapes combine the technological aspect of audio design with physical beauty, many arguments spring forth over the topic.

The name of the game for enclosure shapes is standing waves. Standing waves occur when sound waves build up at a particular frequency as a result of the resonance of the speaker enclosure. The standing waves can null out other audio waves and produce a weak response at a particular frequency or frequencies. As a result, the frequency response of the enclosed speakers will be uneven or lacking, particularly at the bass frequencies. Because of the negative effect of standing waves, it is desirable to prevent the speaker from being in a location (in the enclosure) where it is equidistant from the speaker walls. Thus, the shape of a cube, with one speaker mounted in the center of one side, is one of the worst possible geometric configurations (Fig. 7-3).

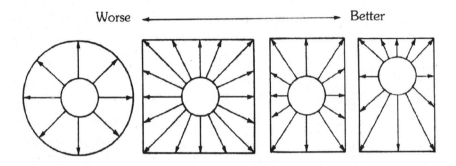

Worse ← → Better

Fig. 7-3 The distances from the speaker to the enclosure wall.

For some time, I assumed that a perfect cube would be one of the best enclosure shapes because the waves would all reflect back at the same time, aiding the movement of the speaker and making the sound stronger and tighter. Whoops, nearly the opposite is true; those reflected waves are fighting against those that are currently being produced by the speaker. As a result, the best sound occurs when the waves are permitted to reflect back at different distances.

One of the best speaker enclosure shapes is a rectangular box with the speaker mounted off center. This speaker shape is so popular because it is effective, and because it is the easiest and least expensive to implement. With the speakers mounted across the front panel, very few of the waves will reflect back at the same distance. Because the shape is so simple, standard boards and joints can be used for the enclosure. The simple parts and construction make rectangular boxes the favorites for both home construction projects and commercially available boxes.

Another nonstandard shape for speaker enclosures (i.e., a non-box shape) is the trapezoid. In case the information from your high-school geometry class has slipped away with the names of the actors from "Eight is Enough" or if you decided not to bore yourself by taking that class in the first place, a trapezoid is any four-sided figure that has non-90° angles at the corners. This shape is becoming more popular for high-end speaker enclosures because there are fewer parallel surfaces, speakers can be tilted slightly up to focus the treble frequencies, and because the high-end companies aren't as restricted by cost per unit as the mass-marketing audio companies.

I have also heard some arguments and read differing (pro and con) accounts of some speaker enclosure shapes, such as the sphere. The sphere is a particularly interesting shape because many people have argued that it is either the very best or the very worst shape for a speaker enclosure. It is sometimes considered to be the worst shape because a number of distances from the speaker would be the same length, so waves would return to the speaker at the same time. This would set up an ultimate worst case for standing waves in a speaker enclosure. However, this standing wave problem would only occur if the speaker were actually in the center of the sphere, so proponents of this shape say that it is actually the best of the bunch. In my opinion, the point is virtually moot: the shape is totally impractical for anyone to build a spherical enclosure (the only real possibility would be to cast it out of Fiberglass), and even if it weren't, the shape wastes space and the enclosure would roll around, unless it was bolted down on a speaker stand. The best part is, if you created such a system that worked properly, it would look like a giant pair of eyes in your living room. Then, you could invite all of your paranoid friends over for dinner and tell them about how the speaker "eyes" appear to follow you wherever you walk.

Another geometric possibility would be the pyramid. This design would be much easier to build than the sphere for obvious reasons. However, on the downside, the pyramid would require much more space than any of the other enclosure designs, so it probably will not be useful to most people. However, some high-end speaker designs are tall, narrow pyramids without the tip (instead having a flat top).

Although a number of different speaker shapes are possible in home audio applications, the most useful are the rectangular and trapezoidal boxes because of the good-quality sound, the ease of construction, and the lower cost. As a result, these two basic types are covered almost exclusively throughout this chapter.

SPEAKER ENCLOSURE DAMPING

As has been mentioned, the volume of and the materials in a speaker enclosure are critical to the sound that the speakers will produce. The sound can, in turn, be either enhanced or degraded by using damping materials inside of the box. Damping materials are sound-absorbing layers that are added to the inside of a speaker box to reduce the reflections and "tighten" the sound. Another quality of damping materials are that they can effectively make a smaller enclosure sound as if it is much larger (to a certain point). Considering the cost of materials and relatively small amount of space that is typically allocated in your living room, damping materials are very popular!

It is somewhat common for speaker enclosures that require very light damping to have the insides of the box covered with a very thin layer of carpeting. However, it seems that larger amounts of damping are required for most speakers—especially now that people are becoming more mobile and living space is shrinking. These days, most commercial speaker enclosures seem to be undersized models that have been padded with damping materials to compensate.

Some of the most common sound damping materials are acoustic polyfill and unbacked Fiberglass insulation. After insulating a few houses with Fiberglass insulation, I try to avoid the stuff, but it isn't so bad to install such a small amount in a speaker enclosure. Another possibility is polyester quilt backing. It has less damping ability, but it is also a bit more fun to work with and you can buy it in smaller quantities than Fiberglass insulation. You can purchase acoustic polyfill at some local audio stores or mail-order companies, rolls of Fiberglass insulation from building supply companies, and quilt backing from fabric stores.

To install damping material, just staple a layer of it to the inside of the speaker box—either to the back wall or just so the sheet is squashed in across the back and covering some of the other inside walls as well. If you don't have a staple gun, then try spraying the inside with adhesive, such as that which is used to hold carpet on an enclosure. Next, put the front plate on the box or insert the speaker (depending on the type that you have) and listen to the way that the bass sounds decay. If the sounds aren't tight, add another layer and try it again. If the bass frequencies seem to be absorbed, remove some of the damping material and try it again. After a few tries, you will have the damping material/speaker enclosures tweaked for optimum performance.

SPEAKER ENCLOSURE DESIGNS AND TECHNIQUES

It might seem as though the this section's topic is a repeat of what was just featured in the last section. Nope, those were all speaker enclosure shapes, whereas this section covers different designs that are all modeled around the rectangular box shape. Speaker enclosure designs can be very complicated, involving multiple speakers in various arrangements, large speaker boxes, tuned ports, etc. Fortunately, some of the best designs for speaker boxes are also some of the least complicated.

THE CLOSED-BOX ENCLOSURE

Because of the absolute simplicity, good performance, and difficulty in botching up the sound quality, I prefer the closed-box (sealed) enclosure. The closed-box enclosure is a simple speaker enclosure that is sealed on all sides so that the air mass behind the speaker is entirely separated from that which is infront it (Fig. 7-4).

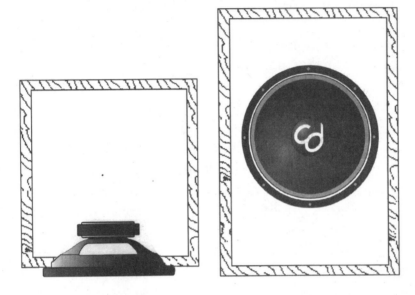

Fig. 7-3 A sealed enclosure. CD Technologies

The volume of each box has a particular frequency range for which a speaker of a particular size will operate well. The box will generally work well for all audio frequencies that the particular speaker is rated for. However, if the box has a smaller volume than is required for the size of the speaker that is in it, the sound pressure will be even higher within the box. As the pressure level increases within the speaker enclosure, the effect is that some of the lower frequencies are dropped out. And, as the size of the enclosure is reduced, the pressure level within the box is increased, and even more of the lower frequencies are cutoff. But not all of the low frequencies are removed, as is the case when a speaker is in a free-air position.

Instead, some of the frequencies are removed and others peak, which results in a "boomy" bass sound, instead of a tight, clean bass sound.

As a result of this action, larger speakers require larger box volumes to be able to accurately reproduce the low frequencies properly. Because of this speaker law, very small woofers, such as the 8" models, are quite popular among people who want to have bass, yet can't or don't want to waste the speaker and enclosure space that would be required to support a larger system, such as one for 12" or 15" woofers or subwoofers.

Because speaker enclosures can "stiffen" the sound waves and cause the low bass to drop out if the area inside is too small, you might want to make the box larger than is specified. I have heard some varying opinions on the subject of larger-than-specified box enclosures. Some people have said that the lower bass frequencies will drop out and others have said that they won't, but that a larger box has little "bass boost" over one with the specified box size. The arguments are usually pointless because you probably wouldn't want a few massive, oversized enclosures in your living room anyway. And it's pointless to build a huge enclosure for your subwoofer because the room that you would be sticking it in is probably too small to adequately reproduce the bass frequencies.

Regardless, by varying the size of the enclosure, you will produce a different sound, perhaps one that is more to your liking than the specified enclosure volume. So, it is very helpful to use speaker enclosures that are near the proper volume so that you can get the maximum sound quality from your system.

Unfortunately, the volume of a closed-box speaker depends on a number of different factors: Q is the magnification of the resonance factor of any resonant device or circuit, Q_T is the total Q factor of the speaker, f_S is the free-air resonance of the speaker (frequency), and V_{AS} is the compliance of the speaker. These calculations and few other factors are used in a number of different equations to determine the exact best volume for a closed-box enclosure.

In order to design a closed speaker box, you must know three of the terms from the previous paragraph: f_S, Q_T (often listed in manufacturer's specifications as Q_{TS}), and V_{AS}. These values should be available from the manufacturer, and they are often printed right on the box (or in the manual or product information sheets), next to the other specifications, such as the power ratings.

For a sealed box design, all you really need to know is "the bigger, the better" until the box volume exceeds (time to get out that calculator):

$$Maximum\ box\ volume = 1.1 \times V_{AS} \times Q_{T2}$$

The total volume will be in cubic feet if V_{AS} is in cubic feet or in liters if V_{AS} is in liters. If you need to covert this information:

$$1\ cubic\ foot = 28.3\ liters$$

Making the box much larger than this is a waste of particle board.

For more advanced mathematicians, you can now calculate how the bass will be (for any size of box) using:

$$Cutoff\ frequency = 0.8 \times f_S \times \sqrt{V_{AS}/box\ volume}$$

For this equation, V_{AS} and box volume must both be in either cubic feet or both in liters. These equations are just approximations, but they should be accurate to within 10% of the actual value.

For example, unless you are an audiophile or a hard-core experimenter, you might be better off using a chart of approximate specifications. To get the simplified volume specifications for closed-box speaker systems, see Fig. 7-5, which shows the approximate volumes for most speakers that would be enclosed in a home audio system. The sizes listed are only per a single speaker. If you are constructing a three-speaker tower, determine the volume for each speaker and add the total. You might even want to envision the assembly as three different (assuming that you are using a woofer, midrange, and tweeter) enclosures connected together.

In all, the only major concerns with building a closed-box enclosure are to achieve the proper volume inside, and to make it solid and airtight.

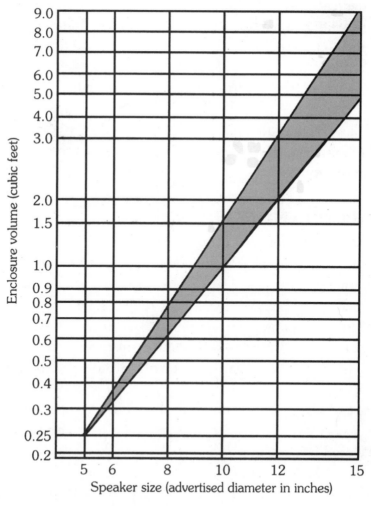

Fig. 7-5 The box enclosure volume for any given speaker.

CLOSED-BOX ARRANGEMENTS

A number of different speaker arrangements are possible with the closed-box speaker design. Two subwoofers can be placed in one box, side by side, to double the bass force of a sub box. Or the full-range of speakers (woofer, tweeter, and midrange) can all be placed in one box (as mentioned in the previous paragraph). Or different arrangements of woofers can be placed in the box, such as the many variations on the push-pull theme, where two woofers are mounted in line to "drive" each other. The possibilities are numerous, so if you want to read further on the subject, try reading a dedicated speaker book, such as those by David Weems (listed earlier), subscribe to *Speaker Builder* magazine, or see the DIY Speakers homepage on the Internet:

http://uts.cc.utexas.edu/~speakers/index.html

The folks who run this page also run The Bass and DIY Loud-speakers mailing list—an invaluable source of technical information on the topics.

APERIODIC ENCLOSURES

Because of the amount of pressure that exists in a closed-box enclosure, some people have experimented with removing that pressure without making the box "leaky." The result is the aperiodic enclosure, which is a closed-box design with a screened hole that is covered with an acoustic damping material (Fig. 7-6). Thus, the pressure inside of the box is released, yet the box is still acoustically sealed. Normally, the pressure vent is a square or rectangular hole that is anywhere from approximately 1" x 1" (2.54 cm x 2.54 cm) to 3" x 3" (7.62 cm x 7.62 cm). Although the aperiodic enclosure is a serious standard speaker enclosure, it is outperformed in nearly every way by a comparable closed-box enclosure.

The pressure vent is typically located in the back of aperiodic enclosures for cosmetic reasons. Because the amount of damping

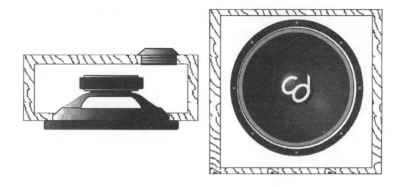

Fig. 7-6 An aperiodic enclosure. CD Technologies

material will determine how acoustically tight the box really is, you should experiment with how much material you use over the hole so that you can tweak the sound to your liking. Likewise, you should also tweak the amount of damping material that is in the box. For the most part, the same procedures and rules that apply to closed-box enclosures also apply to aperiodic enclosures, except that the internal pressure has been released.

In general, the aperiodic enclosure is not a favorite of audio enthusiasts and some people look upon it disparagingly.

PORTED-BOX ENCLOSURES

Complicated ported-box enclosures have been in the audio world for decades. Audio enthusiasts choose ported-box speaker enclosures over the other types because they believe that these designs have an edge in frequency response over the others. Not being an audiophile, I would choose the closed-box enclosures for the sake of simplicity, when building my own boxes. In my opinion, the extra work and frustrations would not be worth the price to pay for slightly better audio quality. But, of course, they are worth the price for some people to pay, so for these people, and for the sake of covering the most popular types of enclosure designs, they are included here.

SPEAKER ENCLOSURES

A typical ported-box enclosure is a type of speaker enclosure that features a port in which a tuned pipe can be fitted (Fig. 7-7). If a tuned pipe is used in the design, its diameter, length, and the way in which it is mounted are crucial. In the second type of ported-box enclosure (a double-chamber reflex), the top part of the enclosure is exactly the same as the typical ported box. However, it is also ported into another, smaller enclosure, which also has a separate port to the outside. Thus, the speaker "sees" the chambers as being either separate area or as a united air mass, which permits it to be much more flexible in terms of frequency response.

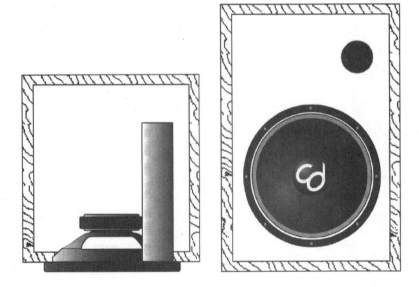

Fig. 7-7 A ported enclosure. CD Technologies

The last type of ported-box enclosure is another design that uses a parasitic speaker. If you read the section that covered multiple-driver speakers in Chapter 6, you might remember that one type of speaker array used a parasitic tweeter without a magnet or voice coil to capture and reradiate sound. The parasitic ported-box enclosure uses a parasitic speaker (often called a *passive radiator*) instead of a port to function. This style of enclosure would be very interesting and inexpensive to experiment with, except that most audio manufacturers do not sell parasitic speakers. However, Madisound does have several of these models available for home experimentation.

One design that uses a tuned port, yet isn't normally considered to be a common ported-box enclosure, is the bandpass enclosure. In this design, the speaker is not visible—the sound can only reach the outside via the tuned port (Fig. 7-8). I can't say that I know of many people who are building bandpass enclosures, but it is a very popular style among the commercial subwoofer system designers.

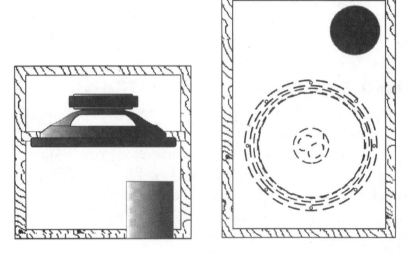

Fig. 7-8 A bandpass enclosure. CD Technologies

The tuned port in ported-box enclosures alters the resonant frequency of the enclosure. By adding a port with a larger diameter, the resonant frequency will be increased. You can see the same effect by making an "owl whistle" with your cupped hands. To raise the pitch of the whistle, you merely open your outside hand, which covers the back of the enclosure. This open area that is covered by your back hand operates as a variable simple port to alter the pitch of your whistle. The speaker duct is only used to tune air within the enclosure, not to focus the energy from the speakers. As a result, the duct can either run straight toward the back of the enclosure or it can be bent upward. Also, the frequency of the box can in turn be lowered by adding a length of pipe (or a square-shaped duct) to the port. As a result, the port roughly determines the frequency of the box and the duct is used to fine-tune the system.

In addition to the variables that are encountered in determining the proper specifications for a closed-box enclosure, the port size and duct length are also necessary to determine the proper specifications for a ported-box enclosure. Many pages could easily be filled just with the material constants, duct specifications, and design parameters. Instead of covering every aspect of ported-box enclosures, some basic design information is covered in the following section.

PORTED-BOX DESIGN AND EQUATIONS

The same variables that were necessary to determine the size of the closed-box enclosure are also required to find the proper specifications for the ported-box enclosures. If you haven't already read the section on determining the closed-box speaker enclosures, read it, and find the f_S, Q_T, and V_{AS} for your speakers. If you are planning to use a ported box, you must use the following equation to roughly estimate the box size.

$$\text{Use a port when the box volume} > 2 \times V_{AS} \times Q_T^2$$

If you can tolerate having enclosures with a volume of this size or larger, then you will probably benefit from using a ported box. Otherwise, you should probably stick with the closed-box enclosure. As was the case with the closed-box enclosure, the box should be as large as possible until it reaches its maximum volume. Once again, pull out that calculator:

$$\text{Maximum box volume} = 11 \times V_{AS} \times Q_T^2$$

The result is in cubic feet if V_{AS} is in cubic feet and it will be in liters if V_{AS} is in liters.

You can now calculate how low the bass will be for any size of box using the following equation:

$$Cutoff\ frequency = f_S \times \sqrt{V_{AS}/box\ volume}$$

For this equation, V_{AS} and box volume must both be in either cubic feet or liters. These equations are just approximations, but they should be accurate to within 10% of the actual value.

Once you have chosen the box volume that you feel would work best with your speakers, then you must design the port itself. First calculate the box frequency (the frequency that the port is tuned to):

$$Box\ frequency = 0.39 \times \frac{f_S}{Q_T}$$

To calculate the length of the port:

$$Port\ length = \frac{2117 \times D^2}{box\ frequency^2 \times box\ volume} - (0.732 \times D)$$

In this equation, the port length and the port inner diameter (D) must be in inches and the box volume must be in cubic feet.

Most ports for these enclosures are made with 2" or 3" PVC pipe because of its low cost, strength, availability, and ease of use. Calculate the port length for each diameter of pipe that you are considering and choose one that is not too short (less than 3" or so) or too long (won't fit within the box or comes within a few inches of the back wall of the box).

TRANSMISSION-LINE ENCLOSURES

A transmission line is a cable, usually coaxial cable, where a radio signal flows (either transmitter to antenna or antenna to receiver). Thus, the coaxial cable that connects TVs to a cable system is transmission line. In terms of speaker systems, a transmission-line enclosure is one in which the air pressure is forced to travel through a long maze until it is relieved through a small duct at the bottom of the enclosure. Transmission-line enclosures have some of the same advantages and disadvantages that were mentioned in the last section on ported-box enclosures. They are said by some audiophiles to have superior bass response and clarity, but they are very complicated, esoteric, and difficult to build. You might have a blast experimenting with building transmission-line enclosures, but I feel as though I would be wasting my time experimenting for any slight advantage in sound quality that would be gained.

As stated in the previous paragraph, the transmission-line enclosure is a box that requires a long passage for the sound pressure to travel through. If you have considered using a transmission-line enclosure, think about the potential specifications of a system of this sort. These enclosures are almost always large—usually very long. Some transmission-line enclosures might be taller than you are! Also, the transmission lines in these systems are normally filled with acoustic damping material. Large amounts of damping material tend to settle to the bottom of the box

SPEAKER ENCLOSURE CONCLUSION

This section on speaker enclosures just skims the surface of the topic because its breadth and complexity. What is included here is intended to help you gain some understanding of speaker enclosures and to be able to build simple, solid, high-quality boxes for your house. For additional information on designing speaker systems, enclosures, and crossovers, read *Designing, Building,* and *Testing Your Own Speaker System with Projects (3rd Edition)* and *Great Sound Stereo Speaker Manual with Projects* by David B. Weems. They are excellent resources and should give you a number of ideas if you are an audiophile and experimenter. A great periodic source of information for the audiophile is *Speaker Builder* magazine, which features numerous designs.

BUILDING SPEAKER ENCLOSURES

Building a speaker for good sound is not overly difficult—just follow solid construction practices and tighten everything up a bit more from that. In order to build most of these boxes, you will need to have at least a few tools, but a full-blown workshop isn't a must. The only tools that you must have to construct a simple closed-box enclosure are a saw (either a hand saw or an electric table saw), a screwdriver, a tight-fit hand saw, a caulking gun, an inexpensive soldering iron, and a hand drill. If you use a hand saw, you will probably also need to use a mitre box. Depending on the techniques that you plan to use, you might need more tools, but these are the only must-haves.

First, you must determine the box volume that your speakers require. Then, determine the height x width x depth specifications that you plan to use. Particle board is available in a number of different sizes, shapes, and styles, but my favorite type is that which is used for inexpensive shelving. This type has a harder finish, so it is less likely to flake apart while you are building the cabinet. Also, if you can design the cabinet's sides to be either 8" (20.32 cm), 10" (25.4 cm), or 12" (30.48 cm) wide, you will only have to cut the ends of the boards, not the lengths.

Another consideration is the finish of the cabinet. Typically, speakers are finished with veneer, although I've seen a few that have been painted with a high-gloss enamel. If you like the paint option best, be sure to test it on a piece of particle board before

mauling the exterior of your cabinets. This way, you will be sure
that the finish will live up to your standards. Use a type of board
that contains the finest (smallest) bits of wood possible so that
you don't have to fill, patch, and sand the cabinets before painting
them. After you have finished the cabinets, apply at least one coat
of sandable primer and lightly sand it with a fine grit (220 grit or
higher) sandpaper. When it feels perfectly smooth, lightly coat it
with spray enamel. After a few coats, being sure that the paint
doesn't run, the project should have a professional look.

If you choose the more traditional wood-veneer route, how much
veneer is required to cover the cabinet? You will need to determine the necessary square feet of veneer required to cover the
cabinets. In addition, you must know if the sheets are wide and
long enough to cover a speaker side in one piece, and if you can
cut all of the sheets out of the veneer that you order (i.e., so that
you aren't left with a 2-foot and a 1.5-foot piece of veneer to
cover a 3.5-square foot speaker side). Veneers aren't very easy to
find and many of the manufacturers sell their products only to
other manufacturing companies, not to individuals. The best hope
to find veneers are via mail-order, where a number of different
types of wood finishes are available at prices that range from
about $0.70 per square foot for poplar to $9.10 per square foot
for ebony! Flexible Materials and Brookside Veneers both manufacture veneers that are appropriate to cover speaker enclosures.
The Hardwood Store sells many different types of wood veneers
by the square foot.

Before you progress too far with the design and assembly of your
speakers, you need to decide whether you want to use sections of
grille cloth over the front of the cabinets. Grille cloth isn't necessary, but it will prevent the speakers from getting dusty and it will
also protect the fragile cones against accidents. Grille cloth is
essential if you have kids or if any ever visit your house. ("Watch
mommy scream when I pour my juice here!") Despite the apparent

necessity of grille cloth, I've rarely seen the standard black or brown sheets for sale. One of the few places I've found it is Parts Express:

http://www.parts-express.com

Surprisingly, the old black and gold patterned grille cloth from radios of the 1930s–1950s is very common. Most antique radio stores carry it, and even specializes in it (who would have imagined!):

http://www.libertynet.org/~grlcloth

If you can't find any material that is sold specifically as grille cloth and old-time radio cloth is too gaudy, you can substitute regular material. However, remember that the material must be more than just thin—it also must be virtually transparent to sound. In other words, it should be both thin and very sparsely woven.

Once you have the cloth, you will need to attach it to a rectangular frame. The easiest construction methods would be to use wood for the frame, and to attach the cloth by stapling it to the inside of the frame. To hold the frame onto the cabinet, drill matching holes in the frame and the cabinet. Then glue dowel rods into the frame so that they extend out from it. After the glue has dried, the dowels that extend from the frame will fit snugly into the holes of the cabinet.

JOINTS

Wood corners can be made in a number of different ways, but not all of the styles are appropriate for speaker enclosures. For example, the very popular dovetail joint is not effective because the particle board is not strong enough to hold together at the dovetails. Also, a pretty joint is not particularly useful when you plan to cover it with veneer anyway. The most useful joints are the butt joint, the rabbet joint, and the beveled joint.

The beveled joint is one in which the edges have been cut at 45° angles and then are glued and sealed. The joints must be sealed, so you must either use a table saw or a hand saw with a mitre box so that the joints are tight (Fig. 7-9A).

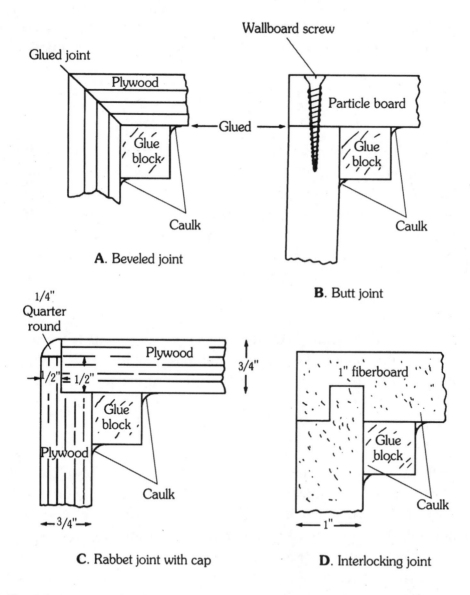

Fig. 7-9 A variety of different carpentry joints for speaker cabinets.

The rabbet joint has the edge of one board butted into a grooved board. You should also use two or three wood screws in each corner for extra strength. You can easily remove the rectangular-shaped groove from the corner with two passes on a table saw. However, the rabbet joint requires more work and tools if you only have hand tools. You can make the cut that is perpendicular to the board with the hand saw. Then, use a finer toothed saw, such as a hack saw, to cut through the board edge and meet the perpendicular cut. You should avoid removing the corner piece with a chisel because the edge will be rough and the joint won't provide a tight fit (Fig. 7-9B).

The butt joint is the simplest and one of the most common joints in carpentry work. It is simply two boards that have been butted, glued, and screwed together. Unfortunately, the butt joint is also one of the weakest joints and the edges must match almost perfectly in order to achieve a strong and airtight joint. If you don't cut the edges perfectly straight, you might need to use a disc sander to get a tight fit (Fig. 7-9C and 7-9D).

When you build any box enclosure, you should screw the corners together so that they hold solidly and don't pull apart after years of use.

For the sake of having both a sealed enclosure and structural integrity, you should build a small wooden frame inside of the enclosure (Fig. 7-10). Glue and screw in small, square or rectangular lengths of wood that are approximately 1" x 1" (2.54 cm x 2.54 cm) around the entire inside front and rear edges of the speaker enclosure. To prevent the particle board from splitting or cracking, be sure to drill countersink holes that are approximately two sizes smaller in diameter than the screws that you will be using. Then, another strip of wood should be glued into each corner. After the glue dries on the entire speaker cabinet, use a tube of all-purpose caulking to seal all of the edges of the wooden

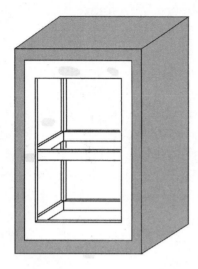

Fig. 7-10 A speaker cabinet frame

frame to prevent air leaks and vibrations within each of the pieces. Be especially careful to make sure that the corner joints are sealed tight. You could probably get away with skipping the inside frame (except for the corner pieces) and screwing the front and rear panels directly to the sides of the enclosure. However, although the particle board is strong, it is also brittle. By screwing through the front panel and into the particle board edge, you will risk having the edges chip apart and strip out the edges where the screws would fit in. So, the wooden frame is a must if you want your box to last any length of time.

The front and rear panels are a bit easier to build and assemble to the frame of the enclosure. The worst problem with the front and back pieces are cutting the holes for the speaker and for the terminal block. You have several options for cutting the speaker hole in the front panel. You can use a special drill bit that is used to cut large-diameter holes, you can cut it out with a jig saw, or you can improvise.

If you have a jigsaw, you probably already know how to use it. Many of us aren't lucky enough to own a wood shop, so the improvised method is described next. Draw an outline of the planned speaker holes. Be sure that you use the proper size that is required for each actual speaker and that you don't just trace the outside of the speakers; otherwise, you will have nothing to mount the speaker onto. Then, drill small-diameter holes (about 1/8" or 3.18 mm in diameter) along the speaker outline. Drill enough holes together that the blade of a jeweler's saw or a tight-fit hand saw will fit through. Use the saw to cut the speaker hole out. Using this method will make the outside edge of the hole a bit rough, but you won't see this edge anyway. Then, insert the speaker in the hole and make sure that it fits well. Draw an outline around the outside of the speaker and measure the thickness of the speaker gasket. If you want to have a perfect fit, drill this wood as deep as the gasket is thick with a drill press. You will have tough time drilling out the gasket depth with a hand drill, so if you don't have a drill press, you might just be better off skipping this process and having the speaker slightly raised off from the front panel. Once the hole is cut properly and the speaker fits in just right, apply a light coat of strong adhesive (such as Liquid Nails) to the bottom of the gasket, which will rest on the drilled-out front panel of the enclosure. After the adhesive has dried, seal the edge of the speaker to the front panel with caulking. Follow this process for each speaker that you plan to install in the front panel.

VENEER

Now that the box is nearly complete, you should start working with the veneer. The box surface should be smooth and clean. Pull out your pieces of veneer and be sure that they will cover the area where you want to use them. Also be sure that the grain is running in the direction that you want it to run. Determine where you want to cut the pieces of veneer (the veneer pieces should be slightly larger than the area to be covered), then place a piece of masking tape over the entire length of the cut. Now cut it with whatever instrument is recommended by the manufacturer to cut the veneer you have purchased (often a table saw, utility knife, or even scissors). Evenly apply contact cement to the surface of one side of the cabinet. Place separator sticks near the end of the side and position the veneer on the cement (Fig. 7-11). Either rub the end down or roll it down with a J roller,

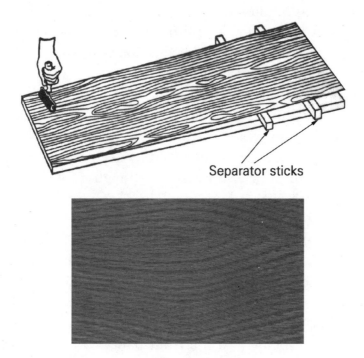

Separator sticks

Fig. 7-11 Applying the veneer to the surface of the flakeboard with a roller (top). A small sample of Flexwood oak grain. Brookside Veneers (top) and Flexible Materials (bottom)

and gradually move the separator sticks to the end opposite of the one you're rolling out from (finally, pull them out from between the veneer and the cabinet).

When you have finished applying the veneer and you're sure that it has solidly bonded to the cabinet, let it dry. Now, use a router with a laminate trimming bit (according to manufacturer's instructions) to smoothly cut away the excess veneer. To prevent the edges from splitting away, start from one end and cut it to about the middle. Then, go to the other end and start cutting so that two cuts meet in the middle. Follow these directions until you have completed applying the veneer.

If you are using an unfinished wood veneer, lightly sand the surface with a fine grit sandpaper, and smooth the routered edges. When it is very smooth, you can finish the cabinet with the product of your choice—wood wax, polyurethane, stain, etc.

FINISHING THE CABINET

Next, the front panel can be attached to the enclosure. Be sure to drill countersink holes before inserting the screws. You will probably need to insert one screw for approximately every two inches around the perimeter of the front panel. That might seem like a lot of screws, but they are necessary to prevent the front panel from vibrating and either buzzing or just leaking and altering the sound of the enclosure.

A number of different types of speaker terminal panels are available from distributors, such as Parts Express. Nearly all of these terminals are panels that require you to cut out a hole in the back of the enclosure. However, only a few require you to drill two small holes to pass the wires through. Then, the terminal block can be screwed onto the back of the cabinet. Some other speaker terminal panels include extras, such as fuses, spring-loaded or screw-on terminals, gold plating on the terminals, and multiple terminals for multispeaker enclosures. Choose a speaker terminal panel that best suits your needs: fused blocks for high power, multiterminals for multispeaker enclosures, gold-plated terminals for high power or audiophile quality, and inexpensive spring-loaded terminals for inexpensive applications.

To complete the speaker enclosure, cut the hole for the speaker terminal panel using the same improvised method that was used to cut out the hole for the speaker. The only difference is that this hole will probably either need to be shaped like a square or a rectangle. To achieve the squared corners, drill the holes in the middle of the sides so that you can cut to the edge of each corner with the saw. If you are using a round terminal panel, you will need to cut the hole out with either a wide-diameter drill bit or a jeweler's saw—the close-quarter hacksaw has too wide of a blade to cut out an approximately 3 to 4" (7.62 to 10.16 cm) diameter hole.

To attach the speaker terminal panel, use a strong construction adhesive and screws. Then, seal the edges of the panel with caulking.

If you are building an aperiodic enclosure, cut another hole in the back panel that is approximately 2 to 3" (5.08 to 7.62 cm) in diameter, although it can be most any shape that you want. Attach a piece of strong (but fine) plastic mesh over this hole

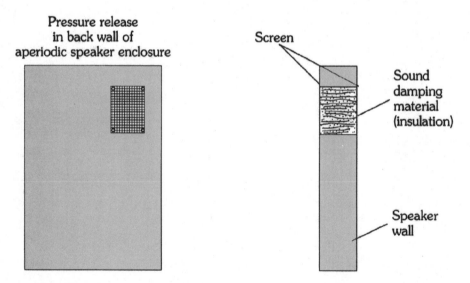

Fig. 7-12 The aperiodic hole

with either staples or with wood, small screws, and a strong construction adhesive (Fig. 7-12). Then, cover the hole with about a 1" thick sheet of acoustic damping material and attach it with a strong adhesive.

After the caulking and glue have dried, wire the speaker to the speaker terminal panel. To wire between the speaker and the speaker terminal panel, use the same gauge of wire that you are using for the speaker wire between the amplifier and the speaker. If this is an audiophile installation, be sure to use a type of wire with the same quality (if not the same brand of wire) as you're using throughout the rest of your living room. Chances are that your speaker will require standard female slide-on connectors. Make sure that you purchase terminals that are made to be soldered onto the same gauge of wire that your system is using. Measure out enough wire so that you can easily pull the back off of the cabinet if you need to get inside to fix a problem. Then, solder the connectors onto the wire and attach them. Line the inside of the cabinet with a bit more acoustic-damping material than you thought was necessary.

Drill the sink holes for the screws and install the corner screws in the back of the cabinet. Do not use a strong construction adhesive on the back panel of the enclosure or you will never be able to pull the box apart without wrecking it. Connect the speaker to your system and listen to the sound. Then experiment with removing and adding more acoustic-damping material. Listen for any rattles or hums in the speaker cabinet and also listen to the decay of the bass frequencies. If the cabinet is loose and vibrating, tighten it. If the decay is not clean, add more acoustic-damping material; if the bass sounds weak, try removing some of the material or try a thinner sheet of acoustic-damping material.

Of course, other designs will require other, more specific, construction methods. However, these basic methods will help you to build some of the simpler designs, and if you care to build a monster-ported masterpiece at a later time, this example will help prepare you.

CONCLUSION

Now that the speakers have been purchased and the speaker enclosures have been constructed, you only need a good set of crossovers to make the most of the sound.

8

FILTERS & CROSSOVERS

Filters and crossovers are two often misunderstood pieces of audio equipment. Although the various computations and applications for crossovers can be very difficult and complicated, the basic concept of what crossovers do is quite simple. A crossover is an electronic circuit that channels audio frequencies to the speakers where the sound can be best reproduced. This system of high-pass and low-pass (and possibly also of bandpass) filters is used to direct low-frequency audio to the woofers, mid-frequency audio to the midrange drivers, and high-frequency audio to the tweeters.

Not many people really consider the crossovers in the stereo system that they are putting together. That's because crossovers are typically built right into the speaker cabinets. The only exception to this rule is in the case of car stereos, where crossovers are built into a cabinet, often with equalizer control potentiometers. The car stereo crossovers are often built into boxes because the bass, midrange, and tweeters are often placed wherever they will fit, not in one speaker box. Space is not a problem in speakers for the home, so crossovers are built right in. Because commercially produced speaker systems already contain crossovers that were designed specifically for the speakers within, you don't need to touch them. As a result, this chapter is only relevant if you are interested in building your own speakers, or if you have a peculiar curiosity in audio.

CROSSOVER USES

As mentioned earlier, a crossover consists of high-pass, low-pass, and possibly bandpass filters. The two primary practical purposes of crossover networks are to prevent the high-frequency speakers (i.e., the tweeters) from being destroyed and to make the audio system sound better.

Tweeters are built to handle high-frequency audio, which consists of much smaller, faster vibrations. Whenever these smaller speakers, which often have stiff speaker cones, are subjected to the large, powerful low-frequency waves, the voice coils will often quickly overheat and blowout. On the downside, you have two (or more) dead tweeters. On the upside, you've now got a pair of powerful refrigerator magnets. The only way to protect the tweeters is to use a crossover network to prevent the lower frequencies from reaching them.

Another problem with not using a crossover is that the audio simply doesn't sound as good. Speakers just can't reproduce audio across the entire human-hearing frequency range—even as several speakers that are each assigned to a different part of the frequency range. Without the crossover network, each speaker will attempt to reproduce across the entire range. Although this system will sound better than just one speaker of comparable quality, it won't emit satisfactory sound because the speakers will be playing frequencies beyond their particular ranges, where distortion becomes noticeable. By cutting out the areas where the audio is rough and "assembling the pieces," you can produce a sound that is much better.

That sounds easy enough; just pick up a high-pass filter for the tweeters, a low-pass filter for the woofers or subwoofers, and a bandpass filter for the midranges. Then, you're all set. The problem is that there are a number of variables. For example, at what frequency should each filter cut off? Also, the cutoff rate (also known as a *skirt* because of its image when graphed) of each type of filter is somewhat gradual. How steep you want the skirts to be will change the type of crossover that you plan to purchase or build. And where should the crossover points be and how should they overlap?

As was previously stated, the use of crossover networks causes other problems, but they are almost essential to attain good audio and safe speaker operation. These are the scientific anomalies that books are made of and companies survive upon. In all, crossovers can be a real pain to deal with, and it's a whole lot easier to pick up commercial speakers with built-in crossovers than it is to buy parts, guesstimate the values, and experiment (Fig. 8-1). Crossovers are one of those

Fig. 8-1 Notice the crossover box between the woofer and the midrange drivers in this pair of Polk SDA SRS speakers.

things that are best left to people with about intermediate-level (or above) electronic experience (i.e., typical electronics hobbyists) and a great deal of patience.

BUILDING AND BUYING CROSSOVERS

Companies such as Parts Express, Scosche, Sound Quest, Crutchfield, etc. offer several types of capacitors, power resistors, inductor coils, and even PC boards so that you can build your own crossovers. If these don't quite suit your needs, some of these companies have tiny in-line units (with or without tiny enclosures) and larger assembled crossovers that are open, carefree, and enclosureless (Fig. 8-2).

Fig. 8-2 A small separate crossover box from the 1950s.

BASIC CROSSOVER THEORY

As stated in the last section, the goal of any crossover system is to transmit different chunks of the audio frequency range to the proper speakers. For the end result, the unattainable optimum is for all of the signals and speakers to fit together perfectly, as if it were one perfect speaker that was receiving audio directly from the system. This isn't easy and it's been known to make some audio tough guys scream for their mommies.

BASIC CROSSOVER COMPONENTS

Crossovers seem to have built up a large mystique among many audio enthusiasts—particularly among the newcomers to the hobby. To some degree, at least, the aura of crossovers seems to rival waxing audio cables for a "slicker" sound or building a "flux capacitor" to power your system. In reality, passive crossovers are quite simple, as far as assemblies and parts are concerned. It is the effects of the crossovers and the crossover points that are difficult to control. Most crossovers just consist of inductors or capacitors in series or in parallel, depending on the speaker arrangement.

ORDERS OF CROSSOVERS

The different orders of crossovers have nothing to do with secret societies, although somewhere in the world, there is probably a group of guys who have a secret chant and handshake, and a silly hat, who get together to drink beer and talk about crossovers. They might even go bowling together and sell raffle tickets for crossover networks. Even if these guys aren't so noticeable in your community for you to have heard them talking, they have surely discussed the merits of the first-order crossover. The first-order crossover was evidently so named because it is the simplest of all passive crossovers. For a set of two speakers (a woofer and a tweeter), only a single capacitor and an inductor are used (Fig. 8-3).

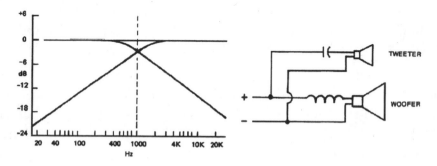

Fig. 8-3 A first-order crossover network. AudioControl

The capacitor is used as a high-pass filter to prevent damage to the tweeter and an inductor is used as a low-pass filter so that the woofer won't sound bad in its attempts to reproduce the higher frequencies.

In a system such as this, just half of the first-order crossover, a high-pass filter (a capacitor) could have been used to protect the tweeter (Fig. 8-4), but then again, this would be just a low-pass filter and not a crossover. Even so, you might feel that your woofer/tweeter combination sounds fine without any crossovers. In this case (and for the sake of saving some money), you could just insert a single capacitor as a high-pass filter to protect the tweeter.

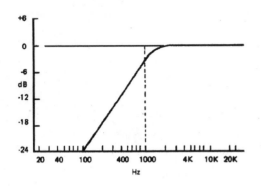

Fig. 8-4 A 1000-Hz high-pass filter.
AudioControl

Nearly all crossovers produce a cutoff slope that is a multiple of 6 dB per octave. The orders of crossovers are all very exact, and as a result, you can multiply the number of the order times the 6-dB per octave figure to find the cutoff slope for any of the basic crossover designs. So, the cutoff slope for the first-order crossover is 6 dB per octave (1 x 6 = 6). This is a very light, gradual cutoff rate and it is either praised or degraded by audio enthusiasts. Supporters of first-order networks praise the simplicity and low cost of the system, and also the easy-to-control phase characteristics and the natural-sounding frequency division. Skeptics see the very gradual cutoff slope as being slightly better than not using any crossovers at all, and they would probably also say that you get what you pay for.

As you now know from the previous descriptions, the second-order crossover is more complicated than the first-order type, and it has a cutoff slope of 12 dB per octave. As far as the actual parts count goes, the second-order network doubles the number of parts that were used before—the high-pass and low-pass filters each consist of a capacitor and an inductor (Fig. 8-5). The 12-dB per octave cutoff rate tightens up the frequency division and it also provides more protection for the tweeters than the first-order systems. The three well-known types of second-order crossovers consist of the Butterworth filter, the Bessel filter, and the Linkwitz-Riley filter.

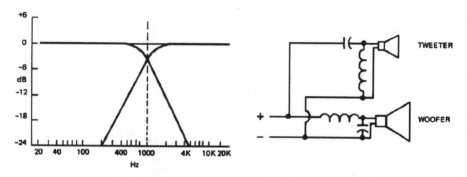

Fig. 8-5 A second-order Butterworth crossover. AudioControl

Unfortunately, the increased complications of the second-order crossovers create a few esoteric electrical problems. The major problem is that the signals to each speaker in the crossover network arrive 180° out of phase. When the same signals arrive in opposite phase (180°), they will tend to cancel out. In this case, the best that you can hope for is a "hole" in the sound between the two speakers. In the worst case, the frequencies will cancel out and the frequency response of the system will be hindered (probably sounding "thin" or "tinny"). If you have installed a second-order crossover system and you don't like the sound (or even if you just like to experiment), try connecting one of the speakers out of phase and see if the sound improves.

Of course, the increasing complexity of crossovers also increases the complexity of the problems that result from using these systems. Now that the phase has been corrected, the frequency response distorted and there is a peak in the response at the crossover frequency of the Butterworth version. Take your pick—

either a null or a peak at the crossover frequency. This is where the Linkwitz-Riley filter fits in. Instead of producing a peak in the frequency response, the Linkwitz-Riley filter has a dip in its overall total power response. As a result of these complex problems, the Linkwitz-Riley filter is probably a better pick for a home or an auto audio system. The second-order Butterworth filters are commonly used in public address and auditorium audio systems because the audio peak is usually in the midrange. Because most of the sounds for voice recognition are in the midrange, this system is perfect for maximum intelligibility, where pure high-fidelity audio is not a concern. Bessel filters also peak at the crossover frequency and dip in the power. Bessel filters are not as commonly used, although some high-end companies, such as Audison, exclusively design their crossovers around this design of second-order crossover.

When you page through the auto audio catalogs, you will rarely see what type of network is being utilized in any particular system. I suppose that most of these companies feel that knowing the filter types won't be particularly useful. Some companies, such as Parts Express, don't list the orders of the crossovers in the component descriptions, but they do list the cutoff slopes of each (which is the most important information anyway).

The very steep skirts of the third- and fourth-order networks are rarely used for crossover applications (Fig. 8-6 and Fig. 8-7). The cutoff slopes are 18 and 24 dB per octave (respectively) and in most cases, they are much steeper than is necessary. After all, the goal of audio and crossover design is to reproduce the source audio as closely as possible and blend the sounds together, not perform laser surgery.

Third- and fourth-order crossovers are sometimes used with subwoofers to prevent the upper bass range from being audible. One of the great assets of subwoofers (as described in previous chapters) is that because the low-frequency sound waves are so

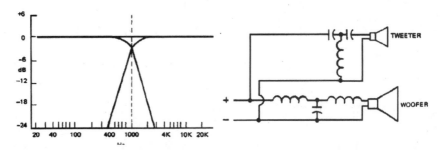

Fig. 8-6 A third-order Butterworth crossover. AudioControl

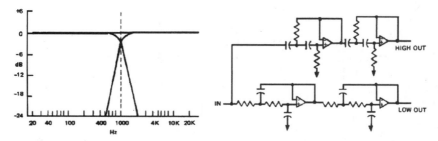

Fig. 8-7 A fourth-order Butterworth crossover. AudioControl

long, subwoofers can be placed anywhere in the room and the bass audio will not sound as if it is coming from one particular direction. However, if the upper end of the bass frequencies are allowed to pass through the speaker, they will "give away" the location of the subwoofer.

Another application for third- and fourth-order crossovers is to reduce "boomy" bass. Like the problem with hearing where the subwoofers are (in the previous paragraph), the problem with boominess also can be traced to having too much upper bass being output by the subwoofers. If you try to lower the frequency of the first- or second-order crossover, you might cut out some of the important low-bass frequencies. The best solution in these cases might be to slice off the upper-bass range with a third- or fourth-order crossover.

In the third-order crossovers, two capacitors and one inductor form the high-pass filter and two inductors and one capacitor form the low-pass filter. In fourth-order crossovers, two capacitors and two inductors are used in both the high-pass and the low-pass filters. Both of these crossovers can become very complicated, when using them in a three- or four-way system. Also, the phase issue reappears. The problem of phase with these crossovers is that the signals do not arrive in phase (as with first-order crossovers) or completely out of phase (as in the second-order crossovers). Instead, the signals arrive at two different points along the waveform. The only way to solve the phase problem is to modify the electronic circuit and probably cause even more negative side effects.

If you want to play it safe, avoid the third- and fourth-order crossover network designs. They are much more complicated, expensive, and frustrating than they are worth.

DETERMINING THE CROSSOVER VALUES

Determining the crossover frequencies for your speakers and the values for the parts of your subsequent crossover might seem like a difficult task—especially if you have no electronics background. But, it really isn't so bad; there's even a table to help you find the values after you determine the crossover points.

DETERMINING THE SPEAKER CROSSOVER POINTS

If you have the frequency specifications or a frequency response chart for your speakers, determining the crossover points shouldn't be an overly difficult task. If you want to protect your tweeters and want a decent-sounding system, but you don't want to waste your time, try the pin-the-tail-on-the-donkey approach. Most of the crossover points in commercial systems are at between 3,000 and 5,000 Hz (to define the border of the tweeters' range), approximately 800 and 1000 Hz (to define the bottom edge of the midrange and the top edge of the woofers' range) and at 100 and 300 Hz (to define the bottom edge of the woofers' range and the top edge of the subwoofers' range).

If you are taking the simple random route with two speakers per corner and a first-order crossover, you would probably want the crossover frequency to be closer to 3,000 Hz for better tweeter protection. The slope of the first-order network is so gradual that dropping the crossover frequency below 4,000 Hz could still allow enough low-frequency audio through to damage the tweeter. If you feel that some of the sound in the midrange would be lacking with such a high crossover rate, use a second-order network (with a much steeper cutoff skirt) instead and drop the crossover lower (to about 5,000 Hz). In either case, it's still a good idea to use a solid-quality midbass or midrange speaker to fill out the rest of the sound. With a good midbass, an average (or better) tweeter, and an appropriate crossover network, you can have a great, natural-sounding installation. Some people even prefer this arrangement because it is simpler and fewer sound-debilitating complications can arise. Also, for the cost of six average speakers, you can buy two really good midbass speakers and two tweeters instead.

The alternative is to dig out the frequency specifications of the speakers that you are using for your system. Normally, good speakers will produce a fairly flat line of response for the range that they are built for. Then, toward either edge of the flat response, the response line will either drop or will begin to spike. Flat response is the key. Spikes, peaks, and sudden dropoffs will alter the overall quality and destroy the realistic sound of the audio. As a result, you can locate potential crossover points by finding where the response begins to get flaky. You need to trim off these rough edges, so whenever possible, configure the high-pass or low-pass (depending on which needs to be used) appropriately. The problems crop up when your speakers are basically mismatched and the response lines get flaky at overlapping frequency regions. If you tried to cut out the areas that aren't flat in a system such as this, you would be left with a gap in frequency response. Depending on the size of the gap and the steepness of the skirt, a gapped-out system can sound really bad—in part because the gap will often occur toward the middle of the hearing range (i.e. where most crossovers are set).

Shown in Fig. 8-8 is the graphed response for the Audax HT110G2 midrange speaker. The response is very flat and it drops off almost as if it already had a crossover installed. However, its

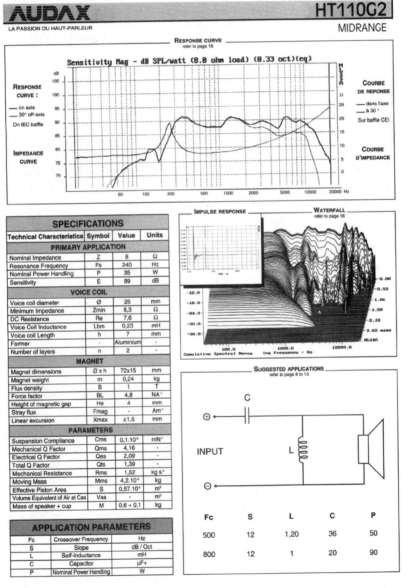

Fig. 8-8 Speaker-response curves for the Audax HT110G2. Polydax

frequency response does carry well into the bass frequencies. The manufacturer recommended parts for a second-order high-pass filter at either 500 or 800 Hz, depending on your preference.

Another problem with rolling up your sleeves and digging into the frequency ratings and graphs is, what if your speakers don't have any sections of relatively flat response across the graph? If the frequency response of a speaker looks as though it had been chewed up by a doberman, you should probably reconsider purchasing the speakers. If you already own the speakers and still want to use them in your system, try to place the crossover frequencies in such a way that you can make the most of what response is there and still cut off some the more extreme response fluctuations. Just try to follow the general guidelines for commercial crossovers that were listed several paragraphs ago. Otherwise, you could wind up with a system that requires eight speakers in each channel. Even if you had all of this stuff on hand, the performance would still be lacking because of the electronic complications involved.

DETERMINING THE PARTS VALUES

Any technophobic Debbie Gibson fan can pull out a few graphs of speaker specifications, draw a few lines, and say "I want the crossover points to be here and here." Actually implementing these changes is another story altogether. You need to determine what parts values to punch in for each component. This task might sound like another "this-is-beyond-the-scope-of-this-book" topic or you might be groaning "Oh no, he's going to bring out an arsenal of equations." Nah. Thanks to some good mathematicians and stereo enthusiasts, the inductor and capacitor component value charts for crossovers have been available for a number of years (Fig. 8-9).

At first, the crossover value charts look more like an aerial bombardiers street map of Grand Forks, North Dakota, than a

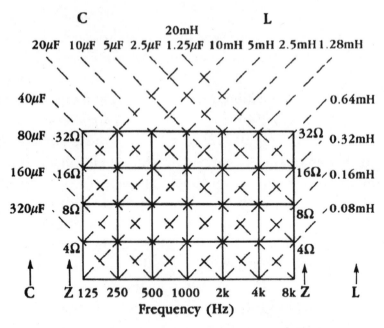

Fig. 8-9 A crossover chart with values for capacitors and inductors.

useful electronic chart. The impedance (in ohms) lines are those that are the horizontal lines on the graph. The frequency range (in hertz and kilohertz) is across the bottom. The capacitance values (in microfarads) are the diagonal lines that run from the upper left corner toward the lower right. The inductance values (in millihenries) run from the upper right corner toward the lower left corner. To read the chart, first find the impedance of the speaker(s) that you are using. Then, find the crossover point that you intend to use on the appropriate horizontal line. Follow the lines from that point toward the inductance and capacitance values. If your intended crossover point falls between two lines, use a little math to guesstimate the appropriate values for each component. The main values in this chart are for first-order crossovers. The italicized values that are listed beside each main value are for second-order crossovers. In case you are scientifically curious, the second-order values were found by multiplying each first-order capacitance value by 0.7 and each first-order inductance value by 1.414. A chart of values is also included to make the value-hunting process even easier (see Table 8-1).

For example, to create a simple first-order crossover for two 4-ohm speakers at 4,000 Hz, the value of the high-pass capacitor would be 10 μF and the value of the low-pass inductor would be 0.15 mH. For a second-order crossover at 4,000 Hz, the value of both of the capacitors would be 7 μF and the value for both of the inductors would be 0.212 mH. The difference between the high-pass and the low-pass filters for the second-order network is that for the high-pass filter, the inductor should be wired in parallel and the capacitor should be wired in series; for the low-pass filter, the inductor should be wired in series and the capacitor should be wired in parallel.

Sure, most any electronics components could be used in your crossovers, but the parts that are used in audio crossovers are strange because the values aren't standard. For capacitors, the voltages are much higher and the capacitance ratings are much lower than those used in modern electronics. The typical capacitors used in crossovers are nonpolarized electrolytics and mylar types. The inductors (also known as *crossover chokes* in some company catalogs) are peculiar little coils of wire. Unlike capacitors, the crossover chokes have strange enough values that they are typically made by domestic audio supply companies, specifically for crossover applications.

Values for Parts in Various Crossovers. M&M Electronics

| Crossover point desired | This is a 6 dB/octive crossover | | | | This is a 12 db/octive crossover | | | |
| | 4-ohm speaker | | 8-ohm speaker | | 4-ohm speaker | | 8-ohm speaker | |
	MFD	MH	MFD	MH	MFD	MH	MFD	MH
50 Hz	796.7	12.7	398.1	25.5	998.0	32.0	499.0	64.0
75 Hz	530.8	8.5	265.4	17.0	665.3	21.3	332.7	42.7
100 Hz	398.1	6.4	199.0	12.7	499.0	16.0	249.5	32.0
125 Hz	318.5	5.1	159.2	10.2	399.2	12.8	199.6	25.6
150 Hz	258.4	4.2	132.7	8.5	332.7	10.7	166.3	21.3
175 Hz	227.5	3.6	113.7	7.3	285.1	9.1	142.6	18.3
200 Hz	199.0	3.2	99.5	6.4	249.5	8.0	124.8	16.0

Continued

| Crossover point desired | This is a 6 dB/octive crossover | | | | This is a 12 db/octive crossover | | | |
| | 4-ohm speaker | | 8-ohm speaker | | 4-ohm speaker | | 8-ohm speaker | |
	MFD	MH	MFD	MH	MFD	MH	MFD	MH
225 Hz	176.9	2.8	88.5	5.7	221.8	7.1	110.9	14.2
250 Hz	159.2	2.5	79.6	5.1	199.6	6.4	99.8	12.8
275 Hz	144.8	2.3	72.4	4.6	181.5	5.8	90.7	11.6
300 Hz	132.7	2.1	66.3	4.2	166.3	5.3	83.2	10.7
400 Hz	99.5	1.6	49.8	3.2	124.8	4.0	62.8	8.0
500 Hz	79.6	1.3	39.8	2.5	99.8	3.2	49.9	6.4
600 Hz	66.3	1.1	33.2	2.1	83.2	2.7	41.6	5.3
700 Hz	56.9	0.9	28.4	1.8	71.3	2.3	35.6	4.6
800 Hz	49.8	0.8	24.9	1.6	62.4	2.0	31.2	4.0
900 Hz	44.2	0.7	22.1	1.4	55.4	1.8	27.7	3.6
1000 Hz	39.8	0.6	19.9	1.3	49.9	1.6	25.0	3.2
1100 Hz	36.2	0.6	18.1	1.2	45.4	1.5	22.7	2.9
1200 Hz	33.2	0.5	16.6	1.1	41.6	1.3	20.8	2.7
1300 Hz	30.6	0.5	15.3	1.0	38.4	1.2	19.2	2.5
1400 Hz	28.4	0.5	14.2	0.9	35.6	1.1	17.8	2.3
1500 Hz	26.5	0.4	13.3	0.8	33.3	1.1	16.6	2.1
1600 Hz	24.9	0.4	12.4	0.8	31.2	1.0	15.6	2.0
1700 Hz	23.4	0.4	11.7	0.7	29.4	0.9	14.7	1.9
1800 Hz	22.1	0.4	11.1	0.7	27.7	0.9	13.9	1.8
1900 Hz	21.0	0.3	10.5	0.7	26.3	0.8	13.1	1.7
2000 Hz	19.9	0.3	6.6	0.4	25.0	0.8	12.5	1.6
3000 Hz	13.3	0.2	6.6	0.4	16.6	0.5	8.3	1.1
4000 Hz	10.0	0.2	5.0	0.3	12.5	0.4	6.2	0.8
5000 Hz	8.0	0.1	4.0	0.3	10.0	0.3	5.0	0.6
6000 Hz	6.6	0.1	3.3	0.2	8.3	0.3	4.2	0.5
7000 Hz	5.7	0.1	2.8	0.2	7.1	0.2	3.6	0.5
8000 Hz	5.0	0.1	2.5	0.2	6.2	0.2	3.1	0.4
9000 Hz	4.4	0.1	2.2	0.1	5.5	0.2	2.8	0.4
10000 Hz	4.0	0.1	2.0	0.1	5.0	0.2	2.5	0.3

Capacitors with appropriate crossover values are very difficult to find in most electronics supply houses. Also, most inductors for crossover applications are made by audio supply companies, so your best bet when ordering these parts is just to check first with a mail-order audio component supplier, such as Parts Express. With a company such as this, the parts are labeled specifically for crossovers, so you know that the components are appropriate.

CROSSOVERS FOR THREE-WAY SPEAKER SYSTEMS

For the sake of simplicity, the systems described in the book thus far have been for two-speaker systems.

The common crossover points for two-way and three-way crossover networks were covered in the first paragraph of the section "Determining the speaker crossover points" earlier in this chapter (Fig. 8-10). Combine this information with the tips for determining the crossover point in a two-way speaker system and you're all set. The only peculiarity of the three-way crossover is that you have to lump both a high-pass and a low-pass filter on the midrange speaker (Fig. 8-11). One strange problem that you could have if you don't really think about what you're doing is getting the values reversed. For example, if you set the crossover rates at 500 Hz and 4,000 Hz, the necessary values for the high-pass and low-pass filters are 80 μF, 1.28 mH, 10 μF, and 0.16 mH. If these are reversed, then none of the audio will reach the proper speakers and everything will be cut out from the midrange. If you install a crossover network and think that you might have blown the speakers out because the audio is low and unbalanced, check your crossover values to make sure that they aren't reversed.

MIXING AND MATCHING DIFFERENT CROSSOVER ORDERS

There's no rule that says that "You must use the same crossover networks in a system or everyone in Wisconsin will turn into slabs

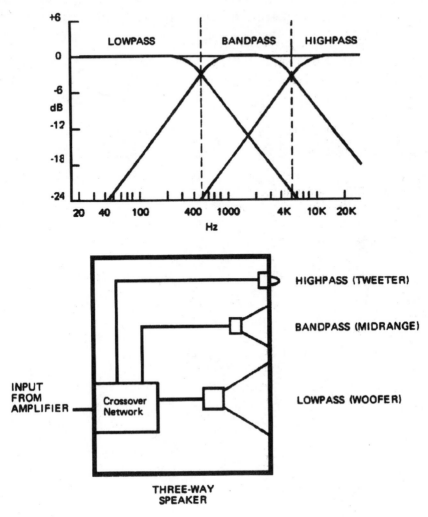

Fig. 8-10 Response rate for a three-way crossover (top) and the crossover arrangement for the system (bottom). AudioControl

of Monterey Jack and the Milwaukee Brewers will win the World Series." Of course, you would only be able to use dissimilar crossovers in three-way or four-way separate speaker systems because the two-way systems have only one crossover.

Really, there's nothing special about using different crossovers in the same network. A number of different commercial crossover networks use a first-order crossover at the lower frequency (bass/midrange) and a second-order crossover at the higher frequency

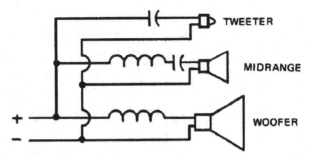

Fig. 8-11 A three-way crossover schematic. AudioControl

(midrange/treble). This system allows the audio to be smooth and natural across the important lower frequencies, and it still can quickly crossover the high frequencies to the tweeter to prevent it from being damaged (Fig. 8-12).

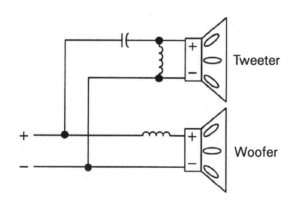

Fig. 8-12 A combination crossover with a first-order lowpass filter and a second-order high-pass filter.

NOTCH FILTERS

No speaker has perfect specifications. In addition to the problems of having a frequency response that drops too quickly after either end of the graph, some speakers have high response peaks. The peak or peaks look like a big stalagmite pointing up from the floor of a cave. The problem with having such peak responses is that one little section of frequencies is much louder than the others. You might find these peak responses annoying.

One solution to these audio stalagmites is by using notch filters and contour networks. Unlike high-pass, low-pass, or band-pass filters, notch filters notch out a tiny segment of the audio frequencies. Notch filters are commonly used in good-quality shortwave radios because the control allows you to notch out narrow-bandwidth sources of interference. A perfectly tuned notch filter in a speaker system can be used to tame those peaks. The only problem is that notch filters are really touchy—just having the component values off slightly will notch out frequencies just above or below the peak. This subject is impractical for the beginner or intermediate audio hobbyist, so it is not further covered here. For more information, see *Designing, Building, and Testing Your Own Speaker System With Projects* by David B. Weems.

RESISTANCE AND L PADS

I have heard some stories about how a few do-it yourselfers built their own really hot speaker systems. They were very excited about the great sound that would soon be filling their neighborhood. Instead, they found that although the audio was clean, it was very shrill and high-pitched. What to do? This looks like a job for Resistance Man—a masked superhero, who installs carbon and wire-wound electronic resistors during the day and who protests the government at night (maybe that was a dumb, cheap joke, but at least I didn't make any jokes about Crossover Man!).

Resistors and L pads are not part of the crossover network, but they can do plenty to control the individual speakers. Also, they are simple electronics that are built into the same physical areas that the crossover networks are constructed, so L pads and crossovers are often mentioned in the same breath. A resistor is an electronic component that limits the flow of a signal through a wire.

If you are a daring, experimenting-type person, you can use resistors to reduce the volume from one particular type of speaker (e.g., the tweeters) in a multi-speaker system. Just wire a resistor with a low-value (such as 10 ohms) in parallel across the terminals of the overpowering speaker.

The problem with wiring a resistor in parallel across the inputs of a speaker is that the value of the resistor will change the value of the crossover point. With some work and experimentation, you can tame the overpowering speakers and tune the crossover frequency, but it would probably require a large effort, which might not be worthwhile.

If you decide to go ahead with the experimentation, the second major obstacle is that you don't really know what value will work properly. There is no standardized method for determining these resistor values, like there are for determining crossover values. Part of the trouble is that speakers vary in efficiency, so unless you check the efficiency of each speaker to make sure that they match, one of the speakers will overpower the others. Matching efficiencies usually isn't a great idea anyway because chances are that you either will not get the best quality or the best prices that you would find if you just got the best speakers that you could afford and matched them later. That is where the resistances are helpful in balancing out the system. The fixed-value resistors are very inexpensive (usually only a few cents apiece), but you will need to experiment with plugging in a number of different values so that you can pick the one that is most suitable for the system and your ears (Fig. 8-13).

Another possible solution might depend on the type of capacitor that you used in your crossover. Although a capacitor is obviously built to add capacitance at a specific point in the circuit, it also has other values, such as resistance and inductance. Different types of capacitors have different ratings of resistance, inductance, etc., even if their values of voltage and capacitance are the same. Depending on the type of capacitors you are using, you might be able to clear up your problems with overly "bright" tweeters by using a different type of capacitor (one with more inherent resistance). This theory might border on a "snake-oil"

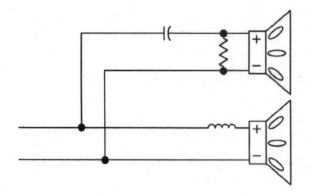

Fig. 8-13 A first-order crossover with a resistor in parallel at the tweeter to reduce its output.

remedy, but if you already have the components, it might be worth a try just to see what happens.

The L pad is handy because it is not virtually permanent, like soldering in the resistors, and it can be tuned to the proper resistance to limit the audio of the speakers. The L pad is a component with two separate sources of variable resistance. When it is installed, one resistance element is connected in parallel to the speaker and the other is connected in series. When the L pad is tuned, it can reduce the output to the driver while maintaining a steady impedance. In all, the L pad is a variable resistor (potentiometer) that is able to maintain a steady impedance.

Most L pads are configured to tame shrill sound from either tweeters or midrange speakers (which are typically more efficient than woofers), and some even have both types built into the same front panel. So, if you want to control the speakers with an L pad, you will need to find a place to mount the L pad, then wire the speakers to it from their separate mounting locations.

You should never try to use an L pad in conjunction with woofers and subwoofers. The system would require massive power resistors, and the effective Q of the system would be increased, which would make the sound "boomy." And because of the differences in efficiency, there is no reason to tone down the woofers.

OTHER COMPONENTS

Up to this point, Chapter 8 has only covered crossovers, filters, and L-pads. A different, unrelated group of equipment is used to process the audio before it reaches the speakers. These include DSPs and equalizers. Although both general groups of equipment are different, they both process audio and are thus included here.

DIGITAL SIGNAL PROCESSORS

Digital signal processing (DSP) has been one of the hottest aspects of all types of audio over the past few years (Fig. 8-14). Among other things, DSP is used to reduce interference in some applications, and to control time delays in others. In auto audio applications, DSP is primarily used only in coordination with various time delays to achieve different acoustic effects.

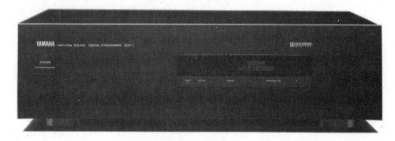

Fig. 8-14 The Yamaha DDP-1 digital sound processor. Yamaha

Some amplifiers and preamplifiers have five preset sound-field configurations: concert hall, live night club, cathedral, stadium, and disco. In each of these settings, the reflected and direct sounds come from different general directions, are at various intensities in relation to each other, and all vary in time response.

Whenever you listen to a studio recording from a band, it generally sounds as if it were recorded in a studio (although this varies, depending on the overall effect that the producer was attempting to create). With the DSP unit, you can make the acoustics within your living room sound like a cathedral, no less!

In addition to the available presettings, you generally have some manual control over the settings of the DSP so that you can set the audio to appeal to your personal tastes. Of course, the DSP could ruffle the feathers of any strict audiophile, who would hate to see the sounds manipulated in ways that weren't intended by the album's producer. Of course, like anything here, you are not required to buy into everything—especially if they violate your morals and sensibilities. I don't have a DSP unit either—not because of a need to uphold the laws of aural purity, but because the enjoyment that I would receive doesn't balance its cost.

EQUALIZERS

In contrast to the new, high technology of the digital sound processor, the equalizer has been in common use for several decades. The equalizer is a sort of analog sound processing unit that controls the strength of the different audio frequency bands. Instead of working with the bits of a digital medium, the standard equalizer is simply an array of variable slider resistors. Each resistor is a different value and has control over a particular audio frequency band. As a result, you can boost the audio response at lower or higher frequencies. Or if there is some hiss or other high-frequency noise, you can reduce the levels on the highest-frequency control to effectively cut back the effects of the interference.

Like many other features, equalizers appear in conjunction with various pieces of equipment. Occasionally, a three- or five-band equalizer is included on a portable stereo system to allow the user to have a few extra controls over the final audio output (Fig. 8-15).

Another type of equalizer is the amplifier equalizer. These units were fairly common in the late 1970s. Many of these units were used for small PA systems for schools or churches, but would often get kopped into service with someone's stereo system. The amplifier equalizer is typically a black box in the shape of a typical amplifier, with about 10 slider potentiometers in the front

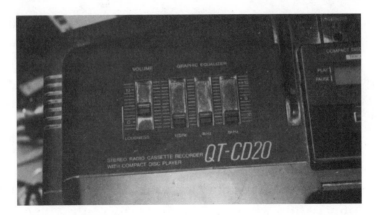

Fig. 8-15 A simple three-band equalizer on a CD/cassette "box."

panel. These units might be a great buy for a small PA system, but they are best avoided in your stereo. I don't really consider these models to be real equalizers, either.

I consider the real, grass-roots equalizer to be a black box with anywhere from about 5 to 12 slider potentiometers on the front panel (Fig. 8-16). These units almost never do anything but equalize the signals.

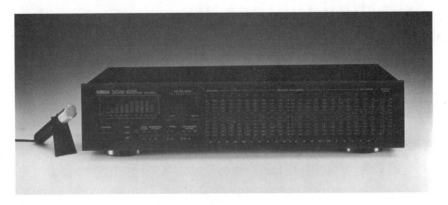

Fig. 8-16 A Yamaha EQ-550 10-band stereo graphic equalizer. Yamaha

Equalizers are incredibly useful because they can help alter the sound of a recording and to emphasize or deemphasize certain audio frequencies. I always liked to jack up the high frequencies on some of my third+ generation tapes to try to perk them up a bit. However, to repeat a piece of advice that I have heard a number of times, equalizers are not a replacement for good-quality audio and they should not be used as such. If you need to alter the sound of a cassette with an equalizer, then you should re-record that cassette.

Another audio problem can actually occur as a result of the equalizer settings (and this is one reason why audiophiles avoid them). If you raise all of the potentiometers to their maximum position, the output will ripple (the severity of the ripple depends on the quality of the equalizer). This effect (Fig. 8-17) certainly adds credibility to the belief that anything extra added between the signal source and the speaker can only distort the sound.

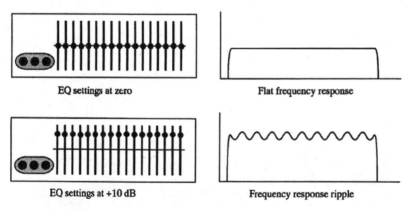

EQ settings at zero

Flat frequency response

EQ settings at +10 dB

Frequency response ripple

Fig. 8-17 Maximum equalizer settings can induce output frequency-response ripple. AudioControl

CONCLUSION

Crossovers are essential for any system, both to improve the audio quality and to protect the tweeters. Signal-limiting resistors and L pads are very handy audio-balancing components, although they aren't necessary in all systems. Although a great amount of mystery and alchemy surrounds all of these components, they are all fairly simple to construct and use, so long as you keep it simple and follow some of the recommendations, such as using the crossover values component chart.

9

INSTALLATION

Did you know that your speaker output does not match the frequency-response graphs that the manufacturer promotes? It's not a scam; the manufacturer is being honest. Those speaker ratings are only the maximum output under selected conditions. The room that your stereo system is placed in can significantly affect the output of your speakers. You can regard the manufacturer's published frequency-response graphs for your speaker as being the maximum (in terms of smooth, lifelike response) that can be reproduced. When you take the speakers out of the box and place them in your room, they might output sound in a manner very similar to the published graphs—or they might sound terrible, with all sorts of peaks and dips in the response.

It might be a bit disconcerting to realize that you just spent hundreds (or thousands!) of dollars on speakers for your "listening center" and they might perform just as well in your house as other models that cost less than half the price. Fortunately, there are a number of different cures and tweaks for these frequency-response dilemmas; although the solutions are technical in nature, you can generally be clueless about acoustics and electronics and still be able to make your speakers sound as good as possible (hopefully up to your standards).

THE SOUND STAGE

One very important aspect of audio that is almost entirely based on the speakers and their stereo separation is the *sound stage*. The sound stage is the positioning of the sound, as you hear it (Fig. 9-1). The positions that affect the sound stage are front and

HOME SYSTEM

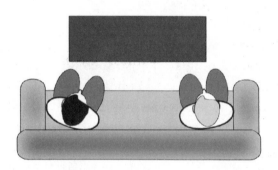

Fig. 9-1 The typical soundstage for a home audio or home theater system. CD Technologies

back (depth); up and down (height); and left and right (width). The sound stage is very important when designing and installing any audio system because it is the key to making music from your system sound real and lifelike.

The combination of the physical speaker locations, the stereo effects of the recordings that you listen to and the combination of audio signals in the air creates the sound stage, which is much different than the physical speaker locations alone. When you have two (or four, in a surround-sound system) widely separated speaker locations, the audio will not sound like it is coming from each of the sources. Instead, it will spread out and fill the room. If all of your speakers are mounted in the front of the room, the sound stage will be decidedly to the front, which is generally good; without rear speakers, the sound will not be as realistic because the audio will lack depth. As a result, it is best to have a balanced set of speakers around the room. With some creative speaker placement and acoustic design, you can create several different sound stages.

For example, as I write this, I am listening to a cassette recording on a portable stereo (affectionately known as a "box" around these parts) that is about 4' (approximately 1.3 m) away at a 45° angle to my front left. The sound stage is small and to my lower left. Although the music is clear and in stereo, it does not sound like a real band—it sounds like some music that is coming from a small box a few feet away from me. This sound stage is very narrow and unbalanced and is what you should try to avoid.

On the other hand, I can go out to my car and experience an entirely different sound stage. With the wonders of faders, I can move the sound stage around me. My personal favorite type of sound stage is to place the settings so that the sounds are hitting me from all angles and it seems as if I am in the middle of the band, but still am facing most of the members. The speaker system consists of one speaker in each side of the dashboard and one in each side of the rear deck. The speakers in the rear deck are built to handle more bass than the speakers in the front. As a result, the sound is three-dimensional—a sort of artificial quad sound. The front/back ratio is set so that the audio from the front and back is almost the same volume from where I am sitting in the driver's seat. Thus, bassier instruments sound as if they are coming from the back somewhere, but everything else seems to be coming from very slightly in front of me. By setting the faders this way, I am sacrificing the audio that would sound as if it was coming from far in front of me (and as a result, all of the points of origin for up-front sounds seem to be very close). Many sound experts would say that I have shortened the frontal sound stage too much with my settings, but I like it this way and it's my system.

Back to the home audio system. To create a proper sound stage, you should have the two speakers mounted near the same wall, both facing out, toward where you will be sitting to listen to the stereo. The speakers should both be separated by a considerable amount of space, which depends, in part, on how far away you will be sitting. For example, in my office, I have the speakers only about 4' apart, but I am only about 2' in front of them. For a better stereo effect, I have the speakers angled in toward me. The result is good stereo separation (which unfortunately varies if I move my head a few inches in any direction), but a small, tight soundstage. It's not an optimum audio situation, but I like it. The sound isn't bad by my standards, and it enables me to listen to music at a decent volume, without bothering my wife or kids. Also, they can still communicate with me, as would not be the case if I were consumed with the desire to have a proper soundstage and music that filled the room.

My parents have a terrible sound stage in their living room (Fig. 9-2). Unlike the ultra-modern, technology-oriented home-decorat-

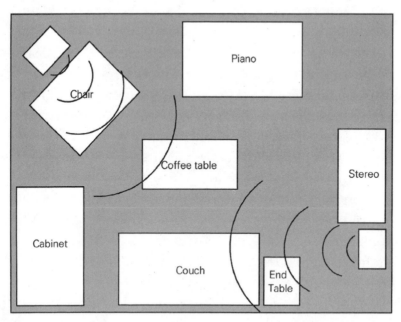

Fig. 9-2 A terrible soundstage: the sound from one speaker is absorbed and muffled by the stuffed chair, and there's no place to sit to hear clean stereo audio.

ing tastes of most audiophiles, my parents have furnished their home with plenty of antiques. They also follow through with the

Colonial Williamsburg (where technology, such as TV antennas are banned) concept that technology is inherently ugly. When they purchased a component stereo system years ago, they refused to have either the cabinet or the components visible in their house. I built a Shaker-style stereo cabinet that could tuck all of this equipment away. But what about the speakers? My parents grudgingly allowed them to be visible—one was placed in a corner beside the stereo (the corner was not one of the room's focal points) and the other in opposite corner of the room, partially behind a padded chair! Both speakers face each other. The end result is a terrible sound stage: the effect is best if you stand in the middle of the room, between the speakers. In any of the places to sit in the room, the audio from one speaker is overwhelming, or you have a sort of "slightly more stereo than mono" soundstage occurring in front of you. For more information on a better alternative than placing your speakers behind furniture, see the section "Hidden Speakers" near the end of the chapter.

Hopefully, these real-life examples will provide you with some ideas about how you want to develop (or how you want to avoid developing!) your soundstage around your current living space.

FREQUENCY RESPONSE

In addition to affecting the soundstage, the location where you place the speakers can also alter the frequency response that you hear. For example, if you angle the speakers in toward your main listening location (probably a comfortable chair or couch), the treble frequencies will be a bit stronger and the sound will be a bit brighter. This can be good or bad. If your speakers already sound a bit too bright, you should probably leave them facing straight out from the wall, or angle them in slightly and compensate with the equalizer or treble control (Fig. 9-3).

Another factor that affects the treble frequencies is the height of your speakers. For best results, the higher-frequency speakers

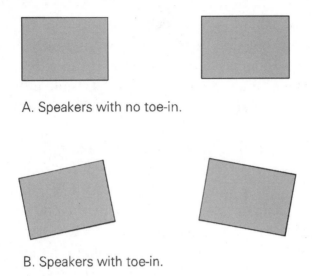

A. Speakers with no toe-in.

B. Speakers with toe-in.

Fig. 9-3 Speaker toe-in.

should be closer to ear-level. This is why so many of the high-end speaker systems are very tall and why the tweeters are always on top. A problem related to this phenomenon is occasionally experienced by people who move frequently and don't spend much time with their stereo systems (such as college students). Sometimes the big, block speakers will accidentally get turned upside down. All of the treble stays along the floor, and the bass is given free reign, resulting in a boomy, muffled sound.

The opposite effect occurs if you place your speakers back toward (within a few feet) of a wall. The bass frequencies are reinforced by the walls. The overall effect is that the bass range could be extended lower in frequency (some of the very low bass becomes audible) and higher in amplitude (the bass frequencies that were audible before can become louder). This effect can be very helpful, but there are a few potential drawbacks:

     1. If the speakers are already too boomy for your tastes, reinforcing the bass frequencies is no help.

     2. If the effect is greatly heightened, it can skew the overall

frequency response of the speakers. In this case, the nice, plateau of the frequency response is warped with peaks and valleys throughout much of the range of audibility.

All speakers are constructed in different ways and with different final results. The only way to be sure that your system sounds as close as possible to the way that you want it to, is to experiment. Sit where you would plan to be for your most regular listening and move those speakers around. Move them closer to the wall, away from the wall, closer together, further apart, angle the speakers in, and let them fire straight out. If possible, even try moving everything to a different wall. Play around for a while, give it a few hours, and see what you think sounds best. When you have found *the* location, stop and enjoy a few songs.

ROOM REFLECTIONS

One potentially serious problem for the listener is that of sound reflections. As you know, sound will readily reflect from flat, hard surfaces. If you have two hard, flat surfaces that are parallel to each other, the sound waves will emanate from the speakers, bounce off one wall, reflect off the parallel wall, reflect back to the opposite wall, etc. until the sound dissipates. A worst-case condition occurs in a house: a typical room features three parallel walls, all of which can wreak havoc on an audio signal.

You have probably experienced this type of echo when you walked into a completely empty room (with a hard floor), basketball court, or racquetball court. If you talk in a typical empty room in a house, the echo is very fast, making your voice sound a bit fluttery. This echo should quickly dissipate. If you talk loudly on a typical indoor basketball court, the echo will be long and strong; you should be able to shout "Bach!" and hear at least one repeat of the word before it dissipates. The college that I went to contained one poor, much-oversized, all-concrete racquetball court. This thing was like a terrible echo chamber. If you smacked a ball off a wall, the sound wouldn't dissipate for at least 10 seconds. If you wanted to talk to people on the court and be understood, you had to wait for the other noise to dissipate, walk to within a few feet of them and speak quietly.

From these examples, you might have picked up some elementary principles of room acoustics (if you didn't know them already):

  1. Some building materials reflect sound waves more efficiently than others.
  2. The size of the room affects the time delay of the echo.
  3. These audio reverberations will distort a natural sound.

Although you can find varying amounts of echo (called *reverb* or *delay* in recording applications) in any recording, this effect must be eliminated in a home listening environment. If you would have a stereo playing in a completely empty room, the reflections would cause some frequencies to be amplified and others to be canceled out. The sound would be choppy and not at all natural. If your only option was to listen to the stereo in this sort of environment, you would be better off either buying a real cheapo stereo or purchasing a decent stereo and investing in a good pair of head-phones (Fig. 9-4).

Fortunately, unless you are in prison, these aren't your only listen-ing options. Another positive aspect of this scenario is that you don't have to make the parallel surfaces nonparallel (massive remodeling!). Instead, you can experiment with interior decorat-ing to dissipate sound. Carpeting on the floor automatically elimi-nates the parallel echoing surface between the floor and the ceiling.

Now, you've got two more sets of parallel surfaces to conquer. A large bookcase will successfully dissipate much of the sound en-ergy because there will no longer be one flat surface, but, rather,

Fig. 9-4 If your home environment isn't conducive to listening or if expensive speakers and amplifiers aren't in your budget, why not opt for a good pair of headphones? JVC

many jagged edges. Along the same lines would be a wall of slatted, bifold doors or shutters. Some of the other absorptive possibilities that might fit in with the decor of your house are a woven blanket or rug (Southwestern style), a quilt (Colonial or "country" style), or even a large bear skin (Adirondack style). Some high-end audio companies sell sound-diffusing materials for your house, but they are terribly expensive and, in my opinion, they are butt ugly. Some of the possibilities are sections of wooden grating for the walls and huge carpeted columns that are placed in corners to dissipate corner reflections. Using typical audiophile supplies, your listening room would look slightly more homey than the rooms from the set of "Battlestar Galactica."

Between the preceding solutions and the addition of a couch and a few padded chairs, you will probably find that the sound in the room is not noticeably degraded by room reflections. It might not sound as good as if you had covered the walls and ceiling with acoustic tile, but these solutions listed here are much more practical, nicer looking (by most people's tastes), and far less expensive.

Some audio pundits have stated that you need to have a separate listening room that has been designed specifically for your audio pleasure. In all of the examples of listening rooms that I have ever seen, the room is empty, except for a large stack of high-end audio equipment, some commercial sound-diffusing devices and one or two chairs. Considering the cost of the equipment and the extra room, this might be fine if you regularly earn $75,000+, but who would have the time to just sit in a room and do nothing but listen to music a few hours per day? Even if you don't have a spouse or children, the responsibilities and the commute of such a job would eat up most of your time. From what I can determine, the only way the anyone could fully take advantage of such a system is if they were independently wealthy, were well-paid musicians, or were audio engineers. Because this book is entitled *Home Audio*, not *Audio Systems for the Rich & Famous*, dedicated audio-listening rooms aren't covered in this book.

Audio room tweaks are both an art and science, but the end result is that you need to move the speakers and sound-deadening objects around the room for the best results. If you would like to check more into the theories behind room acoustics as they relate to audiophile stereo systems, see *The Complete Guide to High-End Audio* by Robert Harley. For a look at the subject from the perspective of a professional recording engineer, see *The New Stereo Soundbook* by F. Alton Everest and Ron Streicher.

RATTLE AND HUM

As is the case for other audio components (especially tube amplifiers and record players), speakers are susceptible to vibration. You don't have to worry so much about them being induced into altering or creating a sound, but causing something else to make an unwanted sound. The worst of these are vibrations in different objects caused by the sound energy.

For example, if you crank up the volume, the speaker cabinets might hum a little or a loose window pane might buzz at certain resonate frequencies. The options here are fairly obvious: fix the glazing in the windows and mount the speakers so that they will stop vibrating. The first is an easy fix, but the second can be a bit more difficult.

A speaker box might be buzzing for a few different reasons:

1. The enclosure might not be solidly mounted on the floor.
2. The enclosure might have a crack or a loose piece inside.
3. The speaker might have become loose from the enclosure.

Always be sure that the enclosure is well mounted on the floor first. This can be a real problem if the floor is uneven, such as the case with slate, tile, or old pine floors. In the first two cases, rubber feet or rubber mats are the best and least-expensive solutions. Solid speaker stands should also cure the problem, but they are much more expensive. With pine floors, these solutions should all be effective, but metal cones or spikes (available from high-end stereo companies), mounted on the bottoms of the enclosures, are also effective. These cones screw into the bottoms of the speakers and acoustically join the box to the floor. This solution is a possibility only if you don't plan to ever move the speakers—the cone points will cut the finish and bore into the wood.

If, even after you know that the speaker has a solid mounting, it still audibly vibrates, pop off the grille cloth covers and try to tighten the speaker mounting screws with a screwdriver. Does the buzzing persist? If so, is it with both speakers or just one? If it is just one speaker, assess how difficult it would be to pull the back off the speaker enclosure and dig inside. If you own $2,300 speakers that appear to be sealed, don't mess with them! Find a professional to check the problem; that way, they will be liable if they further damage, rather than fix, your speakers.

If you have older $200 box speakers and it appears that you can get in fairly easily, unscrew the access panel and pull it out gently—especially if any wires are connected to it. Check for cracks in the bracing pieces and in the corners, and look for loose or fallen screws or lugs. With luck, a screw is rattling around in the bottom. If one of the corners or bracings has separated, run a bead of glue or caulking across the afflicted joint.

If the problem persists, check over the three general problems again or start looking for an entirely different problem (see Chapter 15, which covers some common stereo repairs).

EQUIPMENT STANDS

Now that you have the speakers arranged, and the room is set up for sound, the next consideration is system placement. Where do you place that equipment? The most common solution is to stuff those black boxes in a stereo cabinet or in an entertainment center. This might be the most common, but it is also frowned upon by audiophiles. What is the best solution?

Audiophiles dislike low-cost consumer audio equipment cabinets because they are not solid; loud stereo volumes, traffic noise, or people walking through the house will cause vibrations to be transmitted through the cabinet and into the equipment. Vibrating equipment will perform at a lesser quality than that which is rock solid. As a result, audiophiles insist on specialty audio equipment stands that are built to dampen vibrations.

The obvious solution is to go out and find a really tough stand that will prevent vibrations from being transmitted into your equipment (Fig. 9-5). Before you spend a thousand dollars on a stand with airshocks, think a bit about the equipment that audio-

Fig. 9-5 A typical metal stereo component rack for a home audio or home theater system. Wee Bee Audio

philes use. Many audiophiles go for records over CDs and nearly all vote for tube amplifiers. Both of these are incredibly sensitive to vibrations: the tone arm and needle of the turntable and the elements of the vacuum tubes of an amplifier.

As a result, you should choose a solid cabinet for your system, but if you don't have a turntable or tube amplifier, you shouldn't be overly concerned about damping the vibrations. Just find something fairly solid. For example, a standard stereo stand, such as the types that are packaged with complete stereo systems, will work, but they are often a bit wobbly and, in my opinion, ugly. For the best bet in flexibility, quality of construction, and looks, I believe that it's best just to place all of the stereo equipment in a good-quality home entertainment center. Here, not only does it look nice, but it is also most functional: you can play audio from your video system back through your amplifier and speakers, and keep all of your equipment in one place (Fig. 9-6).

Fig. 9-6 The all-in-one-cabinet look of the Yamaha CS-R4000 stereo system.
Yamaha

But if you have either a tube amplifier or a turntable, vibration control and elimination is essential. You should first go to a specialized stereo shop and check out their equipment racks. Be sure that you do this in person, rather than just ordering something through a catalog. Some of the most commonly available supposedly "high-end" stands are far from sturdy. A few that I've seen have so many long, thin pieces of sheet metal that I would guess that the stand would "sing" if you turned the music up too loud! In terms of vibration alone, the typical entertainment center would be much better than a poor-quality stereo rack.

The hallmarks of a good stereo equipment rack are dense, heavy materials and a means of dampening vibrations. The best racks all have the same general design. Three or four steel post legs are aligned vertically and solid shelves are bolted on. The shelves consist of either solid sheets of steel or flakeboards. Some of the flakeboard shelf units have shock-absorbing materials around each shelf to dampen the vibrations. Others fit into a metal frame or are simply bolted to the vertical posts.

The metal posts are the second variable that determines the quality of the stereo rack. The best are made with a thick metal and use methods to dampen vibration. Some legs are connected in segments, thus partially isolating one segment of the post from the next. In the best rack systems, you can fill the hollow posts with sand or metal shot. This makes the rack tremendously heavy, which is important for three reasons:

1. The rack will be acoustically coupled to the floor.
2. It is unlikely that anything will knock the rack over (especially if the legs are filled with lead shot).
3. You probably won't be frequently rearranging the room and moving the rack around.

BUILDING AN EQUIPMENT STAND

One problem with going equipment-rack shopping is that, like anything in high-end audio, it's expensive. Most of the good equipment racks cost anywhere from $300 to $500, which seems mighty pricey for a small set of shelves, constructed from such exotic materials as steel and flakeboard! Rather than spending your hard-earned dollars on such a mundane aspect of audio, you might consider just building your own rack system.

Of course, building a rack system requires some tools, space, and experience with building furniture-related projects. Constructing equipment racks is a bit beyond the scope of this book because it requires prior knowledge and use of many different tools and techniques—even including (depending on the design and materials used) welding. Because of the advanced techniques and because it would require too much space to show step-by-step how to construct an equipment rack, I'll just toss out a few ideas to whet your appetite and start you thinking about some designs. If you decide to experiment with rack construction, follow standard safety procedures. Although prior experience is not required for most construction techniques, you must be trained in welding and have proper equipment to weld a stereo rack.

The problem with building an audiophile-quality equipment rack is that the frame should be constructed from something hollow and metal. The post legs for a commercially built equipment rack are thick metal pipe. The dilemma is, if you can't weld the pipes together, how can you build a rack?

One possibility is to use short segments of threaded plumbing pipes for the rack legs and flakeboard book shelving for the shelves. Drill out holes that are the same diameter as the pipes in each corner of the shelves. The holes should be in exactly the same location in relation to the edges of the shelves so that they are all perfectly aligned.

Get four of the small sections of pipe and cap one end of each. On the other end of those pipes, screw on a pipe nut. Spin each one down about three inches, but adjust them so that all are even. Stick the pipes into the holes of one of the shelves; the nutted end should go into the shelf holes. Turn it over so that the pipe ends are on the floor. Push the shelf down so that it is resting against the pipe nuts. Next, screw on a pipe joint on the top of each of the pipes that are sticking up through the shelf. Now, move this little bit of the rack over to where it will eventually be sitting permanently. Check to be sure that the shelf is level where the rack will be sitting (many floors are not level, so it is important to place the rack where it will be sitting). You can straighten out the shelf by raising or lowering the pipe nuts, as is appropriate.

After you have the shelf leveled, screw in the next set of pipes. Then, screw in the pipe nuts, push the shelf on, level it, and screw on another set of pipe joints. Keep going until you have installed as many shelves as you feel should be in the rack (it should contain no more than about five shelves and be no higher than about four feet tall). After you have moved it into place, you can fill the legs with sand or shot. Then place an end cap on the top of each pipe. Except for the paint, you're finished.

SOME OTHER IDEAS

You can probably think of a few ideas to improve this rack system or design something with a totally different structure. Would the shelves be better isolated from floor vibrations if you placed a large rubber washer between the pipe nut (under the shelf) and the shelf? Could you receive the same (or better) results by placing a rubber mat on top of each shelf, then putting another shelf on top of the mat? Could you modify a consumer shelving unit to yield similar results?

HIDDEN SPEAKERS

An alternative to speaker racks and having large speakers sitting around your room is to hide the speakers. As mentioned much earlier in this chapter, putting the speakers behind a couch or stuffed chair will devastate the sound. You must be careful with speaker placement—this is audio, not an Easter egg hunt!

The first option in fitting speakers into the decor of your house is in-wall speakers. In-wall speakers are assemblies (speakers and crossovers) that are attached to a metal frame with a metal grille cover. The assembly then mounts into the wall between the studs. For even less obtrusiveness, most of the metal grilles can be painted to match the color of the walls in the room. The speakers are designed to use the standard 8-feet long 3.5-inch wide gap between the wall studs as an enclosure, so the sound is good, despite being a compromised arrangement.

I heard one interesting story relating to choosing in-wall speakers. One man decided that in-wall speakers were his only solution. He went comparison shopping and discovered that one set of expensive in-wall speakers with a high-end brand name appeared to be very similar to an inexpensive set from Radio Shack. He chose the cheap speakers and installed them and was pleasantly pleased with the results. A few weeks later, his "know-it-all" brother-in-law was visiting and listened to the speakers. He said, "Are those (insert high-end brand X) speakers?" "Yep." And the brother-in-law smugly leaned back and said "I knew it; you just can't get that sound with cheap speakers." (To the best of my knowledge, neither man was employed by Radio Shack!)

Another alternative is to reduce the size of the speakers. Instead of floor-standing speakers, maybe you would be nearly as happy with a pair of miniature or bookshelf units. Polk, for example, manufactures a pair of miniature speakers that are designed to be placed on a mantle with other objects. The Polks blend in really well, becoming nearly invisible! If you find the sound to be adequate and the price tag to be within your budget, this might be the route to take—especially if you live in a town house or condo, where cutting holes for in-wall speakers might be discouraged.

Conclusion

With a room mostly designed for sound, chances are that you have your audio system about ready to go. But there's still the matter of getting the audio signal to the speakers, and connecting audio, video, and data lines. See Chapter 11 for more information on wire, cabling, connectors, and transmission systems.

10 COMPUTER AUDIO

Where and how you listen to music affects everything from what you do while you are listening to the type of music that you listen to. For example, some people listen to upbeat music while in the car on the way to work in preparation for an active day. Then, they listen to light jazz or classical music when they return home to unwind.

Years ago, listening to music meant sitting in front of the radio or to a turntable connected to the radio. This period lasted for decades, until the hi-fi revolution of the 1940s and the open-reel tape popularity of the 1950s. From this point on, it became listening to audio (or stereo), and the location was your hi fi or stereo. The system then contained an amplifier, receiver, a turntable, and an open-reel tape deck (later including the CD player, cassette deck, and a few other less-popular media. The hi-fi/stereo system lasted for years and is still a valid listening center. But, by the 1980s, the typical stereo system had morphed into something different—the home theater. Here, you could sit back, catch an album, then catch a movie, complete with hi-fi sound.

An entirely new listening system has been developed in the 1990s—one that has developed separately from the audio sources of the past. As you know from reading the title of this chapter, it is the computer stereo system.

Considering the state of the home computer in 1985, it is just amazing that computerized audio systems could be a possibility in less than 10 years. At that time, most home computers were running at a fraction of the speed of today's machines. The most common computer storage devices were cassette players and low-density single-sided 5 1/4" floppy disks. Even by the late 1980s, it was just exciting to be able to play Dig Dug or Pac Man on a computer and hear a really tinny version (sounding like today's song greeting cards) of the video-game theme songs.

Computers are the next big thing in the audio world because of the development of smaller ICs and higher-capacity hard drives. The increase has been blistering: nearly every year the processor speeds are doubling. At this writing in 1997, it's MMX technology, in 1996, it was the 200-MHz Pentium; and by the end of 1995, it was the 133-MHz Pentium. In addition, the price cuts are staggering. That Pentium 200 computer might have cost $4,500 when it hit the market, but it's now well below $1,500. The 486 DX4-100 (roughly half the processor speed of a Pentium 100) might have initially sold at the same price as the Pentium 200, but now its $700 or less.

The same kind of increases in processor speeds and price cuts are occurring in the rest of the computer industry. CD-ROM drives, sound cards, RAM chips, software, etc. are all becoming faster and less expensive. *Multimedia*, the catch word of the 1990s, is no longer used to impress your friends. It's so common that everyone just expects multimedia from a computer.

Now that multimedia has become passe and computers are filling homes and offices around the world, the emphasis is not on the novelty of multimedia, but whether a computer can be at the heart of an audio system. The answer is, of course, yes (with a few reservations).

The type of system described in this chapter is a digital/analog combination with a multimedia computer, an amplifier, speakers, and a cassette or DAT tape deck. Everything is centered around the computer (in terms of use and applications) and the computer system (in terms of location), which is why it is considered separate from a "traditional" audio system.

A standard multimedia computer audio system would consist of a computer with a CD-ROM drive, sound card, and amplified speakers. Such a configuration will work fine, but the sound quality and flexibility could be upgraded considerably for little cost. That is the focus of this chapter—not to build a 64-channel digital audio workstation, but to dramatically improve a system that most people take for granted.

HARDWARE

The following computer and audio hardware is either necessary or helpful when constructing or improving a computer sound system.

MOTHERBOARD PROCESSOR

In the early to mid 1990s, the speed of a computer often prevented users from successfully installing and using multimedia upgrade kits. Many people were concerned about the amount of RAM required and the minimum processor speed. If you have purchased a computer that was manufactured since 1993, chances are that the computer will have no problem with the processor speed. The MPC Level 2 specification requires a minimum speed of a 25-MHz 486SX chip.

HARD DRIVE

If you are just playing CDs on your CD-ROM drive, then the amount of available space on your hard drive is irrelevant. That situation only changes if you are saving audio as computer files (typically .WAV files) or mixing/editing audio. You just don't need a little bit of empty space; you need a massive hard drive! A 30-second chunk of sound, recorded on your computer in stereo at

CD quality (44.1-kHz sampling rate) will require 5.25 megabytes of space on your hard drive! Recording a typical 45-minute-long album onto your hard drive would require 472.5 megabytes! Lucky for us, the cost per megabyte of hard-drive space has dropped incredibly over the past few years (Fig. 10-1).

Fig. 10-1 A typical computer hard drive. Maxtor

Even though a 160-megabyte hard drive is required for a computer to pass the MPC Level 2 specification, few new computers are sold with less than 10 times that much available space! As of this writing, most new computers are being sold with disk drives that range in capacity from 2 gigabytes (2,000 kilobytes) to 4.5 gigabytes (4,500 kilobytes). That might sound like a tremendous amount of available space, but if you perform much multimedia work (audio, still images, and video), that space will be filled out faster than the extra room in your jeans at the beginning of winter.

SOUND CARDS

Sound cards are the heart of the computer sound system. They act as a digital-to-analog (D/A) converter, analog-to-digital converter, MIDI interface, and a central "station" for interconnections: line in, mic in, audio out, and MIDI in/out. In short, they make it possible to output or input audio (Fig. 10-2).

Fig. 10-2 If good computer sound is a priority, the sound card is the first place to start: The Turtle Beach Multisound Pinnacle sound card. Voyetra

Current models of sound cards all use wavetable synthesis, as opposed to some other methods of deriving sound, which had been used in the past. At this point, the only thing that you need to know is that wavetable sound cards will produce realistic audio, and some of the other now-defunct types (such as FM synthesis) produced video-game-type sound. FM synthesis sound cards might be nice for playing "Asteroids," but they aren't much good for playing back music CDs.

The D/A converter part of the sound card works on the principles that were covered in Chapter 3, which covered digital audio from CDs and MiniDiscs. For more information on D/A and A/D conversion, see Chapter 3. To be completely superficial and nontechnical, let's just say that the D/A converter changes all of that binary code into great music.

MIDI FUNCTIONS

In addition to acting simply as a D/A and A/D converter, the sound card also acts as a MIDI interface. *MIDI* is an acronym for *Musical Instrument Digital Interface*. The acronym is a perfect description: the sound card acts as an interface between the computer and other synthesized instruments (such as keyboards and drum machines). With the MIDI-capable sound card, the computer is capable of sequencing the instruments, controlling their operations, and editing the sound. While all of this is occurring, the sound card is working as a D/A and A/D converter and is "giving the instruments a voice." The sound card controls the sound of the different instruments, so the instruments played back through one sound card will sound different when played back through another. For example, the Ensoniq Soundscape Elite sound card features 128 different MIDI instruments, including 7 different drum kits and 61 different drum programs to choose from.

Because the sound card provides the instruments' sounds, choosing a sound card is like choosing all of the instruments for a band, if you are planning to work with a MIDI. Typical computer purchasing involves checking through the *Computer Shopper* and a few local computer sale flyers to see if you can find the best price. You just can't do that when looking for a sound card for MIDI applications. Even looking at the specifications or the number of instrument "voices" available on the card won't show you what it actually sounds like. The only way to hear all of the sound cards on the market is to listen to each in action. Such a screening simply isn't possible via mail order or at a local store. However, the Wavetable Sound Card Test Drive Internet Web page is a great help to any MIDI hobbyist or professional who is on the lookout for a sound card. This page features downloadable MIDI audio files that were recorded using different sound cards. From listening to the dozen or so files that are posted on the page, you can get a good taste of what different sound cards sound like for MIDI applications. You can download them from:

http://pubweb.nwu.edu/~jll544/sndsmpl.html

If you are serious about MIDI and would like more information, see *Making Music With Your PC: A Beginner's Guide* by Warren

Sirota, *A Musician's Guide to MIDI* by Christian Braut, *The MIDI Manual* by David M. Huber, *Random Access Audio* by David Miles Huber, and *Computer MIDI Desktop Publishing Dictionary* by Albert DeVito.

The Web pages on the Internet are just loaded with good MIDI information. Rather than list all of the different pages here, check a page called *MIDI Links*. That's all it is, tons of different links to MIDI-related Web pages:

http://www.csee.usf.edu/~gould/midi.html

SPECIFICATIONS

Of course, when you are considering building an audio system around your computer, you have to be concerned with the quality of the sound output. You won't be able to go into a computer store and listen to every model of sound card with a great amplifier and pair of speakers, so you'll have to rely on the specifications (and possibly a review or two) if you want to be satisfied.

Sound cards are intended for different computer applications. Some focus on a billion different instrument sounds for MIDI. Others provide neat gimmicks that you can use to manipulate audio (such as reverb, chorus, and specialized audio software). Still others simply strive to be inexpensive. But a few work hard at providing high-quality audio output. You can see this in the specifications.

One company that has consistently worked toward producing audiophile-quality sound cards is Turtle Beach. For example, their MultiSound Pinnacle sound card features the following specs:

* S/N: > –97 dB
* THD: < 0.005%
* Stereo crosstalk: 90 dB at 1 kHz
* Frequency response: 10 Hz to 22 kHz

As you can see from the specifications, you can assume that this sound card has a better sound than many of the CD players currently on the market. In addition, the MultiSound Pinnacle can also record as high as 20-bit audio with a frequency of 48 kHz. This higher-resolution audio is even better than that which is available via CDs (16 bit at 44.1 kHz)!

But the most exact tests are from the ears of audiophiles, not the meters of test equipment. Of course, this is only one review, but the November 1995 issue of *Audio* featured an article entitled "The Promise & Problems of Computer Sound Boards." Although the author had a few problems with the sound cards that he tested, he gave them a thumbs up for multimedia purposes. He gave the Turtle Beach Monterey card a better review and said, "Generally, I was impressed." Not bad for a high-end audio magazine.

CD-ROM DRIVES

Essentially (when playing audio CDs in a computer), the CD-ROM drive performs as a CD transport (Fig. 10-3), and the sound card works as a D/A converter. Although the CD-ROM drive is an

Fig. 10-3 A typical computer CD-ROM drive installed in a minitower with the tray open and a CD in place.

246

important component of the computer audio system, it is not necessary to get an expensive CD-ROM drive simply to play back audio CDs. To comply with MPC Level 2 specifications, the drive must have a data transfer rate of 300 kilobytes per second. The base figure for determining the transfer rate ("speed") of a CD-ROM drive is 150 kilobytes per second, which would be a 1x CD-ROM drive. Thus, a 4x drive would transfer data at 600 kilobytes per second, an 8x at 1,200 kilobytes per second, a 10x at 1,500 kilobytes per second, and a 12x at 1,800 kilobytes per second.

The speed of a CD-ROM drive determines how fast the data (audio, visual images, etc.) hits your screen and speakers. So, if you are playing a CD-ROM on a 12x drive, it will be capable of transferring data six times faster than a 2x drive. A high-transfer-rate CD-ROM drive (faster than 2x) is not necessary for playing back audio CDs because they can play back all of the available data per second. Unlike analog media, digital systems can't improve the definition of a signal by recording it at a faster speed. Everything that is played back is contained on the tape, disc, or hard drive; nothing is missed. Instead, to get more music information into a digital medium, you must increase the sampling rate and the bit depth. So, if you want your CD-Vs by the artist formerly known as an unpronounceable symbol formerly known as Prince to load faster, you've got to get a faster CD-ROM drive. If you want your audio CDs to sound better, get a better sound card or amplifier/speaker system.

CD-ROM RECORDERS

The ultimate in safe data storage is the CD-ROM. The data is physically burned right onto tracks in the aluminum sheet that is enclosed within the plastic disc. With this type of storage, you don't have to worry about sitting a disk on a speaker and it getting erased. Any sort of tape drive that magnetically records data to tape is at risk. Not only is it sensitive to heat and electromagnetic radiation, but recording tape, diskettes, and hard drives will naturally degrade over time. This isn't as much of a problem for personal recordings on analog tape; the music might just sound a bit bassy or have a brief dropout. If any degradation occurs in a digital file, it can completely fail.

Another excellent reason to save data on CD-ROMs is viruses. Unless the data is permanent (once-write only), it can potentially be destroyed or altered by computer viruses. Although regularly backing up the data on your hard drive with one or more tape cartridges or SyQuest disks might be a good idea, it can later be corrupted by a virus. The CD-ROM might perfectly store files, but you have to be careful; if you aren't careful and save everything to CD-ROM, you might have permanently saved a virus. The only way to avoid this and other computer virus problems is to get a good computer antivirus program, such as those produced by McAfee and Norton. Then, you can be sure that your files are clean before permanently storing them.

For computer storage, the CD-R is an unbeatable combination of low-cost, permanent storage. The really great aspect of using the CD-R in a CD-ROM recorder is that it can produce audio CDs as well as computer CD-ROMs. The only difference when producing them is the software; you must have specialized software to make audio CDs. Most of the CD recorders on the market are sold bundled with audio-CD production software, but not all are. If you decide to spring for a CD-ROM recorder, be sure that it contains all of the software necessary to produce audio CDs. Otherwise, you'll have to track it down, and probably pay more money in the long run.

The most beneficial aspect of CD-ROM recorders for the audio fiend is that they can be used to record digital music virtually perfectly—from either DAT, CD, or from your hard drive. Thus, you can record and produce CD-quality audio on your computer and record it to CD. Or you can record demos or other music from DAT to CD for an indistguishable copy.

AMPLIFIERS AND SPEAKERS

Amplifiers and speakers are some of the biggest rip-offs in the computer industry. The quality is generally bad, the ratings are often incorrect, and (except for surplus) the prices are incredibly high.

The typical computer multimedia on the market today includes a pair of amplified speakers. The plastic boxes each contain one speaker that is about 3 inches in diameter and a small amplifier. Some of the better systems will also toss in an amplified subwoofer. Such systems typically cost anywhere from about $25 to $600. These systems either sound so bad that you wouldn't want to use them or are so expensive that you couldn't afford to.

I've heard a few computer systems with these types of speakers that sounded fair when you sat right in front of the computer with the speakers angled perfectly. Of course, with such small speakers, the bass was virtually nonexistent, but they didn't sound too bad. But if you moved just a few feet away, the sound became tinny, like sitting a pair of headphones on the floor and listening with the volume jacked up. Despite the weak audio, some have killer specifications. One set of amplified speakers that I saw last year at a computerfest were rated at 160 watts. Yeah right, a 160-watt amplifier built into the cabinet where a 3" speaker is housed. Those speakers would have been lucky to even survive 160 watts peak output power for a few seconds. I would be surprised if those speakers were good for more than about 10 or 20 watts rms, and who knows what that amplifier was capable of!

The bottom line is that multimedia speakers are inferior by design and are price inflated. Plastic enclosures are never used in home audio applications, and amplifiers are never built into speaker boxes. A 4" "subwoofer" built in an 8" plastic box? Give me a break. These are extreme no-nos in home audio, and they are just as serious flaws when used for computer multimedia.

Fortunately, the problem is easy to solve. Just avoid specialized computer multimedia speakers and amplifiers. Instead, dig into the junk box. Your best bet on a cheap (or free) system that's better than most of the computer speakers on the market is an old junker music "system." That's right, the old 1980-era phono/radio/cassette system with the crappy speakers will knock the socks off of most multimedia speaker/amplifier combinations. The amplifiers were built to handle about 15 to 25 watts of power with somewhat low distortion—certainly not a Linn LK100, but substantially less expensive. Although the speakers are substandard, they are larger than multimedia speakers (not a true sign of better fidelity, I realize), and have flakeboard cabinets with a larger internal volume. A better alternative would be to find a good 1970s or early 1980s-era receiver for $20-50 (Fig. 10-4) and add some cheap, used bookshelf speakers. You could really beef up your computer's sound for about $100.

Fig. 10-4 A cheaper and better solution to using amplified speakers is buying that classic 70s receiver from your neighbor's yard sale.

With my computer, I use a set of speakers from a cheap, old system that was about to be thrown away, two car stereo subwoofers, and a Harman/Kardon amplifier (Fig. 10-5). Except for the amplifier (which I hadn't been using regularly), all of the audio components were free. To find a system on the market with a comparable sound and the ability to crank up the volume, I would have expected to pay $300 or more. These stereo systems

Fig. 10-5 My computer audio system.

are really cheap and easy to find because they are so old and no one wants them if the cassette player breaks or if it is an 8-track/ phono/radio combination (the latter is larger and might eat up too much space at your computer desk).

RADIO AND TV CARDS

Miniaturized computers, dedicated to a single application (or sometimes several applications) are used for all sorts of appliances—everything from microwaves to radios and TVs. Considering the plummeting cost of computers, sometimes it is less expensive to develop all of the hardware on a plug-in board for a computer, write software for the application, and let the personal computer do the rest. On the other hand, high-tech gadgetry pulls in lots of money, so some of the computer boards on the market are more along the lines of expensive novelties than something practical. Regardless, this section is about some of the communications boards that can be popped into your computer.

The most popular of the boards are the video converter boards, which allow you to connect your TV, VCR, or camcorder to your computer and play it back on your monitor. These are a bit out of the coverage of this book, so see its companion, *Home Video*, if you are interested in more information.

An Australian firm, Rosetta Laboratories, launched a product called *WiNRADiO*, which claimed to be "the World's first wide-band communications receiver card on a PC card." Placing a sensitive receiver inside a computer seems to contradict common sense. What are these wacky Aussies going to do next, tell me to bury my antenna underground? The noise interference generated by the PC is enough to wreck your radio listening. Yet, Rosetta Labs opted to eliminate this interference by putting an entire shielded radio inside a personal computer (Fig. 10-6). Provided that the shielding is good enough, the effect should be much the same.

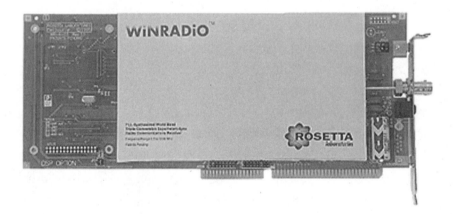

Fig. 10-6 One of the first radios on a computer card: The WiNRADiO from Rosetta Laboratories. Rosetta Laboratories

Several advantages of having a communications receiver inside a PC are:

     * The user interface (in WiNRADiO's case, running under Windows) can be very user-friendly and can contain many more features and functions than could be fitted on a stand-alone fixed-panel receiver.

     * Some very advanced features, such as spectrum analysis,

expensive on a stand-alone receiver, can be made cheaply with a PC-based radio.

 * The PC mass storage facilities (hard disk) mean practically unlimited memory capacity for frequency storage. A direct integration with a database is also possible.

 * A single radio card can have many different software "personalities," developed to suit your particular preference or application.

 * A close integration of a radio and PC can mean an easier development of enhanced functions (for example, real-time signal enhancement and decoding facilities).

I won't get into many of the technical details, but here is a rough sketch of how the receiver fits in with your computer system. WiNRADiO is available on a standard full-size PC-bus (ISA) card, which requires a single slot on your PC. A BNC connector is used to connect an antenna, and a standard audio jack is used to connect speakers or headphones (so, a sound card is unnecessary, although if your computer has one, the audio will be fed to the speakers, like any other multimedia application).

The WiNRADiO is the ultimate in computer-based communications receivers. It can receive almost anything, except video. The 0.5 to 1300 MHz includes such services as the AM (MW), shortwave, and FM (VHF) broadcast bands; audio from VHF and UHF TV stations; amateur radio bands; and two-way communications.

Although not for the audiophile, the WiNRADiO does provide an excellent look at a veritable smorgasbord of radio communications. Considering the price, how much territory it covers, the type of new technologies involved, and all of the different functions, the WiNRADiO performs fantastically. My only problems have been with images; I receive some local FM stations in many places in, above, and below the FM broadcast band. This is a fairly serious affliction in the FM band, but overall the performance is fairly solid.

Be sure to visit the Rosetta Labs Web page for new releases:

http://www.winradio.net.au

AUDIO SOFTWARE

To do anything with a computer, you must have software (computer programs) to do it. Software is the interface between you and the computer; via the software, you tell the computer what to do and (if the software is well written) the computer will tell you what it is doing and what your options are.

Every different computer application requires software, which only consists of codes on a disk. Thus, the process of developing new software is simple; the engineers must only create the code for the application. Unlike other manufacturing fields, they don't need to have a prototype constructed, then have molds and dies cut, and other equipment set up. And, if the computer engineers want to add or alter some features, they just need to write the code and use the new information as the master for copying. If an engineer in car manufacturing were to implement such a change, several of the machines would need to be altered to produce the new parts, and the production protocol would also need to be changed. Because of these differences in processes, computer programming can be developed at little cost and updated regularly; this means that many different programs are available for nearly any different application.

Computer audio-related software can be broken down into the following general categories: CD players, audio players, and audio editors. CD players simply allow you to play audio CDs in your CD-ROM drive. Nearly every new computer sold since about 1992 has contained a CD-ROM drive and CD player software, so you might not have a reason to try other software. But, you might be interested if you want some special features with your player. In addition to the simple features, such as play, stop, pause, skip, and being able to move to any part of the song, some of the available CD player features include shuffle mode, intro mode, the ability to follow created playlists, jukebox mode, and auto eject. One player even sports a spectrum analyzer! A number of CD players also contain a database whereby you can identify CDs and include song titles and other information; these players will automatically display the artist information and allow you to control aspects of the playback by the artist or song title information.

Audio players can be further broken down to the subcategories of Internet and computer audio players. Internet audio players are used to play back the different high-compression audio files that are placed on Web pages. The most common Internet audio players are those for RealAudio and TrueSpeech. Unlike .WAV and .AU files, which require you to download audio to your hard drive, Internet audio players allow you to listen to programming in real time. A number of radio stations are now live simulcasting their programming via the Internet, so you can finally check out that Brazilian heavy metal station you've always wanted to hear! Aside from playback, Internet audio players contain no features.

Standard computer audio players will typically allow you to play a number of different formats of audio and/or MIDI files. Most include some novelty features, such as looped playback (the file is played over and over in a loop), alarm (using audio files to wake you up at a predetermined time), or spectrum analyzer. Still, the most important feature of computer audio players is the ability to play back as many different formats as possible.

The final category is that of audio editors. The category of computer audio players is somewhat small because many people like having the ability to edit and record audio, as well as play it back. Audio recorders are fantastic tools because they give you the ability to edit as precisely as if you were cutting tape on an open-reel deck, yet it is much faster, less permanent, and allows you to listen to your work before permanently editing it (the mighty Undo command!). Audio editors vary fantastically in their number of features and general quality. They vary from little shareware clip-and-paste programs to full-blown multichannel professional mixing/editing programs that cost thousands of dollars.

If an audio editor seems to be in your future, check your priorities. If you plan to record audio from a band for possible release, you would want it to have multitrack options, many different audio effects that you could manually adjust, pitch control, and a spectrum analyzer might be useful, too. If you are recording music by yourself or if the band uses sythesizers, then MIDI compatibility is a must, too. If you just want something that you can use to record messages for your answering machine, try a shareware editor that includes some features (especially audio effects), yet seems intuitive. Also, the ability to play back many different types of audio files will be helpful because you will probably use the editor to edit or play back some of the files that you find and download from the Internet.

If you are interested in any kind of audio software for your computer, you must find the Audio Software Web page. This page is divided into CD players, audio players, and audio editors, and it features brief reviews of the software, plus links to the Web pages where you can download shareware or demo programs. This page is a must for anyone interested in these players/editors:

http://www.com.org/~fournl/windows95/audio.html

CONCLUSION

Today's multimedia software will enable you to perform many different audio tasks with ease, most of which were previously impossible or were very expensive. Better yet, some of the sound cards now available offer audio quality that is as good or better than many of the comparably priced consumer audio systems.

11 WIRE AND MORE

The most forgotten part of any audio system is what actually transmits the power and audio signal from one part of your system to another. Wire and cabling are often forgotten because they are about as boring as a Paul Anka record. Why would you waste your time and money working on wires when you could purchase and spend your time on some really cool equipment? I have no idea. I would much rather play with all of the buttons and displays!

When you get right down to it, the subject of wire and cabling is very important. With a bad choice in wire, you could decrease the quality of the sound or pickup interference. Although it is unlikely that a poor choice in wire will cause a house fire or an electrical hazard, the difference is in efficiency and overall sound quality.

WIRE

Other than one peculiar exception, wire is always used to transfer audio and electricity between the various components. Few people think about the different qualities of wire and the efficiency as a signal travels from one component to another. However, wire is made from several different materials (of many different qualities) using different drawing methods. Also, wire can be made either with one single wire, with many strands, or with bundles of strands; it can be shielded to prevent other signals from causing interference; and multiple wires can be encased within either a round or a flat cable (Fig. 11-1).

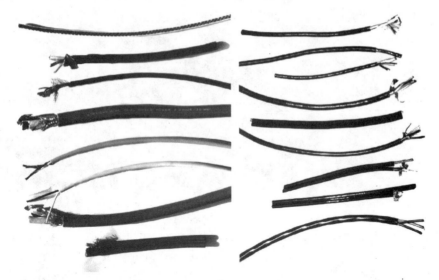

Fig. 11-1 A number of different types of speaker, interconnect, and power cables.

Most audio and power cables are made from copper. But if you use wire that was intended for some other electrical application, be aware that it might be made from another element or elemental combination, such as aluminum or copper-coated steel. Generally, copper is the only element to use to transmit audio and power signals through your house. Aluminum is fine for use in electric fences or in long radio antennas, where low cost is more important than high efficiency.

As stated in the previous paragraph, copper is an excellent conductor of electricity. Silver is a better conductor. However, its cost is obviously prohibitive for most electrical applications.

WIRE SHAPES AND STYLES

A number of problems can occur when different components are connected together via wire. Two major problems are resistance and skin effect. Skin effect is the scientific property by which electricity travels on the outside (the "skin") of a conductor (Fig. 11-2). It has nothing to do with rashes, blushing, acne, leprosy, or a host of other dermatological problems. Skin effect causes dif-

Fig. 11-2 A visual representation of skin effect. © AudioQuest

ferent problems in different applications. For example, when transmitting at radio frequencies, if a station is outputting too much power into too small of a conductor (one that has too little surface area per watt of power), the resulting heat could cause the radio antenna to burn up. However, at audio frequencies, skin effect is a completely different monster. Instead of the "bigger is better" maxim that rules for radio conductors, larger diameter wires can cause other problems that result in high-frequency distortion. This distortion problem occurs in both solid and multistrand conductors.

Resistance is another problem that plagues electrical circuits. As stated in another chapter, resistance is the opposition to an electrical signal flow. Although the resistance through a wire will cause a slight decrease in the signal strength, it will also cause some distortion.

Solid (single-strand) wire has a much higher resistance than stranded wire. You can see that problems occur with this type. If the diameter of solid wire is too large, the signals will distort as a result of skin effect. Yet, if the diameter is too small, the resistance of the wire will cause distortion. Worse yet, the two boundaries overlap and you can be stuck with some sort of distortion, no matter what the wire gauge is.

Now that your dreams of using solid-conductor house wiring for your audio system have been dashed, it's time to move onto the different types of stranded wires. The typical speaker wire is usually something along the line of "zipcord," which consists of two insulated parallel conductors of stranded wire. Unlike parallel twisted hookup wire, the two independent zipcord wires are connected along a seam that runs the length of the wire.

Returning to the problem of skin effect in speaker cables, some companies try to reduce this dilemma by gradually turning the wires throughout the length of the cable (Fig. 11-3). By doing so,

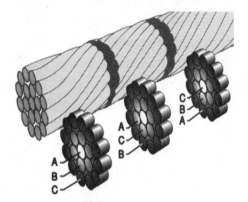

Fig. 11-3 Separate wire strands running throughout a cable length. Notice how they shift position in the cable to reduce skin effect.
© AudioQuest

wires that are in the center at one point are later shifted to the outside, where most of the current is being transmitted. This technique greatly reduces the negative results of skin effect. To further eliminate the negative effects, sometimes either stranded bundles or solid wires are gradually turned around an insulating core. As a result, each of the wire strands within the bundles or surfaces of the single-strand wires is being slowly turned, so the anti-skin effect is doubled. Sometimes, these solid wires or bundles are insulated and kept a certain distance apart to prevent them from interacting (Fig. 11-4).

Another type of audio cable uses several parallel solid conductors or stranded wire bundles (Fig. 11-5). The purpose is much the same as the theory behind the bundled wires from the last paragraph. Like the other types of wire, the parallel multiconductor ribbons are made with a variety of wire types, spacing distances, and jacket and insulating materials.

Fig. 11-4 Insulated wire bundles. © AudioQuest

The last general category of audio wire is that of shielded cable. Shielded cable is any cable that shields the wires inside and prevents various types of electrical interference from entering the lines. Shielded cable is especially important if your electrical system/appliances are noisy or if the speaker cables will be running parallel to power cables. Likewise, some power cabling is also shielded to prevent electrical impulses from emanating out from the cables.

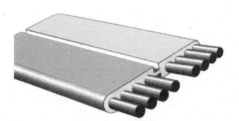

Fig. 11-5 Parallel flat cable.
© AudioQuest

One of the most common forms of shielded cable is coaxial cable, which consists of a center conducter that is surrounded by an insulating dielectric material. A layer of braided copper-wire shielding wraps around the dielectric (it makes a sort of cylindrical copper plaid pattern) and it is covered with an outer insulating jacket (Fig. 11-6). One of the most visible applications of standard coaxial cable is for cable television. Coaxial cable is always used to route the television signals from the source to the home (at least in all of the television cable runs that I've seen). A number of different types of coaxial cable have also been designed for audio-specific purposes (Fig. 11-7).

If you are installing long cable runs throughout your house, you should consider shielded cable. Long cable runs are susceptible to

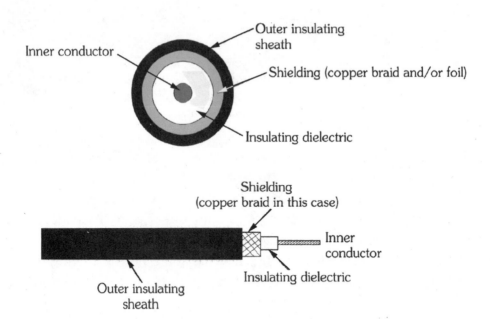

Fig. 11-6 A breakdown of coaxial cable, showing the separate parts.

picking up noise from parallel runs of electrical wires (known as *crosstalk*) or from other devices. Crosstalk was discovered in the 19th century, during the early days of the telephone. Long parallel lengths of telephone wire would sometimes receive audio from the opposite wire. Shielded cable will typically eliminate this interference.

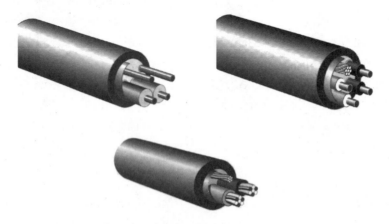

Fig. 11-7 Several different types of coaxial cable that are intended for audio purposes. © AudioQuest

So which cable is best for your stereo system? In general, the aforementioned cables are all of much better quality than what you would typically find packed along with your speakers or at a local electronics store. Most of the specialty cable companies specifically produce their cabling for audiophiles (such as AudioQuest, Straight Wire, Kimber, Tara Labs, etc.), so their products won't be low grade, to say the least. Because the quality of these products is so much better than common hookup wire, the differences between the specialty cables probably won't be important to anyone except audiophiles.

SHOULD I PURCHASE HIGH-END AUDIO CABLES?

The science of cabling audio is quite esoteric and it is one of the most-argued-over topics in the controversial world of audio. Claims about the cabling run from being an audio cure-all to being an absurd case of snake oil advertising. I won't tell you to spend a large sum of money on high-end cables, but I won't say that these cables won't help in some specific applications.

The problem is that when the cables use precious metals, for example, they are bound to be hugely expensive. And if you can't afford a few thousand dollars for your stereo system, why would you blow several thousand on the audio and power cables? Many of the high-end wire companies rely on two factors (proverbs?) to sell their products:

1. More expensive is better.
2. A fool and his money are soon parted.

So, is it foolish to spend your money on expensive audio cables? Not necessarily, but that depends largely on how much money your have and are willing to spend on your audio system. And how much is expensive? Well, Transparent Audio sells their

MusicWave Reference cable for a list price of $4,100 per 8-foot pair! It would be foolish for me to outfit a system with this cable because it would quickly be reposessed, along with my house and cars! It wouldn't be foolish for someone who could easily afford a $200,000 audio system.

Like everything with high-end audio, if it is important for you to have the best and you have the money, then buy it. Otherwise, if the different grades of audio cables are a concern to you, then do some comparison shopping. Check the cables in different systems if you have a chance. Or, talk to some salesmen at different local stereo installation shops and see if you can do some comparative listening. If you are lucky, you might be able to test the same system using different audio cables. Of course, beware of some of the sales tricks, such as turning the volume up higher on the one amplifier so that the system will "sound better." If you have some friends that have trustworthy opinions on audio, then you should talk with them if you can't find any reference audio cabling.

After these tests, choose the cabling that sounds the best for the lowest price. Even if you can notice a difference, the better cabling might not be worth extra cost.

Also, consider the equipment that you have and that which you hear the cable being auditioned with. What grade of components are used in your current equipment? Unless silver and gold are used throughout your amplifier (i.e., it originally cost at least $3,000, there's no reason to waste your money on silver wire. For that matter, Radio Shack's cheapo ($3.99 for 60 feet) was rated highly in the latest "Recommended Components" edition of *Stereophile*. If the differences are negligible, I wouldn't even pay $10 per foot (relatively inexpensive in the audiophile market) for better-grade wire.

Finally, if you are desperate for something decent at a good price, go to a few local hamfests (mentioned in further detail in Chapter 1).

I've found some really great deals on partially used wire spools. Last fall, I bought a new 500-foot spool of #14 stranded copper wire with a plastic-covered rubber coating for $12. A few months earlier, I found a mostly used spool of silver coil wire. It is finely stranded #18 silver (or silver alloy) wire with a Teflon coating that was probably used for coils in high-voltage applications, where other insulations would have burned off. My spool, with approximately 200 feet of wire, cost $4! This stuff wasn't originally sold for $100 per foot new, but it certainly wasn't cheap!

FM TRANSMITTERS

The one peculiar exception to using wire for transporting signals from one location to another is practical for large houses or just for the convenience of transporting a signal from one room to another. Or you might want to transport the signals from your CD player to some place out in your yard, especially if you have a multidisc changer and want to crank out at least a few hours of music.

A number of problems plague long cable runs. The potential for interference grows significantly as the wire length increases, the signals passing through the wire can weaken (important for line-level audio), and the costs can be prohibitive. If you can avoid using wire, why not?

The easiest way to link audio from one source to another is via a radio link. You get a transmitter and transmit the audio to a receiver in a different location. Easy! This concept has been used for years for rock bands, who were tired of tripping over everyone's audio cables. They just went "wireless."

Guitar transmitters operate on special radio frequencies, outside of the broadcast bands, to minimize interference. Because they were designed for the professional application (playing electric guitar or bass in a band), this price of this equipment is high. For that matter, the transmitting frequency isn't really appropriate; it would be much easier to use a transmitter that operates on a standard broadcast frequency so that you could use your stereo system or a portable system to receive the signal.

Back in the 1960s, a few companies realized the usefulness of very low-power transmitters for the broadcast bands. A few companies, such as Knight, built little "phono oscillators"—tiny transmitters that were intended to carry audio from your turntable to any broadcast radio in your house. These little transmitters were originally sold as kits, with one or two tubes, for operation in the AM broadcast band. These units evolved over the years, switching over to FM and transistors, and the applications changed, as well.

Today's versions of the old phono oscillator are tiny little FM transmitters that are typically intended as "home broadcasters" or bugging devices (Fig. 11-8). Some people even broadcast to their

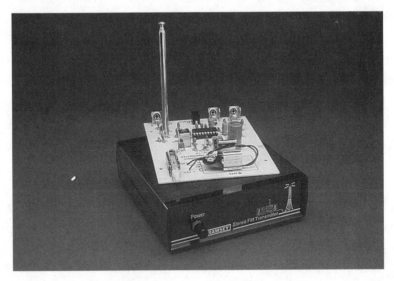

Fig. 11-8 An alternative to long cable runs? The FM-10A FM transmitter kit.
Ramsey Electronics

neighborhoods with them, but those applications, along with bugs, are well beyond the scope of this book. Aside from the typical kits that are available for these applications, a number of different manufacturers are now offering small FM transmitters (called *FM modulators*) along with their in-car compact disc changers. In general, these units are found only in the higher-priced changers. However, Sound Barrier does offer the CD-10FMC 10-disc changer for a list price of $399, which is considerably less than the other models with FM transmitters.

If you are interested in purchasing one or more little FM transmitters for use around the house, be sure to ask for recommendations. Some of the transmitter kits are very unstable (the frequency drifts), so you will have to constantly retune your receiver. Others have limited frequency response, so the highs and lows might be lacking. Still others have poor stereo separation. Your best bet is finding a decent "FM modulator" from a car stereo dealer or mail-order store. These units are typically made specifically for good audio and frequency stability.

As mentioned earlier, the best applications for little FM transmitters are to eliminate long runs of cable throughout your house. Some people connect the audio output from the TV to the little transmitter so that the audio from TV and cable-only stations can be heard throughout the house. This is particularly useful for listening to a TV station for some timely event that you can't hear anywhere else, such as the audio from ESPN or CNN (I think Nickelodeon would lose too much without the video).

I doubt that anyone will make this mistake, but be sure to use an FM-band mini transmitter, not one constructed for some other frequency range. Not only will the audio likely be poorer, but the results are less predictable. For example, a few years ago, an amateur radio operator in North Carolina decided to build a mini shortwave transmitter to transmit the local FM rock station from his house to his workshop. His transmitter was a tiny 5 watts, but it was powerful enough to be illegal to use. Before long, agents from the Federal Communications Commission arrived at this man's house to close the station—it had been heard as far north as Boston! And these distances weren't a fluke; I heard the station for hours at a time while listening in Pennsylvania.

MAKING CONNECTIONS

Making good connections is quite important if you want your system to sound as clean as possible. High-end audio connections are made in a bit different manner than connections for nearly any other electrcal application. Normally, either the wires are "tied off" together or they are soldered and possibly weather-proofed. Some solder and a few wire nuts would be all that you would need to install the wiring on most electrical systems.

However, this is a far cry from connections in the audio world. If you want to see some looks of terror and/or absolute disgust, talk to a professional installer about how you connected your system of equipment from Audio Research, Martin-Logan, and Parasound using only 18 wire nuts! That's worse than ordering caviar from an exclusive French restaurant and dousing it with cheap ketchup.

Fortunately, you shouldn't have to make any splices in your audio lines. You should be able to run a wire straight from one audio component to another (Fig. 11-9). The only extra work that you

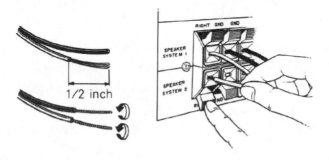

Fig. 11-9 Preparing speaker wires for connections in push-block terminals.
Harman/Kardon

might have is soldering or crimping connectors onto the ends. Be aware of the so-called "crimp-on, no-solder connectors" on the market. Audio connectors are available in three general categories: really cheap "crimp-on, no-solder connectors," solderable connectors, and really well made "crimp-on, no-solder connectors." The really cheap "crimp-on, no-solder connectors" are best avoided. Most of these are flimsy and require solder or the joints will become electrically intermittent. The solderable connectors are of decent quality and are useful for most non-audiophiles. The last group typically consists of well-made connectors with screw terminals. These connectors don't require solder and most audiophiles would warn against it so that you don't add another barrier for the audio signal to pass through.

If you need to splice a cable together and are using solder to strengthen a joint, remember that solder should only be intended as an electrical connection, not a mechanical one. Although solder will strengthen any joint, it does not handle physical stress very well. Some audiophiles will say that solder is not much of an electrical connection either. The antisolder folks claim that because solder is a mixture of lead and tin (neither of which conduct electricity nearly as well as copper), the signal loss and distortion will be severe at these joints. This is a valid point for high-end audio. But, the point is that an audiophile would only use single runs of cable from one audio component to another. If you are even considering using spliced wire, you probably will not be bothered by the slight audio degradation of using solder on a joint. If this is the route you want to take, take your time and solidly crimp the wires together before soldering, so that the wires still make very close contact with each other. The solder would then serve to make the joint a bit stronger (both electrically and physically) and it would also help to waterproof the joint.

Wire nuts are a poor method to connect the wires together because the joints are not especially reliable. A few years of vibrations, being moved to accommodate the vacuum cleaner, etc. will cause these connections to become even less reliable. Most people who connect wires in stereo systems use these splices because their wires were too short to reach from the speakers to the amplifier. If this is the case, just get the correct length of wire so that you can avoid future problems with your system.

CONNECTORS

Choosing the proper connectors for your system isn't a big deal, but the subject does bother a few people who are trying to eke out the most from their stereo. The concern about the connectors is that the metal might be of poor quality. Better grades of metal have a higher conductivity, and the better the conductivity, the higher percentage of signal will be passed from point A to point B. As a result, most audiophiles use only connectors that have been plated with precious metals, typically gold, but occasionally silver. Gold is most often used for audio applications, and silver is typically used for radio (antenna connectors, etc.). Choosing connector metals is like choosing cables, if your equipment is really high end and uses silver throughout, go with gold or silver connectors. If not, skip the unnecessary extra cost.

The most important concern for audio enthusiasts, with respect to connectors, is that they are built tough. The really cheap RCA plugs use a thin metal (that I assume has inferior conductivity) with a small clip-on plastic protective cover. These plugs can easily be ripped right from the wire or become intermittent. The next-better grade of plugs is solid enough to survive years of use in a system. These plugs use stronger metal parts and the plastic or bakelite-type protective cover screws onto the plug. This type of plug is also available with gold plating on the conductor. Don't worry about purchasing the real high-end style of plugs. These typically use a metal screw-on cover (this much isn't overkill) and a metal spring to wrap around and protect the wire from breaking inside the cord. These plugs are intended for musicians or recording studios, where quality metals are necessary in an interconnect that is constantly plugged in and pulled back out. You won't be pulling the plug in and out nearly this much, so save a few bucks and opt for something a bit less tough.

SOLDERING PROBLEMS AND DANGERS

This section is tossed in for those who want to save some money. If you have money that you aren't sure what to do with, you can purchase the best audio cable that you can find, with the plugs already attached. If you don't, compare the prices for a length of cable and a bag of plugs. With a little work and patience, you can whip out some interconnects that are as well-built as something that was commercially assembled. Of course, you might find a set of discounted commercial interconnects for cheaper than the individual components.

Soldering isn't difficult, but it seems as though many people with interests in audio have never soldered before. To make a solder joint, have the connection (wires, terminals, etc.) in the position that you want them to be in. Then, preheat the soldering iron until it reaches a very hot temperature and can melt solder easily. If you try to solder as the iron is still warming up, there is a much better chance that you will make a cold solder joint or that you will overheat the wires and melt the insulation. Next, heat the joint from underneath and place the tip of the solder against the joint from above. The solder will flow into the connection (Fig. 11-10). Some people try to solder by melting the solder against the tip of the iron, but solder is always attracted to the heat, so the solder will stick to the iron and it won't flow into the joint. By using this method, you will surely get a cold solder joint.

The previous two paragraphs covered the problems; now here is the danger (mostly when working on equipment, not audio lines). Be very careful when soldering that you don't overheat a component that is in the circuit. For example, never solder a connection in a speaker line while the speaker is still connected. It probably won't be a problem if you are soldering at the other end of the

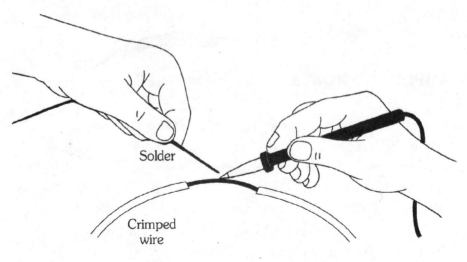

Solder

Crimped
wire

Fig. 11-10 Making a solder joint.

wire because the heat will dissipate along the way, but if you are anywhere near the end of that line, you could quickly zap out the speaker. If your refrigerator already has its fill of powerful magnets, you now have a handy cassette eraser!

This soldering situation can also be dangerous to parts other than speakers. Heat is especially damaging to transistors and integrated circuits, but chances are that you won't be soldering around those parts anyway.

System planning and assembly

As has been stated earlier in this chapter, the wiring in an audio system is one of the most forgotten aspects of an installation. In terms of being overlooked, wire rates with the spider in a speaker.

When you are first assembling your audio system (Fig. 11-11), the wiring goes unnoticed. But when the need to rewire occurs, then it's time to scratch your head and wonder why you didn't think about this earlier. Depending on when you are running the wiring, it can be anything from very easy to extremely difficult to install or replace.

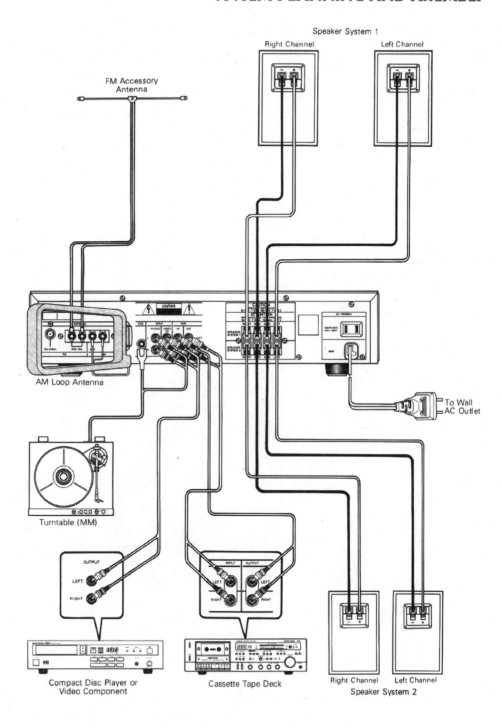

Fig. 11-11 Planning out the wiring for a system can become a fairly complicated project. Harman/Kardon

Installing or replacing the speaker wiring can be a major task. Before you start to install the system, you should determine what type of cable you will be using and how much you should purchase. To find the lengths, determine where the speakers and the stereo system will be positioned. Then, use lengths of string or wire to find the exact lengths. Be sure to account for any extra bends or corners that the wire will be making. Allow an extra 6" to 1' (15.24 cm to 30.48 cm) for every long cable run and about an extra 3" to 6" (7.62 cm to 15.24 cm) to be safe. It might seem like a lot of extra work just to measure the wires, but when you deal with custom wiring, that extra foot or two here and there could add up to quite a bit of money. Then, note any specific connectors that you might need, such as RCA plugs (Fig. 11-12), slide-on speaker clips, etc.

Fig. 11-12 StreetWires cables with specialty RCA plugs at the ends.
StreetWires by Esoteric Audio USA

When you plan out the wiring for your system, try to run the audio cables away from the power wiring in your house, or at least use shielded cables to prevent noise from entering the audio cables. Even if you can't place the power and the audio cables on opposite end of the walls (top and bottom, or on either side), at least try to space them a few inches apart. This distance alone will decrease the noise pickup. Before you start running the wires, be sure that you have made any solder joints that are necessary.

The easiest situation would be in a new house that is in the early to mid-stages of construction. Here, the studded walls would be up and the roof would be finished, but the drywall would not yet have been installed. So long as you have accurately determined where you are going to place the speakers and the audio equipment, the rest is easy. First, you would mark the places on the floor where you expect the equipment to be placed. Then, drill holes through the 2 x 4 studs for the wires to pass through. If your listening room will be on the top story of the house, it's best to place all of the horizontal wiring runs above the wall so that you can easily access it through the attic or crawl space.

Some people take pictures or videos of the house while the beams and studs are all within view. This way, they can get back into the walls without cutting into electrical wires or nails. A really great method of viewing the house is to take slides of the walls while the house is being constructed. If you need to get back into the walls, you can project the "skeleton" of the room up on the walls. Neat!

The photo system of wire tracing can be very helpful, but it's not the easiest method. But merely discovering where the wires are placed in the walls doesn't make pulling the wire out any easier. Heavy gauges of wire will often catch on the edges of holes and pull fast, like a knot. To prevent your cable from knotting up in the walls, you might consider drilling holes in the studs, then passing small-diameter PVC pipe through the holes (Fig. 11-13). Rather than just run the wires out through a hole in the floor or walls, use a plastic electrical junction box. Cut a hole in the junction box so that an elbow joint for the PVC pipe will fit into the junction box. Mount the junction box on a stud, put an elbow joint on the pipe, then fit the other end of the joint into the junction box. Now you can easily feed the wire through the pipe, from one

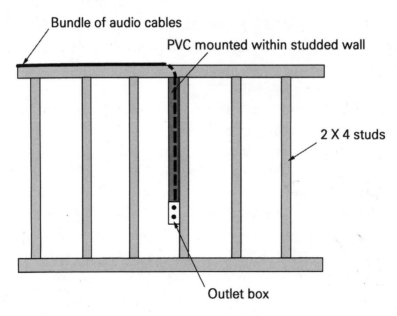

Bundle of audio cables

PVC mounted within studded wall

2 X 4 studs

Outlet box

Fig. 11-13 Running audio cable bundles through studded walls.

junction box to the other. You can either mount jacks onto the junction box plate cover or you can run the wires directly through the cover to the speaker or equipment (whichever is the case).

The real problems occur when you start trying to install system wiring in an already-constructed house. You wind up trying to drill holes in walls, ceilings, and floors, and getting wire stuck or lost. If you have a typical system, you will probably either want to run the audio cables along the baseboard or under the carpet at the edge of the wall. If you choose the former method, you will probably want to staple or tack the cord along the the baseboard. Just be sure that the metal doesn't cut or squash the wires. If you go for the under-the-carpet method, you'll have to pull up the quarterround around the baseboard and slowly work up the carpet around the edges. Then, run the wire along the baseboard, put the carpet back in place, and nail the quarterround back. Be very careful when nailing so that you don't hit the wiring.

It takes a lot of work to try to run wiring through an old house without running it along the baseboard or under the carpet. Part of the problem is that you can never be sure what lies behind that drywall. I have friends who live in an old two-story brick house that was built in the country somewhere around 1900. All of the walls that directly face the outside are brick, covered with plaster. Aside from studding up the inside of the walls, there is no way that you can run wires through the walls.

Even if you are lucky enough to know that the walls are studded and clear of major obstacles, you will encounter other difficulties. For example, you can't easily mount a junction box in the wall if the drywall is already in place; there is simply no space to nail it in. If you want to put one in, you will have to rip out some dry-wall, a piece from stud to stud. Then, you'll have to nail in the junction box, run the wires through the box, cut a new piece of drywall and nail it in, then go through the whole process of tap-ing, applying wall compound, sanding, and painting. That's an awful lot of work, just to make the stereo wiring less visible!

If you want to see some of the problems and questions faced by an audio enthusiast wiring his very large new home, visit:

http://www.mcdata.com/~meh0045/
homewire/wire-guide.html

If you are building a new house and working out the details for the system, this site is a must to see.

GROUNDS

The ground system in a stereo system is often forgotten because not having one won't prevent you from playing back music and hearing it through your speakers. Also, because you have to bury metal in the ground to create a good ground, the subject has attained an almost-new age kind of aura. "You bury stuff in your backyard to improve your stereo performance, eh? (aside) Call the cops, quick!"

Part of the reason that you won't hear much about the ground system for electronic equipment is because good grounds are relatively inexpensive to make; they depend more on getting some metal into the dirt, and less on buying a piece of expensive equipment. So, with little money involved, neither the equipment manufacturers nor the magazines will commercially benefit from writing about hi-fi ground systems.

Grounding equipment is important because cables and connectors receive electrical noise (both natural and man made) and radio/TV signals through the air. Unless these signals are disposed of, the audio will be corrupted—especially in the case of turntables, which amplify the tiny vibrations from the stylus tens of thousands of times.

The only way to dispose of these electrical signals is to dissipate them into the ground or some other large conductive object (Fig. 11-14). The best ground is the earth—especially that which consists of conductive materials (primarily water and salt). Now you need something to connect your equipment to that excellent electrical ground that you think of as a back yard.

The best method is to connect the grounds of all of your audio equipment together with grounding wire (typically, about #12 stranded copper wire or grounding strap). A ground wire is then run from a central piece of equipment (usually, the amplifier) to the ground assembly outside. The actual ground system generally consists of very long copper or copper-coated steel ground stakes driven into the earth, a pattern of wire radials buried several inches down, or a combination of the two.

The ground stakes are available from some electrical supply stores or hardware stores. Although some of the grounds that people install for their house's electrical system are only about 1 or 2

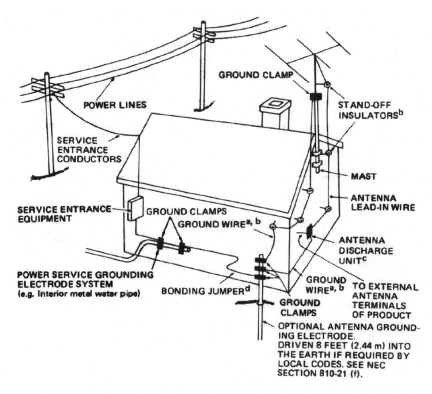

GROUND CLAMP

POWER LINES

STAND-OFF
INSULATORS[b]

SERVICE
ENTRANCE
CONDUCTORS

MAST

ANTENNA
LEAD-IN WIRE

SERVICE ENTRANCE
EQUIPMENT

GROUND CLAMPS
GROUND WIRE[a, b]

ANTENNA
DISCHARGE
UNIT[c]

POWER SERVICE GROUNDING
ELECTRODE SYSTEM
(e.g. Interior metal water pipe)

GROUND
WIRE[a, b]

TO EXTERNAL
ANTENNA
TERMINALS
OF PRODUCT

BONDING JUMPER[d]

GROUND
CLAMPS

OPTIONAL ANTENNA GROUND-
ING ELECTRODE.
DRIVEN 8 FEET (2.44 m) INTO
THE EARTH IF REQUIRED BY
LOCAL CODES. SEE NEC
SECTION 810-21 (f).

Fig. 11-14 An efficient ground system is important for good audio quality and electrical safety.

feet long, a good grounding stake should be at least 4 feet long, and it should be pounded into the ground so that only a few inches stick out above the grass surface. I just hope that you live in an area with nice, smooth dirt. I've spent most of my life living in mountainous areas, and sledgehammering stakes through rocks and clay is a pain, to say the least. Be really careful when pounding these into the ground—they're metal and you're using a sledgehammer! You could easily slice yourself with the stake or mash something (your foot, perhaps?) with the sledgehammer. If you have any doubts about your physical capabilities or if you are accident prone, consider having a professional install the stake or try the next grounding option. Whether you install it yourself or have someone else do it for you, be sure to mark the end of the ground stake with a little flag or cover it with something so that people won't trip and fall on it.

Rather than drive a huge metal stake in the ground, you can run a system of ground radials under the yard. The system merely consists of a number of copper wires, all of the same length, that radiate from a single point, where they are all soldered together. Eight or more radials should be fine for your ground system. Although the length of the wires is specific for radio applications (such as the ground radials for an AM broadcast transmitter), don't worry about cutting them to a specific length—anything greater than 10 feet long should be fine. The wires should all be cut and the insulation should be bared for about 4 inches at one end of each wire. Dig out paths in your yard for the radials, string the wires in place, and twist the bared ends together. Solder it and dip it into liquid rubber (used for insulating the ends of metal tools) to protect the joint from weathering and corrosion. Then, be sure that all of the wires are well covered by dirt; if they aren't, you could hit one with a lawnmower and cause some serious damage!

CONCLUSION

Wire, cabling, connectors, and transmission systems are not the most interesting aspects of audio systems, but they certainly are important. They require some extra work to estimate lengths, plan, and install, so it is important to take your time and think about the arrangement.

12
ANTENNA SYSTEMS

Most anywhere in the United States, you can receive the basic formats of radio programming: classic rock, top-40, urban contemporary, easy listening, country, alternative rock, classical, and some flavor of Christian programming. However, if your tastes vary from what is currently on top of the popularity heap, you might search the radio for something different. If you live in a city, you have a much better chance of finding some programming that you find worthy of listening to. But if you live in the suburban outskirts or in the country, your listening variety will most likely be limited to the basic flavors.

For example, I live about two hours from Washington, DC, and Baltimore, Maryland, so I'm just beyond the fringe-reception area for these cities. One of my former co-workers loved listening to jazz, and the only station where he could find it was on a DC public radio station. He lived much closer to DC than I did, so the reception was marginal (instead of inaudible, as was the case here). He solved his reception problems by purchasing and installing a high-gain FM antenna. Depending on where you live and what you want to listen to, it might be useful for you to work with antennas.

A FEW ANTENNA BASICS

An antenna is any object that is used to pick up radio signals. Of course, most antennas are metallic conductors of a certain length, but antennas can be made from other materials. For example, human skin isn't a very good conductor, but if you hold on to a retracted whip antenna (like those used in portable stereos), the signal will improve because you have become part of the antenna.

Part of the reason why radio theory can get very complicated is because it seems so intangible. However, here are a few of the basics. Every radio signal is a sine wave, and every wave that is on a different frequency has a different length. The frequency is merely the number of waves that occur over the course of one second. As a result, a higher frequency yields a smaller wavelength. Knowing that light (and subsequently all radio waves) travels at 300,000,000 meters per second, you can determine the wavelength of a radio wave at any given frequency.

$$Wavelength = \frac{300,000}{F}$$

Where:
F is the frequency in kHz
Wavelength is the wavelength in meters

From this equation, you can determine that a full wavelength at 540 kHz (the bottom of the AM/MW band) is 555.56 meters long. At 1700 kHz (the top of the AM/MW band), a full wavelength is reduced to 176.47 meters. The FM (VHF) broadcast band is much higher in frequency than the AM (MW) band, so the lengths of the waves are much smaller. The only difference in determining the wavelength from the previous equation is that you must use the constant of 300 instead of 300,000 so that you can use the frequency in MHz. Thus, at 99 MHz (in the middle of the broadcast band), a full wavelength is only three meters long.

The catch to all of these equations and measurements is that antennas perform at their peak if they are resonant to the frequency range that you are listening to. The resonant antenna is an antenna that is either the same length as or is a multiple or division of a given frequency. The most common antennas that are less than one wavelength long are: 1/2, 1/4, and 1/8 wave. An 1/8-wave vertical antenna for 540 kHz would be 69.45 meters high (approximately 225 feet)! Obviously, a 225-foot high antenna in your backyard is a bit impractical for the average homeowner. So, the radio designers go with smaller antennas, typically either whip or dipole antennas for FM band reception, and loopstick antennas for the AM (MW) band.

SIMPLE ANTENNAS FOR AM AND SHORTWAVE LISTENERS

Many AM receivers, whether small portable models or more-expensive component units, contain simple loopstick antennas. On the other hand, most high-performance loops are two feet (or larger) per side. These were used in the back of many of the large, old console radios of the 1930s and 1940s. (Tabletop radios of the day contained terminals so that you could connect an external antenna.) By the 1950s, miniaturization was the key, and standard loop antennas were much too large to install in a radio, so the engineers compensated with a miniature version—a coil of wire wrapped around a pencil-sized stick of ferrite (a ferromagnetic material). Although these little loopstick antennas perform tremendously for their size, they are no match for a good longwire or a full-sized loop antenna.

RANDOM-WIRE AND LONGWIRE ANTENNAS

One of the most common antennas that is used by shortwave and AM (MW) radio hobbyists is the simple random-wire or longwire antenna. This antenna is simply one long (usually 20 feet or longer) piece of wire that is strung in a straight, horizontal configuration. Although the random-wire antenna is not the best choice for heavy-duty shortwave or AM (MW) listening, it is the easiest and least expensive to use.

A short antenna such as this might allow you to receive more stations on the AM broadcast band (depending on the type of antenna that came with your receiver and on the length of your random-wire antenna). If you own a good stereo receiver or a communications receiver, an external antenna will significantly improve AM reception—especially considering that most of these receivers contain no internal antenna.

If you really enjoy receiving distant AM stations, you can improve the performance of the system by using a longer antenna wire. This will make the radio signals at the receiver stronger, enabling you to receive more stations with better audio. If you have a lot of acreage and you are serious about AM radio listening, you might put up a downright huge antenna. Once you have the longwire antenna in the neighborhood of 500 feet long or longer, you will notice that some stations that came in well with a short antenna are no longer audible, and others are now very strong.

This effect is a result of the directionality of longwire antennas. Once an antenna reaches a certain length (based on how low or high the frequency is), it will begin to receive best in one or two directions. In the case of the longwire antenna, it will receive best off of either end of the wire. Another interesting effect is the longer the antenna, the more directional it becomes. In other words, the longer it becomes, the narrower it will "focus" on signals from its front and back end. This effect is really interesting to listen to, and with a very long antenna and a good receiver, it's very possible to receive AM stations from around the world.

LOOP ANTENNAS

The *loop antenna* is a truly odd creature that seems to fly in the face of everything that you know about the way that standard antennas behave. The loop is theoretically a very complicated antenna that consists of several loops of wire wrapped around a box or a box-like form. The loop antenna is so useful because it is very directional; it receives best from either end of the box form and it has very deep nulls at the center of the antenna. As a result, the loop isn't particularly useful on the shortwave frequencies, where there is little adjacent-channel interference, but it is an excellent choice on the medium-wave band, where many frequencies just rumble with the noise of many stations broadcasting at the same time.

Because of the extremely directional characteristics and the very small size of loop antennas, they obviously have some great advantages. Of course, like any other type of antenna, they also have drawbacks. Probably the worst drawback is that they have such a small signal pickup that most people need to connect them to an amplifier just so that the signals are strong enough to hear. Because of the low signals, the performance isn't as hot as a long longwire, V, or rhombic antenna, but many people don't have enough room for these antennas anyway.

Many hi-fi enthusiasts have no interest in AM reception because of the higher amounts of noise and the poorer audio quality of the stations on the band. But, if you are a real experimenter and have an interest in tuning in broadcast stations from around the country or all over the world, a loop antenna (or some very long longwire antennas) is a must. AM reception is of lesser importance to most readers of this book, so no building information is included here. For more information, see *Build Your Own Shortwave Antennas* by Andrew Yoder or *The Practical Antenna Handbook (2nd Edition)* and *Joe Carr's Receiving Antenna Handbook*, both by Joseph Carr.

Several companies manufacture AM loop antennas (Fig. 12-1) for radio hobbyists, but the best-known are those from Palomar Engineers (P.O. Box 462222, Escondido, CA 92046) and Kiwa Electronics (612 S. 14th Ave., Yakima, WA 98902). See:

Fig. 12-1 The Kiwa MW Air-Core Loop Antenna: a serious piece of equipment for those interested in listening to the AM broadcast band. Kiwa Electronics

http://www.wolfe.net/~kiwa

You won't find either of these at stereo shops or hi-fi mail-order companies, but they are commonly available from shortwave radio mai-lorder companies, or you can order them directly from the manu-facturers. Both of these antennas have received good reviews in the hobby radio press for receiving stations on the AM broadcast band.

ANTENNAS FOR FM LISTENERS

For the most part, FM antennas are stock components; you just pick one up from a department store or (if you're feeling really high end) you might stop at Radio Shack to look at their antennas. There are relatively few good, high-end manufacturers of FM antennas. One, Ron Smith Aerials (98 Ash Rd., Luton, Beds LU4 8AQ UK), specializes in high-end FM and TV arrays—from 4 to 92 elements! Some of these antennas are truly complex variations on the beam and Yagi themes (see the following sections).

One of the most common types of antennas in use today for FM listening is the dipole antenna. Unlike the longwire antenna, the length of the dipole is frequency dependent. It must be cut to a particular frequency range (or a clean division of that range) or it will be virtually ineffective.

The most commonly used types of dipole antennas have a transmission line that carries the signal from the antenna to the receiver. Either coaxial cable or twin-lead wire is used for the transmission line of a dipole antenna (depending on the antenna impedance of the receiver).

The transmission line is run upwards, vertically from the receiver, typically at least 1/4 wavelength above the ground. A 1/4-wavelength piece of wire extends horizontally from one lead of the transmission line, and another 1/4-wavelength piece of wire extends horizontally from the other lead of the transmission line. (In the case of coaxial cable, one antenna wire runs to the center conductor, and the other goes to the shield.)

As mentioned, dipole antennas perform best when they are at least 1/4-wavelength above the ground (preferably much higher). So, although you might have plenty of space to install a dipole that is 300 feet long for the top of the AM broadcast band, chances are that you will have a problem raising the whole assembly at least 150 feet into the air. As a result, dipole antennas (Fig. 12-2) are primarily used for receiving or transmitting signals from the shortwave bands up through the VHF bands. (The VHF bands include the FM broadcast band.)

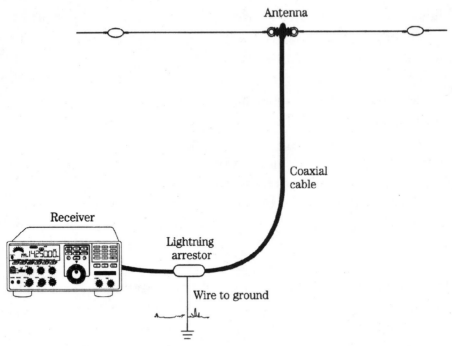

Fig. 12-2 The positioning of a dipole antenna for the shortwave bands. An FM dipole would be very similar.

Dipole antennas are incredibly popular because they are relatively simple, inexpensive, and effective for general receiving applications. Another advantage is that they are nearly omnidirectional. (They receive well in all directions.) Because of these advantages, most modern stereo receivers are prepackaged with a little twin-lead dipole antenna that you can stick on the wall. If you don't have one of these antennas, it's easy enough to either make one or pick one up for a few dollars from Radio Shack or from a mail-order company. The difference in reception quality on the FM band between a simple dipole antenna and a long piece of wire is amazing!

DIRECTIONAL FM ANTENNAS

The advantage of omnidirectionality is that you can receive from all directions at once; the problem is that you can't focus your antenna's signal-receiving capabilities in one direction. If you live far away from any major cities, having a dipole antenna will help you to bring in local stations, but little better than that. If you want to receive stations from more than about 100 miles away, you will need to "focus" the antenna.

To "focus" a longwire antenna, you make the antenna longer. That's fine for random-wire antennas on the AM and shortwave bands, but this method simply doesn't work for dipoles on any band. Instead of adding to the length, you can add separate antenna parts to "focus" the antenna. The most common of these "focused dipole" antennas is called a *Yagi antenna* (Fig. 12-3). The Yagi features a smaller (by 7%) element to one side of the antenna that "pulls" the signals in (called a *director*), and a larger (by 7%) element to the other side that reflects the signals back

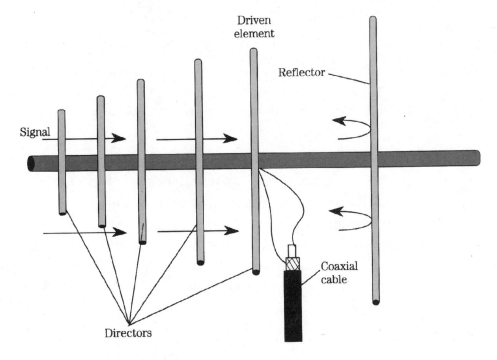

Fig. 12-3 A multielement directional antenna.

(called a *reflector*). The effects that the director and reflector have on the signal reception are interesting because neither is electrically connected to the original dipole antenna (called the *driver* or the *driven element* in a Yagi antenna).

Because of the large size of the antenna assembly, Yagi antennas are typically only used at high frequencies, although very large versions are sometimes used in the upper shortwave frequencies. The size of these antennas, however, is perfect for frequencies in the VHF and low UHF bands. So, Yagis and variations of this antenna are often used for FM and TV reception. Because the antennas are small enough on these frequencies to be rotated, they are always commercially manufactured using light aluminum tubing and installed on a mast.

A three-element antenna will provide significant gain (another way of saying the amount that an antenna has been "focused") over a simple dipole antenna, but the gain can still be dramatically improved. The easiest way to improve reception is to add more director elements. A good indication of how well an antenna will work depends on its size and the number of elements. A few other "tweaks" that many manu-facturers use to improve reception are to slant the elements in to-ward the directors (smaller end) and to stack two sets of antennas.

ANTENNA HEIGHT

As mentioned, dipole antennas and their variations perform better at greater heights above the ground and other objects. Part of this is the nature of the antenna, and part is because the FM signals are primarily received via a line-of-sight path. In other words, unlike AM, you can't receive FM or TV signals if you live in a hollow or if a mountain range is between you and the station that you want to hear.

CONCLUSION

If you are as serious about radio as you are about recorded music, you should inspect some of the antennas on the market. Ignoring this aspect of audio system design is almost like spending a lot of money, carefully choosing a system, then hooking up any cheap speakers. If you include a decent receiver in your system, you will reap much more enjoyment from it if you pair it with a proper antenna.

13

SHORTWAVE RADIO

In North America, few people know exactly what shortwave radio is. It seems like every time that my friends or I mention to someone that one of my hobbies is shortwave, I am invariably faced with the question "So, do you talk to people across the ocean?" When I reply with "No, those are ham radio operators. I just listen to broadcast stations," it seems to suck everything out of what they had to say to me. They usually either leave almost immediately after about 30 bewildered seconds or say "So, you have never talked to anyone on your shortwave radio?" I understand that it's a peculiar and misunderstood hobby, so I don't say "No, do you talk to people on your television set?!" After my usually polite "No, it's just a receiver, not a transmitter," they then leave. Needless to say, people don't stand in line to talk to me at reunions.

The shortwave radio spectrum fills the space from 1600 kHz to 30 MHz, which is a rather large chunk of space. Rather than merely consist of one band, the shortwave frequencies are a patchwork quilt of different radio bands (Table 13-1). The two best-known services on shortwave are the Citizen's Band (CB) and the numerous amateur (ham) radio bands. Otherwise, there are numerous broadcast bands and sections that are dedicated to various utilities. The CB and amateur bands both consist of private hobby two-way communications. The broadcast bands are all filled with a variety of private and governmental stations that broadcast music, news, radio plays, comedy, sports events, and

Local and International Broadcast Bands

540–1700 kHz	AM/MW band
2300–2495 kHz	120-m band
3200–3400 kHz	90-m band
3900–4000 kHz	75-m band
4750–5060 kHz	60-m band
5900–6200 kHz	49-m band
7100–7350 kHz	41-m band
9400–9990 kHz	31-m band
11600–12100 kHz	25-m band
13570–13870 kHz	22-m band
15100–15800 kHz	19-m band
17480–17900 kHz	16-m band
18900–19020 kHz	15-m band
21450–21750 kHz	13-m band
25600–26100 kHz	11-m band
88000–108000 kHz	FM/VHF band

propaganda. Utilities is a generic term for a very wide subject; utilities are often communications between ships, teletype of most any sort (including "wires" from news bureaus), weather faxes, military communications, and even coded number groups from "spy" numbers stations.

Rather frequently, someone will hear about my interest in short-wave and start asking questions. One of the most common is, "You mean your radio can pick up stations from around the world?" So, if I have a radio handy, I usually tune in the BBC (British Broadcasting Corporation) or maybe the Deutche Welle (The Voice of Germany) and let the person listen a little. The next question is usually, "You mean this is coming from England?!" (or Germany, depending on which one I tuned in).

Although most of the people who work with shortwave on a regular basis take it for granted, the distances covered by shortwave radio stations are truly amazing. And it's not just the huge government stations that get out this well. Even small, portable ham stations, minipowered private broadcasters, pirates, and clandestines can be heard around the world.

This chapter merely grazes the surface of the shortwave radio hobby. For more information on the topic, see *The Complete Shortwave Listener's Handbook (5th Edition)* by Andrew Yoder.

DO SHORTWAVE AND HI-FI MIX?

To many people, hi-fi and shortwave might seem like two divergent topics. As illustrated, many people think of ham radio's two-way communications when *shortwave* is mentioned. But the shortwave spectrum contains many broadcast bands that are like an international version of the AM and FM bands. (Receivers that cover these bands are important components in any stereo systems.) There are strong parallels between the AM/FM bands and shortwave, but this still doesn't answer the question of whether a shortwave receiver will comfortably fit in with your stereo system.

The answer is that it can, but should it be in your system? Not necessarily. The shortwave bands are very peculiar by the standards of the more popular broadcast bands. FM is characterized by incredible fidelity and stereo separation, but only at a short range. With a great receiver, FM can sound nearly CD quality. The drawback is that the signal is rarely solidly receivable for more than about a 75-mile radius. Shortwave, on the other hand, can cover the planet, but it is plagued by fading and static crashes (the latter can be devastating to summertime listening). Shortwave listening is made worse by stations who use transmitting equipment with poor fidelity (such as the hummy-sounding transmitters of Radio Cairo). And some equipment manufacturers add to the dilemma by making tinny-sounding receivers that don't adequately represent the audio of the stations that do have a good sound.

The choice of whether a shortwave receiver should have a place in your system depends entirely on your personality. If you have an interest in the "outside world" and you have (or would) listen to a radio station with a weak or fading signal because you liked the program, you might enjoy having a shortwave receiver. If slight imperfections in a recording annoy you, chances are that you would dislike shortwave.

HOW RADIO SIGNALS TRAVEL

It might be best to start with a bit about the basic characteristics of shortwave reception. Shortwave reception is an unpredictable, very complicated beast. The unpredictability is certainly one of the factors that attracted me. It's exciting when you get a chance to hear stations that normally aren't audible in your region of the world.

Long-distance radio reception is possible because of one of the layers of our atmosphere that is known as the *ionosphere*. The ionosphere is many miles above the earth, where the air is "thin"—containing few molecules. Here, the ionosphere is bombarded by x-rays, ultraviolet rays, and other forms of high-frequency radiation. This energy from the sun ionizes this layer by stripping electrons from the atoms in the ionosphere. The ionized layers of the atmosphere make long-distance radio communications possible.

The ionosphere can, in turn, be divided into several layers, but the D, E, and F layers are the ones that affect radio propagation. The D layer is the one that is closest to the surface of the Earth. The existence and strength of this layer depends on and is proportional to the movement of the sun in the sky. As a result, the D layer gradually grows in strength in the morning, is strongest at midday, and gradually decreases until it disappears by nightfall. Also, the D layer is generally stronger in the summer than in the winter. On the lower frequencies (below about 10 MHz), the D layer will absorb any signals that are transmitted into it. A great example of this effect is to tune across the AM (medium wave) broadcast band at midday and then do the same at night. At midday, you will hear local stations and maybe a few powerful cross-state stations. But with nightfall, the band comes alive, and stations from across the country are audible. You have just witnessed the effect of the D layer.

The E layer is much like the D layer, except that it is a bit higher and it has a few redeeming characteristics. The E layer will absorb most radio signals, but it will sometimes refract shortwave signals—especially those above about 14 MHz. So, during the summer months, the higher-frequency amateur bands are particularly "hot" during the daytime when the lower-frequency bands are being eaten alive by the D and E layers. One of the most interesting characteristics of the E layer is called *sporadic E skip*. During the sporadic E skip, some higher frequencies in the lower VHF region, which don't normally skip, suddenly skip for very long distances. Sporadic E skip is somewhat common, but you have to be at the right place at the right time for a good opening. One time I lived in a small apartment and would watch television on a small, beat-up black-and-white TV that my sister had given me. One severe disadvantage to using this TV was that my sister had broken off the whip antenna a few years earlier. So, it didn't receive that well, but we were close enough to Pittsburgh that a handful of stations would come in well anyway. One evening at sunset, channel 4 from Pittsburgh started to fade out and was replaced by another signal. In a few minutes, KHAS, from Hastings, Nebraska, was in loud and clear. About 10 minutes later, KHAS was gone and the regular stations were back.

The F layer makes most shortwave and medium-wave skip possible. This layer is generally about several hundred miles above the e•Earth, and it remains ionized throughout much of the day and night. However, unlike the other layers (under most circumstances), the F layer will refract signals back to the earth. Because the F layer is so high above the earth, signals often skip over very great distances from the F layer—sometimes several thousand miles. As a result, it is easy to hear international broadcast stations with clear signals from around the world.

The ionosphere, skip conditions, and signal absorption have a number of peculiarities. One oddity is that frequencies above the top of the shortwave band will normally cut straight through the ionosphere and travel into space, but the lower shortwave frequencies (as stated previously) are often absorbed by the ionosphere. As a result, there are no perfect frequencies—best frequencies depend on what the intended audiences is, the time of the year, condition of the ionosphere, etc. Another variable that dramatically affects listening is the skip distance. Long skip is not necessarily the most desirable condition. For example, it is common to listen to the 20-meter amateur band (approximately 14 MHz) during the daytime hours and hear a station from a distant country, such as Australia, talking to someone in your state. The problem is that you will probably only hear the station in Australia, not the one in your state! Thus, if you are an amateur operator, you would try a frequency on a lower-frequency band if you wanted to contact someone that close.

The same holds true for broadcast listening. A number of U.S. private stations broadcast on the so-called 41-meter band (approximately 7300 to 7500 kHz). This area is fair to good for only close communications during the day, but at night, the signals get out for thousands of miles. At night (at my location), these stations often drop to about 1/2 strength, and they rapidly fade in and out. The problem is that I am too close to the transmitter for good reception at that time and most of the signal is skipping over me. These problems are virtually unheard of at AM (medium wave) and FM broadcast frequencies, so most people are stunned that they occur on the shortwave frequencies.

One factor makes propagation forecasting and theory very complicated. As you know, shortwave signals are severely affected by the ionosphere, which is (in turn) affected by sunlight. Daylight and nightfall do not occur at the same time throughout the world. This creates some bizarre skip conditions, to say the least. The best way to see what frequencies are coming in at a particular time of day in your area is to either join a shortwave-listening club (so that you can see logs of what other people are hearing) or read the propagation forecasts in some of the amateur radio magazines. However, you can use the simple tune-through-the-dial method to figure out what is and isn't audible. In general, the frequencies below 10 MHz will be best at night and those above 10 MHz will be the best during the day. But the frequencies near this general daytime/nighttime borderline (such as the 31- and 25-meter bands) will overlap and are at least somewhat active all of the time.

This section has been just a very quick, very superficial look at shortwave propagation—just something to help you become acquainted with how shortwave signals reach different parts of the world. As stated earlier, shortwave propagation is much more complicated than this and many important terms and characteristics were left out on purpose. It's just too much to cover in a book on home audio.

SHORTWAVE BROADCASTING

Shortwave listening is fascinating because you can tune in Radio Bras from Brasilia, Brazil, thousands of miles away. Afterwards, you can catch a live soccer match from the BBC or Radio Australia (Fig. 13-1). Then you might listen to a dizzying variety of Western pop, rock, metal, punk, hip-hop, rap, techno, and country music from Radio Kuwait. Finally, you might wind up the afternoon with some commentaries on why communism is so successful, from Radio Havanna Cuba. In times like these, you begin to realize just how small the world really is.

Although the shortwave bands are filled with quite a bit of propaganda and dry rhetoric, there is still a lot of interesting

RADIO AUSTRALIA
OFFICIAL VERIFICATION CARD

Fig. 13-1 A major voice from the South Pacific, Radio Australia.

information to listen to. Other than on the BBC, very little rock music can be heard on shortwave. WJCR is one of the only short-wave stations that plays country gospel music, and they play plenty of it! Some of the other selections include Afro-pop via Africa #1 (Gabon); contemporary Christian and gospel music via HCJB (Equador); pop and classical music from the Voice of Russia; pop, classical, and jazz music from the Voice of America; a variety of salsa, ranchero, Andean, etc., music from the regional South American stations (Fig. 13-2); a variety of rock from the John Peel Show on the BBC; and other regional and folk music from regional stations around the world.

But all is not entirely serious on shortwave. The BBC, Radio Canada International, and the vast majority of North American pirate stations all offer up some comedy programming—often very dry and witty.

SHORTWAVE EQUIPMENT

The cost of a portable receiver ranges from about $40 to almost $600 (U.S.). The shortwave radio market is rather small and

Fig. 13-2 Although the shortwave bands are dominated by the powerhouse Western nations, much more is audible, such as Radio Santa Cruz from Santa Cruz, Bolivia.

only a few dozen different models are available. But obviously the sizes, styles, quality, and features vary considerably. A good receiver isn't very important if you only want to catch the news on the Voice of America. If that's the case, you can probably get by with a very inexpensive receiver. Even if you just want the cheapest receiver to perform the easiest tasks, you should still check out the different features so that you can find a receiver that will best suit your needs. The following paragraphs cover some of the qualities and features of portable shortwave radios that you should examine before choosing a receiver.

AUDIO QUALITY

If you are considering placing a shortwave receiver in with your home stereo system, the audio is a major concern. As shortwave receivers were miniaturized with solid-state components, the audio quality dropped significantly. In the 1970s and 1980s, very few shortwave receivers were manufactured with good fidelity. But, now that size and portability are no longer novel features, audio quality is once again of importance to some manufacturers. Although it is always best for you to check the audio of a receiver yourself (preferably through good headphones because you will be feeding the audio from the receiver to your hi-fi speakers, not to the little receiver speaker), Drake, Kenwood, and Lowe have long-standing reputations for receivers with good audio.

SENSITIVITY

Sensitivity is the capability of a receiver to pull in weak signals. If the receiver has poor sensitivity, weak stations will not be audible. (Strong signals will still be audible on a set with poor sensitivity.) If sensitivity is a real need for you, look at the receiver specifications, which are often printed in the catalogs of the major short-wave mailorder companies. Sensitivity is measured in microvolts, which might seem like a complicated measurement. But there's an easy way to check the sensitivity: the lower the number, the better. For portable receivers, you can't get much better than the Drake SW8 (Fig. 13-3) and the Lowe HF-150, which both have an SSB sensitivity of 0.5 microvolts.

SELECTIVITY AND FILTERS

Selectivity is the capability of a receiver to choose between different radio signals. For example, a very strong signal might be on 6010 kHz and another strong signal might be on 6020 kHz. On a receiver with poor selectivity, both stations would interfere with each other. A receiver with excellent selectivity will have no problem separating signals that are just a few kilohertz apart.

The selectivity of a receiver is based on the filters that it contains. The filters allow a small segment of the radio spectrum to pass through and be heard from your speaker. Most people without

Fig. 13-3 Not only does the Drake R-8 (big brother of the SW-8) have good shortwave audio quality, but it is an excellent receiver, and it looks more like a piece of stereo equipment than a shortwave receiver. Drake

technical backgrounds just assume that when you tune a radio to a frequency, the radio will just "play" whatever is on that frequency. However, radio signals are very wide, often occupying as much as 12 kHz for amplitude-modulated (AM) signals, which are typically used for shortwave and medium-wave broadcasting.

Amplitude-modulated signals consist of a carrier and two audio sidebands. The carrier is just a "blank" signal. You can hear the carrier whenever there is no audio on the station. A good time to hear a carrier is when a station is signing on or off, between commercials, or during long pauses in a talk show. The sideband signals (upper and lower sideband) are on either side of the carrier; they contain the audio. Typically, the total signal power is 50% carrier, 25% upper sideband, and 25% lower sideband. As a result, a strong radio station often sounds best when you tune just above or below the center (strongest) part of the signal. At the center, you will receive more of the carrier than the audio from either of the sidebands. But, if you tune to either side, you will receive lots of signal from one of the sidebands.

The width of the signal and the audio filters have a lot to do with how the radio station will sound in your speaker or headphones. So, how do the filters apply to real life? If a really strong station is operating with a 10-kHz wide signal and your receiver has a 9-kHz filter, the audio will probably sound really good.

However, if you are listening to a weaker signal that is only 5 kHz wide with the same receiver on the 9-kHz filter, the results will be less spectacular. The audio will be crisp and clear, but an extra 2 kHz of noise or splatter from other stations will be audible on either side of the signal, making it very difficult to copy, even though the sound is not muffled at all. For best results on receiving this signal, a 3- or 4-kHz filter would be used. On the other hand, if a 3- or 4-kHz filter was used on the 10-kHz-wide signal, the station's audio would be much more muffled and unpleasant than if the 9-kHz filter was used.

So, what to do? If the filter is very wide, very strong signals will sound great, but weak signals and signals with adjacent-channel interference will be basically unlistenable. On the other hand, if the filters are too narrow, weak signals will be received well (but not with good audio), but strong signals will also have muddy audio.

Most inexpensive radios—especially portables—have either one intermediate width (usually about 4 or 5 kHz wide). The best portable receivers, such as the Grundig YB-400 and the Sony ICF-2010, have a "wide" and a "narrow" filter position so that both strong and weak signals can be received. The tabletop receivers have as many as five different filter positions for the most flexible receiving conditions.

Many portable receivers have only one or two different filters because of their high cost. New filters each typically cost anywhere from $75 to $200 (U.S.). A handful of good filters alone could cost several times the cost of a new portable receiver. Considering that filters are the "windows to the radio spectrum" and that their cost is prohibitive, the filter is one of the most important components that influences your satisfaction with a radio and its compatibility with your budget. When choosing a radio, be sure to check out what types of filters are included. Some table-top radios companies—such as the Japan Radio Company (JRC), Kenwood, and Icom—sell their receivers like cars; basic models will contain fewer or lesser-grade filters; better or more filters are available as options.

The "wave of the future" for radio filter technology is digital signal processors (DSPs). The Watkins-Johnson HF-1000 has an entirely digital front end; instead of traditional crystal or mechanical filters, the filtering is all processed digitally through integrated circuits. The HF-1000 can be set to more than 55 different filter widths! Using traditional filters, they alone would probably cost over $10,000 (U.S.). Instead, as of this writing, the HF-1,000 priced in at "only" about $3,700 (U.S.). Although these prices are tremendous, expect that the technology will become less expensive in the next few years. About five years ago, I heard short-wave experts talking at a convention about how some of the major radio manufacturers would soon be out with digitally filtered portable radios for less than $500. It hasn't happened yet, but such a radio would all but render the competition obsolete.

IMAGE REJECTION

Image rejection allows the receiver to be exposed to very powerful signals without "overloading." An extremely potent signal, such as that from a local AM broadcast station, might swamp the front end of the receiver. As a result, you might hear "images" on frequencies other than the one that the station broadcasts on. Because of the small size and emphasis on low cost, portable receivers traditionally have been notorious for poor image rejection. I have had some receivers that, when connected to a longwire antenna, swamped on a local AM broadcast signal and I could hear that signal in the background wherever I tuned. Very annoying. However, the image-rejection problems have been corrected (or at least improved) in many of the newer portables. Image rejection in tabletop receivers typically ranges from very good to excellent.

SSB/BFO

The *single-sideband (SSB) mode* is a special type of transmission that is much more efficient than traditional AM broadcasting. As mentioned in the section about selectivity and filters, each sideband only consists of about 25% of the total signal that is transmitted from an amplitude-modulated radio station. With SSB transmission, the theory is that if the carrier and the one sideband are unused, all of the audio signal can be concentrated on that one sideband.

It works tremendously well. However, the fidelity is drastically diminished. Because of the reduced fidelity, only a few shortwave broadcast stations operate in SSB, but nearly every amateur operator uses this mode. The other problem with SSB transmitting is that when you listen to an SSB station in the AM mode, it will sound like some cartoon ducks—except less intelligibly. To hear the SSB stations, you need a receiver that either has the SSB mode or has a BFO (beat-frequency oscillator). Receivers with the SSB mode are often easier to tune than those with just a BFO, so this should be a consideration.

DIGITAL OR ANALOG READOUT

Most adventurous people like to explore by going somewhere new, but not by feeling lost wherever they are. For this reason, digital readout (which prints out the numbers on an LCD) is much more popular than analog tuning (which moves a pointer in front of a few rows of frequencies). Because of the small size of most analog portables, few numbers can be written in the dial space, and you wind up guessing at your frequency (+/− 10 or 15 kHz). Fortunately, with the low cost of components for digital tuning, very few analog shortwave receivers of any type are made any more.

One step beyond digital tuning is *Station Name Tuning*, which is available on several Sony portable receivers. With this system, you can tune to some of the popular frequencies around the short-wave bands, and the name of the station will also automatically appear on the LCD readout. In the Sony ICF-SW77, 94 of these memories are preset at the factory and you can program up to 162 different stations into the memories. The station name tuning is an unnecessary extra for me because I always listen to and tune the radio with a few shortwave newsletters, magazines, or books handy.

TUNING RATE

One of the problems with low-cost digital receivers is that most of them don't tune continuously across the bands. Some of the small, portable, digital receivers only tune in 1- and/or 5-kHz steps. Neither of these types of receivers are useful for hearing amateur radio stations, and you might have some problems with hearing some of the broadcasters, such as the Voice of Greece on 7448 kHz or Radio Copan International on 15674.6 kHz. These stations could fall between the tuning steps of the receiver and be difficult or impossible to receive.

For the SSB stations, you might even have some problems with the digital receivers that tune in 100-Hz blocks. If the amateur is transmitting between the 100-Hz steps of your receivers, such as on 7240.15 kHz, the signal will sound "ducky," no matter where you tune. This can be a real problem when listening to some of the pirate broadcasters that transmit music in the SSB mode.

Some of the better receivers tune finer than you can see. For example, 100-Hz readout is common on the better portables, but some of these tune in increments down to 10 Hz or so. As a result, you can tune in SSB stations much better on these receivers (such as the Kenwood R-5000).

Unfortunately, few of the shortwave mail-order companies list the tuning rate in their catalogs. If you plan to spend a little more on your portable and want to have an easier time tuning in the SSB stations, be sure to call the information line and ask a customer service representative what the receiver tuning rate is.

COVERAGE

Most shortwave receivers cover the entire shortwave band (1800 to 30,000 kHz), plus the medium-wave band (known as the *AM band* in most of North America, 500 to 1800 kHz), and some of the long-wave band (usually anywhere from 10 kHz, 150 kHz, or 200 kHz is covered up to 500 kHz). Some receivers also cover the FM broadcast band (known as the *VHF broadcast band* in many parts of the world), a few cover the aero band (108 to 136 MHz), and some cover the aero and public service bands (108 to 172 MHz) with an optional coverter.

Most of the tabletop receivers cover the entire shortwave band, plus a few other bands. (Sometimes medium wave, FM, aircraft, or some of the VHF utility bands are included.) However, many of the portable receivers have an incomplete shortwave range. Many only tune down to about 3500 kHz and up to about 21 MHz. Others only tune the shortwave broadcast bands. Many old receivers covered the amateur radio bands exclusively; these are only useful to amateur radio operators or radio nostalgists. Beware of these "incomplete" radios!

SIZE AND WEIGHT

Even though some of my old 60-pound radios are excellent, they just don't cut it for traveling; they're a bear just to clean around, let alone carry (Fig. 13-4). All of the "portable" shortwave receivers are at least relatively portable, but otherwise the size varies greatly. The largest of the portables, the Drake SW8, is more like hauling a VCR with a handle than a portable radio. The SW8 is basically a tabletop radio that has been built tough for traveling.

In most cases, shortwave radios are chosen for their portability. However, in the case of using a shortwave receiver as a component in your audio system, a portable will be much more difficult to use than a receiver with a front panel or remote-control features. In fact, if you have invested quite a bit in your system, you

Fig. 13-4 If it made the trip on the Kon-Tiki, would it be considered portable? Not by today's standards! Regardless, these National receivers were built to last in almost any environmental condition.

would probably rather spend the extra money just to have a receiver that looks more like a piece of stereo equipment. Judging by this measure alone, the Drake R-8A (and the previous model, the R-8) is the hands-down winner. Of course, the $1,000 price tag is a deterrent to many people who only have a light interest in shortwave, but at least the R-8A is more than just a pretty face; many shortwave listeners consider it to be the best receiver in the under-$2,000 price bracket.

WHERE TO BUY A RECEIVER?

If you have looked over some of the shortwave books and magazines, you might already know what receiver you want to buy. Now what? Chances are that the only local store that carries any type of shortwave radios is Radio Shack. Radio Shack carries a full line of portable receivers, some of which are made by Sangean. Some other primarily nonshortwave companies, such as Sony, are getting some of their receivers into such chain stores as Sears. So, with some searching around town (provided that you at least live in a small city) at the various electronics stores and stereo shops, you might locate about half of the available portable receivers.

The problem is that you won't see many of the good receivers. Radio Shack receivers *are* available at every one of their branch stores. A few Sony, Panasonic, and Magnavox receivers are somewhat common because these companies all make consumer video and audio equipment. One of the specialty dealers might decide to pick up a shortwave radio or two, just to see if they'll sell.

But some of the equipment manufacturers specialize in shortwave equipment. You won't find their receivers everywhere. Drake is legendary for innovative, high-quality U.S.-made shortwave and satellite receivers, but their equipment is rarely available outside of specialty shortwave shops and mailorder distributors. Lowe's description is much the same as Drake, except that the company is based in England.

Another drawback of picking up a receiver from a local store is that it will probably be close to the list price. The major short-wave mail-order companies sell so many radios that they can offer portables for anywhere from $10 to as much as $200 off of the list price. The only exception to this rule is Radio Shack, which generally offers its radios at good prices and sometimes has excellent sales. Of course, because Radio Shack only sells its own receivers, you have to be yearning for a Radio Shack receiver. If you are, be sure to check all of the local stores for special sales and especially for the closeouts. During the closeout sales, receivers are often sold for 50% or less of the original price!

If you're as cheap as I am, you might be on the lookout for a used receiver. But the prospects of finding one are slim. Used shortwave radios are almost never advertised in the classified sections of newspapers or "shopper-type" papers. I go to plenty of hamfests/computerfests, where all sorts of amateur radio equipment, computers, consumer electronics, and parts are sold. Not many portable receivers even turn up here, but if you have a hamfest/computerfest coming to your hometown, it's worth a look.

Other than these rather infrequent used offerings, your only hope for a used portable is to get a trade-in radio from one of the specialty shortwave mailorder companies. Most of these companies service their equipment and offer brief "return-for-any-reason" periods and 30-days-parts-and-labor warranties. Because of their reputation and because most of these companies have been in business for decades, you can purchase a used receiver from them without fear. Two of the largest short-wave dealers with great reputations are Grove Enterprises (which also publishes *Monitoring Times* magazine):

http://www.grove.net

and Universal Radio (Fig. 13-5):

http://www.universal-radio.com

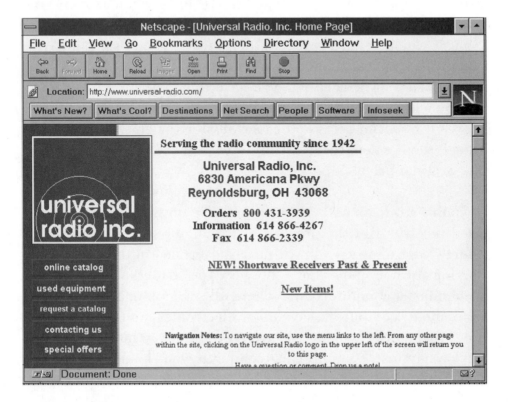

Fig. 13-5 The opening Web page from one of the world's largest shortwave dealers, Universal Radio.

SHORTWAVE INFORMATION

Unlike the AM (MW) and FM (VHF) broadcast bands, you must receive some shortwave broadcast information if you want to keep track of what's on the air. It's like the old "don't know the players without a scorecard" adage.

The difference between these broadcast bands is that the stations on the North American AM and FM bands all stick to their own single frequency and format. The only simulcasts allowed are when one AM and one FM station are owned by the same company and they both air the same programming. The only stations that change formats over a broadcasting day are the few low-power community stations still left and the college radio stations.

Shortwave broadcasters are completely different. Except for the conservative religious stations in the United States and the handful of local commercial outlets in Latin America and a few other scattered parts of the world, the shortwave broadcasters are all governmental branches that periodically deliver a variety of programming that is beamed to different parts of the world. To be able to effectively meet these needs, the typical governmental station will broadcast a program that is anywhere from 30 minutes to 2 hours in length. Then, they will either switch antennas and broadcast to another part of the world or they will switch languages and broadcast another program and switch again. Because some shortwave stations broadcast in as many as 80 different languages, you can imagine the enormity of these operations! Also, as was previously eluded to, these stations broadcast on many different frequencies, in a number of different broadcast bands. For example, according to the 1997 Edition of the *World Radio TV Handbook*, the Voice of America operates 27 different transmitters in North America alone; it also currently operates transmitters in many other countries.

Speaking of relays in other countries, although it is quite possible to hear many stations broadcasting directly from their own country (some stations, such as those as far away as Radio Australia, can be heard quite well in North America directly—even though the transmitter is on the opposite side of the earth), some have relay agreements with other countries, and these programs can often be heard with tremendous signals. For an example of distant transmitter sites, the Voice of America, BBC, and Deutche Welle all have transmitter sites on the island of Antigua in the Caribbean. As far as relay agreements are concerned, The Voice of Free China (Taiwan) has a relay agreement with WYFR (California), Radio China International (Mainland China) has relay agreements with Radio Canada International, the Voice of Russia's North American service has been relayed for years from Radio Havanna sites in Cuba, and Trans World Radio is heard via numerous transmitter sites around the world (Fig. 13-6).

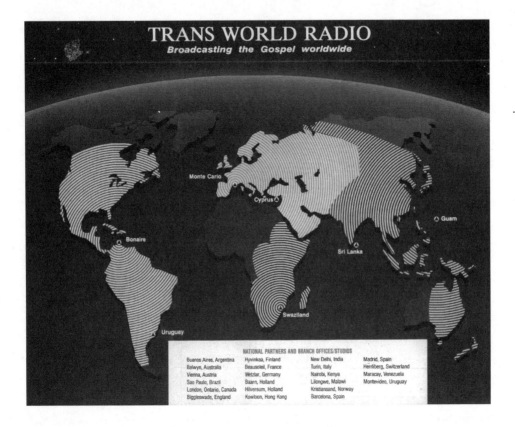

Fig. 13-6 Trans World Radio broadcasts via numerous transmitters around the world.

It was mentioned earlier that frequencies often change. This is because the same bizarre ionospheric conditions that make worldwide radio reception possible also easily affect and disturb radio reception. For example, in the summertime, the noise increases on the lower nighttime bands especially, and the high frequencies often become more reliable. As a result, during the spring, many stations switch to using primarily higher frequencies. Then, during the winter, the lower frequencies become quieter and more reliable, so many stations move some of their frequencies down to lower channels in the autumn months. To make things even more complicated, every 11 years, radio conditions run through a sunspot cycle, which improves reception at its height and damages reception at its lowpoint. During this cycle, there are times when frequencies above a certain point are totally ineffective for reaching an audience, the peak of which is called the maximum usable frequency, and there are other times when frequencies below a certain point will be totally ineffective, the peak of which is called the mininum usable frequency. These conditions force the international broadcasters to have monitors in various parts of the world listening to see if the signals are clear and strong. If not, that station will move its broadcasts to another frequency. Because of these constantly changing conditions, it is important to have current information on hand.

Several different monthly shortwave magazines are available, and a number of different shortwave clubs and organizations offer speedy and informative newsletters. Over the years, I have subscribed to 14 different shortwave magazines and newsletters. They are quite an interesting lot, and I believe they are well worth the money.

Two annual "master reference" books exist on the subject: *Passport To World Band Radio* and the *World Radio TV Handbook*. Both of these references are quite large, thorough, and accurate. The difference between the two is that *Passport* is much easier to use for program listening, but the *WRTH* crams tons of useful and trivial information into the book. These titles complement each other, so I regularly pick up copies of both. If money is a concern, you might consider looking around for older copies of these books. Sometimes I pick up cheap used copies from friends, through the mail from classified ads, or at shortwave gatherings to fill out my collection.

If you want to pick just one newsletter or magazine, you should try one with a large amount of general-interest material. *Popular Communications* (available at newsstands in North America), *Monitoring Times* (available from Grove Enterprises), and *Shortwave Magazine* (available in the United Kingdom, or by mail overseas) are all glossy-covered magazines that cover the hobby well and feature a great amount of basic information. Otherwise, the club newsletters *The Journal* (from NASWA, the North American ShortWave Association) and *DX Ontario* (from the Ontario DX Association) are both excellent for general-coverage shortwave listening. If you live in a different area of the world and you are interested in shortwave periodicals, then you should read the club listings in the *World Radio TV Handbook* and write for information from some of the local clubs.

CONCLUSION

The shortwave bands are an all-too-forgotten region of the radio spectrum. Although the audio is not up to FM standards, you can hear fascinating programs from around the world. Because of the audio quality, shortwave isn't for everyone, but every radio or audio hobbyist should look into the topic.

14

ANTIQUE AUDIO

Baseball cards, cereal boxes, even photos of mushrooms and funguses (no athlete's-foot photos!)—you name it and I'll collect it! It's not that I collect things because I'm bored and need a hobby, not because I can make some money on my collections, and not because someone on a TV faux news show told me that it's cool to collect it. It's just that there are so many neat and exciting things in this world and our lives and memories are intangible. It's too excellent to have a scrapbook or photo album full of mementos of a hobby that you love—a chronicle of fun.

Perhaps it's no surprise that I take lots of photos at home and have a shelf full of photo albums. Likewise, I made a big scrapbook/photo album from my workplace. Other co-workers thought it was great and wanted a copy when they left. A few months later, the entire company was closed, leaving me with the only chronicle. As fast as life changes, if you want to collect a tangible record of these events, you've got to do it right now...as it is happening.

Audio systems have a long history, dating back to the late 1800s, so there's plenty of artifacts out there to track down—everything from equipment to music to advertising memorabilia.

For the most part, the collecting hobby lies adjacent to the hi-fi hobby. Most of the memorabilia (except for recordings and a few pieces of old stereo equipment) can't actually be used in your stereo system. And those old wooden radios might be beautiful, but are you really going to spend hours on end listening to an AM radio if you have a great sound system (and have the option of using a CD player, turntable, or DAT deck instead)? So, this chapter is mostly superfluous to your hi-fi experience—having a big RCA electron tube advertising sign in your living room won't improve the sound of your audio system...but it will look pretty cool.

VALUE

One really great aspect of collecting radio artifacts is that most have little monetary value. Those words would send waves of terror down the spines of antique dealers, pot-of-gold seekers, and profiteers. "Worth nothing?! Then, why collect it?!" Because it's fun, interesting, and it means something to you personally.

The great aspect of collecting virtually worthless items is that you can enjoy the hobby and trade for items that you want without having to worry about investors running the prices beyond your limits.

This isn't to say that everything in audioland has no monetary value—some items (such as old radios) do, but their value is much lower than what they originally sold for. The only sectors of the audio hobby that have really attained a collectible status are specialty rock and pop records, and electronics advertising signs. A rare pressing of a record can easily sell for hundreds of dollars. In general, most older records, CDs, and tapes are worth much less than those that are new. Radio advertising signs, like any old signs, are worth plenty of money. The old metal and neon radio and audio signs typically sell for hundreds of dollars.

TAPES

Some radio hobbyists collect radio programs on cassette. In general, these collectors are fans of old-time U.S. commercial radio—programs such as *The Shadow, The Lone Ranger, Amos*

& Andy—and the many soap operas of the day. Fortunately, these programs were archived. Literally hundreds of different programs are available from radio program dealers.

For more information on purchasing these programs, contact:

BRS Productions
P.O. Box 2645
Livonia, MI 48151

Wayne Caldwell
P.O. Box 831183
Richardson, TX 75083

Satellite Broadcasting, Inc.
4580 E. Mack Ave.
Frederick, MD 21701

A fantastic Internet Web page with links to many other old-time radio tape dealers and traders is the Original Old-Time Radio (OTR) WWW Pages. Also, this site contains plenty of history and information about these programs. This is a must-see for any fan of old-time radio:

http://www.old-time.com/vendors.html

I don't know anyone who collects other radio programs. I have traded some radio hobbyists for recordings of "Axis Sally" and "Tokyo Rose," but that is about the extent of international short-wave broadcasts on tape. However, tape collecting among pirate radio hobbyists is booming. Some listeners (including myself) have snippets or full-length programs from hundreds of stations on cassette. Although some of the recordings are off-air, many are copies of the studio program that was originally broadcast. If you are interested in tape trading (unless you have some really rare, preferably pre-1980 pirates), please don't contact me; try the audio page that is affiliated with the Free Radio Network Internet page:

http://w3.one.net/~folk/tapes.html

RADIOS

Of the different categories here, collecting old vacuum tube radios is by far the most common. It can also be expensive: communications receivers typically remain in the $100 to $400 range, but rare and novelty mediumwave radios from the 1930s and 1940s can easily exceed $1,000.

The prices for old radios are driven up by the profitable antiques and collectibles trade. Just a few years ago, old tube radios were just considered to be junk. Now they are filling stalls at antique malls around the U.S. This sudden interest in collecting radios seems to be spurred on by the recent popularity of antiques/collecting and also in art deco designs and pop culture (Fig. 14-1).

At least a dozen books have been written on the subject, including some large-format, color coffee-table books. One of the nicest books for collecting standard medium-wave radios is *The Collector's Guide to Antique Radios (Second Edition)* by Marty and Sue Bunis. Some of the more popular editions include:

* *Radios: The Golden Age* by Philip Collins
* *Radio Manufacturers of the 1920s* by Alan Douglas
* *Radio! Radio!* by Jonathan Hill
* *The Collector's Guide to Transistor Radios* by Marty and Sue Bunis
* *The Portable Radio in American Life* by Michael Schiffer
* *Radios of the Baby Boom Era*
* *Radios Redux* by Philip Collins
* *Radio Art* by Robert Hawes

Fig. 14-1 A late 1930s Philco art deco console radio.

If you are interested in buying or selling old-time mediumwave radios or memorabilia, the ultimate resource is Antique Radio Classified, which is a very large monthly newsletter that consists almost entirely of radio classified ads! For more information, write to: ARC, P.O. Box 802, Carlisle, MA 01741 or see their Internet Web site at:

http://www.antiqueradio.com

Visiting radio's past

If you are interested in radio collectibles and the history of radio, you will certainly want to visit one or more of the radio museums. Most of these museums are small, private collections dotted around the country. The curators are often radio hobbyists, maybe amateur radio operators, and are usually very knowledgeable about radio. The driving force behind the museums is often simply radio, not money, so you can expect a good time (Fig. 14-2).

Fig. 14-2 A room of the Bellingham Antique Radio Museum, packed with mostly 1920s tabletop battery radios. Bellingham Antique Radio Museum

When you go to visit a radio museum, be sure to take along a camera (ask on arrival if photos are allowed) and be prepared to ask a lot of questions. Also, be sure to either buy a bunch of postcards or grab a bunch of brochures to send to your friends or along with your reception reports. They make a great conversation piece and help personalize a reception report.

The following list includes information for a number of radio-related museums:

ARRL Headquarters
225 Main St.
Newington, CT 06111
203-594-0200 (tel)
http://www.arrl.org
Schedule: Open Monday through Friday, 9:00 a.m. to 5:00 p.m.

Antique Wireless Association Museum
59 Main St., Village Green
Rt. 5 and 20
Bloomfield, NY 14469
716-657-6260 (tel)
http://www.vivanet.com/freenet/a/awa
n2rsm@frontiernet.net
Schedule: Open at various times throughout the year.

Atwater-Kent Museum
15 S. 7th St.
Philadelphia, PA 19016
215-922-3031 (tel)
Schedule: Open Tuesday through Saturday, 10:00 a.m. to 4:00 p.m.

Bellingham Antique Radio Museum
1315 Railroad Ave.
Bellingham, WA 98225
206-734-4168 (tel)
http://www.antique-radio.org/radio.html
jwinter@pacificrim.net
Schedule: Open Wednesday through Saturday, 11:00 a.m.
through 4:00 p.m. or by appointment.

CBC (Canadian Broadcasting Corp.) Museum
P.O. Box 400, Stn. A
Toronto, ON M5W 1E6, Canada
416-205-3700 (tel)
http://www.cbc.ca/aboutcbc/tbc/museum/museum.html
Schedule: Open Monday through Friday, 10:00 p.m. to 4:00 p.m.

Centre for the History of Defence Electronics (CHiDE)
Bournemouth University
12 Christchurch Rd.
Bournemouth BH1 3NA, United Kingdom
01202-503879 (tel)

ANTIQUE AUDIO

http://chide.bournemouth.ac.uk/default.html
chide@bournemouth.ac.uk
Schedule: By appointment.

Library of American Broadcasting
University of Maryland
Hornbake Library
College Park, MD 20742
301-405-9160 (tel)
http://www.itd.umd.edu/ums/umcp/bpl/bplintro.html
bp50@umail.umd.edu
Schedule: Open Monday through Friday, 9:00 a.m. to 5:00 p.m.

Manitoba Amateur Radio Museum
Box 10
Austin, Manitoba R0H 0C0, Canada
204-728-2463 (tel)
http://www.mbnet.mb.ba/~donahue/austin.html
ve4xn@ve4bbs.#hwd.mb.can.na
Schedule: Open June through October 1, Monday through Friday,
9:00 a.m. to 5:00 p.m.

Museum of Broadcast Communications
Chicago Cultural Center
Michigan Ave. at Washington St.
Chicago, IL 60602
312-629-6000 (tel)
http://webmart.org/mbc
Schedule: Open Monday through Saturday, 10:00 a.m. to 4:30
p.m.; Sunday, 12:00 p.m. to 5:00 p.m.

Museum of Radio and Technology
1640 Florence Ave.
Huntington, WV 25701
304-525-8890 (tel)

http://www.library.ohiou/museumr&t/museum.htm
Schedule: Open Friday and Saturday, 10:00 a.m. to 4:00 p.m.;
Sunday, 1:00 to 4:00 p.m.

Museum Radio-Wereld

Achterstraat 9
7981 AS Diever, The Netherlands
31-521-592386 (tel)
http://www.xxlink.nl/tourism/museums/493.htm
Schedule: By appointment.

Museum of Television and Radio (Beverly Hills)

465 N. Beverly Dr.
Beverly Hills, CA 90210
310-786-1000 (tel)
http://www.mtr.org
Schedule: Open Wednesday through Sunday, 12:00 p.m. to 5:00
p.m.; Thursday, 12:00 p.m. to 9:00 p.m.

Museum of Television and Radio (New York)

25 W. 52nd St.
New York, NY 10019
212-621-6600 (tel)
212-621-6800 (tel)
http://www.mtr.org
Schedule: Open Tuesday through Sunday, 12:00 p.m. to 6:00
p.m.; Thursday, 12:00 p.m. to 8:00 p.m.; Friday, 12:00 p.m. to
9:00 p.m.

The U.S. Army Communications-Electronics Museum

Bldg. 275, Kaplan Hall
Ft. Monmouth
Red Bank, NJ 07703
908-532-9000 (tel)
Schedule: Open Monday through Friday, 12:00 p.m. to 4:00 p.m.

The Western Heritage Museum of Omaha
801 S. 10th St.
Omaha, NE 68108
402-444-5071 (tel)
Schedule: Open Tuesday through Saturday, 10:00 a.m. to 5:00
p.m.; Sunday, 1:00 p.m. to 5:00 p.m.

STEREO EQUIPMENT

Most stereo equipment isn't particularly collectible. If you find a
cassette player from the 1960s or 1970s, you'll discover that it's
resale value is considerably lower than its retail price when new.
Really, the only audio equipment since 1950 that has much
collector's value are tube power amplifiers, tube preamplifiers,
and radios. Top-of-the-line turntables and open-reel tape decks
have also held some of their value, but few people say "I'm really
looking for a vintage Viking open-reel deck for my audio system."
Instead, they will look for a good open-reel deck that still works
well, such as a 1970s-era unit from Teac or Revox.

There's a good reason why the tube amplifiers and preamplifiers
have become collectible. Not only do some of the best models
perform excellently, but they really look great! To top it off, most
of these tube amplifiers can be found for much less than the price
of a new tube amplifier. The most collectible amplifiers are those
manufactured by McIntosh. McIntosh equipment provided the
ultimate in reliability, customer service, and beauty for tube amplifiers in the 1950s and 1960s. As a result of this combination
and because it is a small, personal company, the equipment has
maintained a cult following for years. For more information about
how such a little company could have so many fans, see:

http://sundial.sundial.net/~rogerr/mcintosh1.htm

Another company with a cult-like following is Heath (often known
as *Heathkit*). This company began just after World War II and

specialized in kits that were created from vast supplies of U.S. Army surplus electronics parts. Heath started manufacturing amateur radio equipment and electronics test equipment early on, but soon began manufacturing a wide variety of audio equipment, as well. Because of its diversity, Heath has a strong following within both amateur radio and hi-fi audio circles (Fig. 14-3). Unlike McIntosh, which offered virtually unbeatable service and performance at a tremendous cost, Heath became popular by

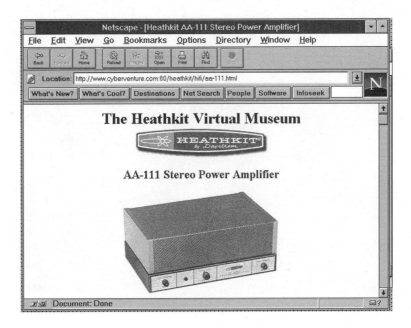

Fig. 14-3 Just one page of the Heathkit Virtual Museum.

offering the best equipment for the money and having excellent customer service. Throughout Heath's existence, you could be fairly certain that any given piece of Heath equipment was better (or much better) than any other comparable equipment of lesser or equal price. There's even a book called *Heath Nostalgia* by Terry Perdue, a large guide to collecting Heath amateur radio equipment, and a fascinating Web page, with a special hi-fi section. The Heathkit Virtual Museum is at:

http://www.cyberventure.com:80/heathkit/hifi

The hi-fi craze that was sweeping through the United States in the 1950s wasn't just held to within our borders. The same type of audio mania was spreading through northwestern Europe. Superb equipment was also being manufactured by Leak (Fig. 14-4), Marantz, Quad, Pye, Radford, Beam-Echo, and others. Unfortunately, this

Fig. 14-4 A classic Leak Stereo 50 amplifier, sitting on the workbench and awaiting repairs.

audio boom isn't documented as well as that of Heath or McIntosh, but one book dedicated to 1950s and 1960s audio in the UK is *Radio! Radio!* by Jonathan Hill. Although little information about the other classic audio companies is lacking, Beam-Echo has returned to making high-end audio equipment, and some background information about their company and products in the 1950s is available at:

http://www.bucc.co.uk/vbp/beam-echo/goldenag.htm

MUSIC AND RELATED MEMORABILIA

After 40 years of commercialized rock and roll, the ultimate in mass-produced culture, billions of records, CDs, posters, buttons, toys, stickers, mugs, and much more, are available in auctions, flea markets, antique malls, and basements. With the success of commercialized rock (including all of the derivations: rap, dance, disco, punk, metal, techno, etc.), other forms of music, such as country, blues, jazz, and classical have also been successfully mass marketed. I won't get into the moral issues of whether mass marketing weakens the music or creates a reaction against it (such as the incredibly strong anti-disco mood of the late 1970s and early 1980s). The important thing for this section is that there are plenty of things to collect, if you are interested.

THE MUSIC

Considering that this book is about audio, the main focus of this section is records, CDs, and tape recordings. Entire books have been dedicated to such topics as Beatles collectibles, so seek out those guides if you want to find out how to best display your vintage "Yellow Submarine" Wheat Honeys box.

CDs

Of course, both new and used CDs are available. The only exception might be a long out-of-print album, which might be available only via second-hand record dealers or private individuals. The main advantage to buying new recordings is that they are still in perfect condition—no scratches and the liner notes or dust jacket haven't been damaged. Those who listen to small, independent musicians know that if you don't purchase the record or CD new, it might become rare and collectible, costing much more than the original sale price.

The benefits of purchasing used music are fairly obvious. The prices are typically much lower (except as noted in the last paragraph). Also, because CD audio does not degrade through normal use, a used CD will sound as good as a new CD. As a result, used CDs retain their value much better than used records or cassettes. In fact, you have to be careful because I've seen some used CDs selling at higher prices than the same titles new, still in their shrink wrap!

As mentioned, you can assume that a used CD will be identical to a new CD in terms of performance. If you want to be sure, take a look at the underside (plain silver-looking) of the CD. Unless it is seriously flawed or damaged, it should play just fine. A friend told me about a bar near Blacksburg, Virginia. In the 1980s, it spent thousands of dollars revamping the sound system and buying 300 new CDs. They didn't want anyone to steal their CDs, so they wrote the name of their bar with a wide, black permanent marker on the underside of every CD. I doubt that anyone stole their CDs! Beware of CDs with flaws this severe, but it is unlikely that you'll come across anything this damaged in most used CD stores.

Presently, most CDs are not collectible, aside from simply being able to listen to the music that they contain. They are too new for most collectors and most of the limited releases are still cut on vinyl anyway. If the complete and total death of records ever occurs, I'm sure that the limited-edition EPs and full-length albums will be available on CD, but right now, it just isn't happening. The only exception to this is bootlegs; for more information, see the following section.

RECORDS

On the other hand, you need to be very cautious when buying used records. Check for severe warps, scratches, dirt, and groove wear. Warps are nearly impossible not to notice (unless you don't pull the record out of the jacket and take a look), but they are also the easiest to correct. Just stack your warped records on something flat and place a few heavy books on top. After a few days, the warps should mostly pull out.

Scratches are fairly easy to see, either by looking directly at the record or by tilting it to one side and looking at it in the light. The question with scratches is not whether they are there, but how severe are they? A deep scratch could cause the record to skip or not to play at all. You won't really know just how bad that scratch is until you try the record on your turntable. The best protection is to avoid any records with deep scratches, unless the record is really cheap or is rare enough for you to take the risk.

Records can be dirty. The damage that the dirt can cause ranges from slight to severe. It depends how often and how roughly the records were handled while they were dirty. I'm not really sure how these records get so dirty, but I've come across a few that were so dirty it appeared that they must have been lying around in a house under construction or on a baseball field. If the records were handled very little while they were so dirty, they should be in at least fair condition. Take the record under a faucet, hold the edges, and let the water do the work of washing away the dirt. Place the record somewhere that it can safely dry without warping (i.e., not on a hot radiator!). After it dries, use a commercial record-cleaning fluid to clean out the rest of the dirt (this method is also best for cleaning lightly or moderately dirty records). Record-cleaning fluids are available from most stereo shops that sell turntables. Now that your record is clean, be sure that the sleeve is clean, too. If it is sleeveless (or if the sleeve is really dirty, buy some plastic or rice paper sleeves from a hi-fi dealer.

Groove wear is the hardest problem to detect, but it is also one of the most harmful. Minor cases of groove wear will be unnoticeable; you should probably just assume that a well-used record (look for plenty of tiny surface scratches from handling) will have at least some groove wear. In severe cases of groove wear, the grooves on the record will have a white defining edge or even leave some white-looking vinyl powder behind! As in the case of scratches, avoid any records with severe groove wear, unless the record is really cheap or is rare enough for you to take the risk.

Records are the ultimate music collectible. Decades of albums are available on vinyl, and record swaps still occur most every weekend around the country. At the swaps, many of the records are very reasonably priced, but some attain true collector value. The main category of records is simply that of bands that became famous. Original pressings of early albums by the Monkees, The Beatles, and others can be worth a bit of money. A related category is that of trend-setting bands that never sold many records (the demand outweighs the supply); for example, I've seen albums by The Seeds, The Music Machine, and The Count V selling for well over $50 apiece.

Picture discs are very popular music collectibles for obvious reasons. Most picture discs are clear vinyl with two full-sized circular photos (one for each side of the record) sandwiched in between. Most picture discs were limited releases in the 1980s from major labels—to promote bands with strong fanship and teen appeal. One of the best picture disc sites that I've found on the Internet is California Albums. Their site features plenty of different records for auction (minimum bid $15), and one large page features just picture discs:

http://home.earthlink.net/~calalbums/pic.html

Not all releases for major bands are common. Some of the most expensive and rarest records to track down are bootlegs. Bootleg records are those that have been produced without permission of the record label or the band (they are illegal) and contain different material than one of the regular issues from this artist. Illegal copies of albums are called *pirated copies* or *counterfeits*. Most bootlegs are live performances, although some contain repressings of rare releases or of studio outtakes that were never released. As you can expect, the sound quality and printing varies from lousy to extremely professional. One of my favorite bootleg stories is that of the band Fugazi. The potential bootlegger went to a show that was sold out and he was not permitted inside. Undeterred, the bootlegger recorded the show from outside the building, amidst the sounds of passing cars! Despite the illegality of producing bootlegs, plenty of information is available. On the Internet, one excellent Website is Hot Wacks, which features the Bootleg Trading Post, articles about bootleg records and CDs, and information about Hot Wacks books:

http://www.bootlegs.com

For more interactive information, go to the Usenet: alt.music.bootlegs

In the 1990s, the only musical niche that still focuses on producing collector records is in the punk rock underground. Here, bands still produce plenty of vinyl, including multi-color vinyl, limited releases, silk-screened vinyl, picture discs, and hand-numbered records (Fig. 14-5). Some really fascinating material exists in this niche—if the music suits your taste. Although small quantities of this music are available via the Internet, the best

Fig. 14-5 A few collector-edition records, including a hand-numbered, blue vinyl 7″ (in the center) and a clear silk-screened record (in the 2 o'clock position).

places to look for advertisements are in the following fanzines: *Maximumrocknroll*, *Punk Planet*, and *Flipside*.

CASSETTES

Unless you find an unbelievable price or a rare release, you should never buy a used commercial cassette recording. Unlike records or CDs, cassettes will degrade over time. They lose small amounts of the magnetic oxide coating every time that they are played, and they are susceptible to being erased or damaged by heat or magnetic materials. In addition to having plenty of cassettes that have begun to lose quality over the years from typical wear, I've had a number that were partially erased by speaker magnets and sunlight. I've even seen some that have had the black cases curl up from sitting in strong sunlight in the back window of a car. It's fine to listen primarily to cassettes, but if the recording means anything to you, first purchase the album on CD or vinyl, then record it to cassette. This method will save you plenty of money in the long run, and will ensure that you always have a clean-sounding copy of the recording.

HI-FI, ELECTRONICS, AND RADIO MAGAZINES

Because radio is such a popular hobby and because its rise parallels the expansion of magazines, you can find a vast amount of print information on the topic. After working in electronics publishing for six years and attending plenty of hamfests (packratting all the while), I have accumulated hundreds, maybe thousands, of magazines. Most of my finds have been fairly recent and common, but sometimes I'll find something that I've never seen before for a good price.

What is a good price? It depends on what you want and how much you need it. Most post-1950 radio magazines sell for anywhere from 30¢ to $1 per issue (Figs. 14-6 and 14-7). Those from 1930 to 1949 will typically go for 50¢ to $10 per issue.

Fig. 14-6 Wiring up for that four-channel sound on the cover of this *Elementary Electronics* from 1972.

The really early magazines from 1910 to 1929 often sell for $5 to $30 per issue. Of course, these prices are based on condition, how common the magazine is, if any famous radio stars or musicians are featured within, etc.

The following is a little glossary of some of the more common U.S. audio magazines that have been available over the years. The list is certainly not meant to be inclusive, but it does contain some of the more common ones, plus a few rare finds.

The Absolute Sound Hi-end audio. Because most subscribers are hardcore into sound, issues are more often available by year or in sets than loose in a box.

Audio Mid-fi audio. Very common.

Electronics Illustrated Electronics projects. This 1950s and 1960s magazine was very similar to *Popular Electronics*.

Electronics Now Electronics projects. This is the 1990s name for *Radio-Electronics*.

Elementary Electronics Electronics projects and radio monitoring. *Hands-On Electronics* was a 1960s and 1970s magazine that occasionally featured some interesting radio and stereo articles. *EE* also did spin-off annuals, such as *Communications World*, *Electronics Hobbyist*, and *Budget Electronics*.

Hands-On Electronics Electronics projects and radio monitoring. *Hands-On Electronics* was a 1970s and 1980s magazine that occasionally featured some interesting radio articles.

Hi-Fi News & Record Review This is a British hi-fi magazine, but it has recently been marketed in the United States and is available in large bookstores. Recent issues should be fairly common.

Mix Professional audio. Not many audiophiles will be purchasing the 128-channel mixing boards advertised within, but the vintage articles and interviews will be of interest to many.

Modern Electronics Electronics projects. A 1980s magazine that occasionally covered radio or hi-fi.

Monitoring Times All-band monitoring. Dating back to 1981, *Monitoring Times* features a large amount of radio information and historic articles. Not yet collectible, so get the older issues while you can!

Popular Communications All-band monitoring. Since its inception in 1982, *PopCom* has featured a large amount of radio information and historic articles. Not yet collectible.

Popular Electronics Electronics projects. This sister publication to *Electronics Now* features more radio-related articles.

Radio Craft Radio projects and monitoring. This 1920s and 1930s magazine later changed its name to *Radio-Electronics*.

Radio-Electronics Radio projects and monitoring. One of the oldest and all-time best-selling radio and electronics magazines. Changed its name to *Electronics Now*.

Radio News Radio/fan magazine. Lots of information about radio stars and listening to the radio. Very collectible. Became *Radio TV News* in the 1950s and later *TV News*.

Fig. 14-7 If classic audio is your hobby, there's plenty of equipment to get excited about on the cover of this Christmas edition of *Radio & TV News* from 1950.

Radio Experimenter Radio projects and monitoring. This hobbyist magazine became *Radio-TV Experimenter* in 1951 and became *Science & Electronics* in 1971.

Rolling Stone Music. Most of the magazines from the mid-1970s on can be found easily and for little or nothing. However, the 1960s *Rolling Stone* issues are extremely valuable.

Short Wave Craft Shortwave radio projects and monitoring. This 1930s magazine from the initial shortwave radio craze mostly featured shortwave radio construction projects, but it also contained a few interesting radio broadcasting articles.

Short Wave Radio Shortwave radio. This 1930s magazine from the initial shortwave radio craze featured some interesting beginner's radio articles.

Stereophile High-end audio from the early 1960s to present. Lots of great stuff here for the collector! This is one of the best magazines for the pure stereo (not radio-related) collector.

Stereo Review Mid-range hi-fi and music reviews. *Stereo Review* has been a top-selling stereo magazine for decades, and back copies are very easy to locate.

If you start collecting old magazines such as these, be sure that you have lots of storage space in locations that are neither too hot nor too damp and protected from insects, if possible. The daily heating and cooling of an attic will damage paper, but it is preferable to a damp basement, where mildew can ruin pages and covers. You need to be especially careful with some of the magazines that are printed on poor-quality paper, such as *Radio TV Experimenter* and *Electronics Illustrated*.

This stuff is like a coarse, pulpy version of newsprint, and only 30+ years later, it is already yellowing and beginning to become brittle. By far the best of the bunch is the type of acid-free paper used by the amateur radio magazine *QST*.

It takes years of mildew and water to destroy the pages, and I have never seen them turn yellow. The only drawback is that a stack of old *QST*s seems as heavy as a stack of bricks!

CONCLUSION

Although most audio collectibles won't improve the sound of your present stereo system, many will help coordinate your living-room decor with all of that equipment.

15

REPAIR

After I have spent weeks (or longer) searching for the perfect equipment for my system at the right price, and assembling it all in my house, the last thing I would want to see is a component failure. Let me correct that; the last thing I would want to see is a telethon with Carol Channing singing nonstop disco songs. The next worst might be Roseanne Barr in the same telethon, except singing pieces from operas, dressed as Carmen Miranda, while playing a banjo. Rest assured that stereo system breakdown rates up there with this company, however.

From an electronics repair point of view, it is both good and bad that the 1950s have passed. In those days, huge, well-built components were screwed and bolted into large steel cabinets. The parts were built well enough that they were expensive but didn't break down frequently. And they were large enough that they could be replaced without difficulty. Today's advantages are much less expensive components and miniaturization; tiny components are crammed so tight that it seems that only a malnourished seven-year-old with tweezers could have assembled the circuit boards. The disadvantage is, in turn, that only that same seven-year-old could disassemble the board without destroying everything else in the process. As a result, in almost all levels of modern electronics, actual repairs are no longer made; instead, the malfunctioning circuit board is pulled out and replaced with another board.

REPAIR

There is very little that you can do to repair failures on these boards, except purchase a few junker units that are the exact same model number as the unit that you own, isolate the problem, and interchange the failed board with one that will work. This should be a great possibility, but chances are that you will not find a number of broken-down units that are exactly the same as yours. If you do find a number of broken units like yours, chances are that you picked a poor model and you might be better off dumping it than trying to repair a cheaply designed piece of electronics.

Most audio components are built using the board-for-board method, except for dedicated power amplifiers (Fig. 15-1). Dedi-

Fig. 15-1 A power amplifier board with heavy-duty parts in a simple PC board layout.

cated power amplifiers, especially the high-quality American-made models, usually use large, heavy components soldered onto thick circuit boards. These amplifiers could be repaired, but they often don't break down unless they have been mistreated. Even then, it is usually the power transistors (usually field-effect transistors) that go through meltdown. If your amplifier contains vacuum tubes, they will slowly wear out, through no fault of your own.

If you can con the manufacturer out of a repair manual, then you will have a much better opportunity to repair your equipment. However, you probably will not be so lucky. Unfortunately, most companies only distribute this information to their authorized dealers, which forces nearly everyone to go to these dealers for repairs...or buy a new unit. In the 1950s and 1960s, a number of American electronics companies provided extensive support for their products with descriptive lists of components, test point information, troubleshooting information and tips, etc. These days, everything has changed and you are lucky if you can get any free information about any electronic gear.

This chapter is primarily intended for people who have anywhere from no experience to intermediate experience with electronics in general or stereo systems in particular. This is not a technician-level book; i.e., it's for consumers, not electronics enthusiasts or repair technicians. You won't be able to use this chapter to discover that voltage regulator Q86 is blown in your particular receiver and that you should replace it. Information of this nature has filled a number of large audio repair books on its own. Instead, this chapter covers a few of the troubleshooting and repairing basics that are relatively easy for the beginner to perform and that don't require the use of expensive test equipment.

TRACKING DOWN THE PROBLEM

Even if you have no intentions of repairing your own equipment, it is important to search out the problem and tell the repair technician where the problem is and what is occurring. This will help the technician find the problem in less time, and it could save you some money.

I saw an episode of *60 Minutes* several years ago that featured a segment that dealt with the integrity of various electronics repair shopkeepers. They had a woman take a VCR with a simple problem (I believe that the drive belt might have been off) into different electronics repair shops in one city. Several of the parts were marked with an ultraviolet pen. The result of the study was that most of the shops were not honest. Some claimed that parts were replaced that weren't; others claimed that they had performed repairs that hadn't been done, etc.

Hopefully, the electronics repair shops in your area are much more reputable than those that were in the *60 Minutes* study. I would like to think that most people who make a career of audio would be above scamming their customers, but this is not a perfect world. Even if stereo installation and repair would be the most honest business on the face of the earth, there would still be a few dishonest people out there. With this in mind, don't torture your repair technicians with accusations; there's no need to ruin their day. But you should always be as informed and knowledgeable as possible on the subject. Nothing will deter getting ripped off on a repair like knowing what has failed where and being able to talk about it with a repair technician.

You should always first check the wiring around where you think the problem is (and possibly over the whole system, if you fail to locate the trouble). Faulty wiring or connections will void the entire troubleshooting process if you don't immediately check these possibilities.

If, for example, your system does not work and no sound is reaching your speakers, check your wiring. Are the units turned on? Is your system plugged into the wall outlets? If you have equipment that plugs into an amplifier, try pulling the plugs out and plugging into the wall outlets instead. Or maybe the system lights up, but you aren't getting any sound out. Have you recently added any components that could have created problems with your system? If you did, check the component's external wiring. Next, check for common-sense things that you might have missed. Did you forget to plug in any audio cables when installing or rearranging the system?

If these problems aren't applicable, check the displays and power-on indicators on the various components. If you aren't getting any sound, does the component even turn on? If not, you should check the connections to the unit. As complicated as today's audio/video components are, it is easy to accidentally plug the input cords into the output jacks (or vice versa). With an overlooked connection, the whole system can go down, or part of it might not work.

Determining faults in a system is a matter of taking educated guesses and almost randomly substituting other components for testing purposes. The rationale is that if one part isn't working, you will be able find that problem by substituting different components one at a time until the system works. From this point, if the problem is in a complicated component, such as a CD player or an amplifier, you might not be able to narrow it down further without using a multimeter, a signal generator, and an oscilloscope, so you might be stuck at this point if you don't have this equipment.

Of course, these tracing examples could be drawn out for 101 different minor problems. Rather than delve into all of these problems, which you probably won't ever encounter, and bore you to tears in the process, this book covers a few basic problems. If you have not had much experience with repairing or troubleshooting electronics equipment, this simplified approach should be more helpful than a deep, all-inclusive look at the topic.

ORGANIZING YOUR WORK

The procedures to disassemble audio electronic equipment are very complicated and you must be very careful or you might wind up with a few "extra parts." As you disassemble the electronic components, don't just dump out parts in a pile (Fig. 15-2). Write down the parts that you have removed and either put them in labeled sandwich bags or in small containers. Better yet, if you have a Polaroid camera or a digital camera, take a photo or two before you start the disassembly process. I have torn apart different components many times and felt that I would know for sure how to put the parts back together. Before long, it seemed that I had the entire project into hundreds of little pieces, and I only remembered how to fix half of the parts in the proper location. You should even draw a diagram of the assembly/disassembly procedures (even if you have a photo) so that you can prevent your projects from remaining hopelessly disassembled.

Fig. 15-2 If your work area is a mess, chances are good that you will hopelessly lose parts and waste plenty of time.

SAFETY PROCEDURES

Safety procedures are never fun because they slow down your progress. I guess I'm just too impatient for safety rules, but it seems as though I have to screw up several times severely before I get the hint that I should be more careful. Then, after a few traumatic experiences, my techniques improve. Fortunately, I've technician or have very little or no experience, read some books that are dedicated to the topic and buy some inexpensive nonfunctioning equipment to experiement with. One of the worst things you could do is to try to repair an expensive piece of equip- ment (such as a $6,000 amplifier) with minor problems, cause more damage to it, and not have enough money to replace it.

If you have had some experience working on electronics gear and feel comfortable about tinkering, be careful and connect the ower only when taking measurements at the manufacturer's listed test points. When testing and taking measurements on a unit, it is much better to remove it from the stereo component rack.

Go to your workbench and connect the unit to a regulated 12-V power supply. This way, you have work space and sufficient light, rather than trying to solder upside down on the floor with molten solder and flux splattering on your carpet and/or the rest of your equipment. It is best if you have an open work area or an electronics workbench that is clean, stocked with parts, and well lit.

Be sure to check for any manufacturer's warranties that you might void by removing the component case and digging around inside. For the most part, if you remove the case of an electronic component, you will void the warranty. Considering that you probably will not be digging around in your new amplifier unless it has malfunctioned, voiding the warranty is bad news.

ELECTROCUTION AND ELECTRICAL SHOCK

The one serious drawback to troubleshooting and repairing electronic equipment, aside from the possibility of damaging it beyond repair, is the possibility of electrocution. Sure, you work with the voltage from the wall everyday, so it might seem relatively tame. It's not. One buzz from the wall could be your last! More than enough to kill you, 110 volts and the corresponding 60-Hz cycles (in North America) are said to be near the optimum frequency for stopping a heart. The voltages in Europe aren't any safer—220 volts at 50 Hz, so you must be excruciatingly careful when working with electronic equipment wherever you live.

If you make a mistake and nothing happens, don't assume that you'll always be so fortunate. For instance, you could be electrocuted by touching a "hot" wire carrying line voltage, but you might actually escape it. This doesn't mean that you should be careless when repairing electronics. Instead, you should take extra precautions to increase your chances of survival if you would touch a "hot" wire. Electrocution is a real possibility if you are well grounded and if you are making a strong contact with the electricity (such as if your skin is wet, if it is entering through a cut, etc.). To prevent being grounded, don't stand in water. Wear rubber-soled athletic shoes and stand on a rubber mat, if possible. Electricity always takes the shortest path with the least resistance to ground. So, if you are standing on a mat and get shocked, you are actually a giant resistor, but if you are grounded through a puddle on the floor, you are a giant conductor. From a safety standpoint, you are much safer being a giant resistor. (However, you are much safer, and happier, not being an electrical component at all!)

Because of the shortest-path-to-ground rule, it is best to avoid having electricity grounding in a path that leads through the heart (Fig. 15-3). For this reason, one commonly used rule in electronics is to work with the left hand in a pants pocket (one of your own). Thus, if you get shocked with a great amount of power, the electricity shouldn't pass through your heart and you won't get killed. It's a simple and effective theory, except for one hangup; it's really tough to work with one hand in your pants. After years of working with your hand in your pants pocket, you probably won't get electrocuted, but your scarred hands and mangled projects will testify to the clumsiness of the arrangement.

As stated previously, be sure to unplug the unit that you are checking (unless you are taking measurements at various test points) so that you don't cause yourself bodily harm. And remember from the operational theory of capacitors that capacitors store electricity until that charge is dissipated. This charge doesn't quickly dissipate while it sits in a circuit; you could easily dig into an amplifier weeks or months later and find out that the heavy-duty capacitors still pack a wallop. The usual method for dis-

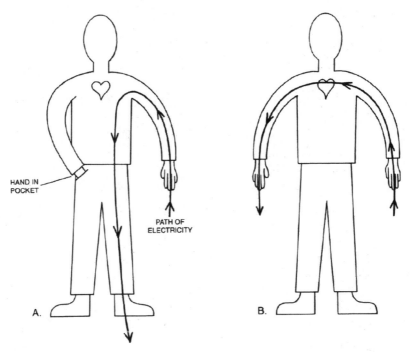

Fig. 15-3 With a hand in your pocket, the electricity will pass through your arm and out from your leg. Otherwise, it will travel through your heart.
Loompanics

charging capacitors is to cross the leads with a large plastic-handle screwdriver (Fig. 15-4). However, to prevent the possibility of having a charge jump over the shaft of the screwdriver and jolt

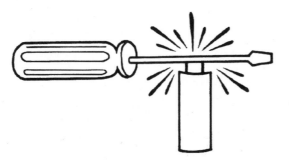

Fig. 15-4 Discharging a capacitor with the old "screwdriver across the leads" method. Loompanics

you, it is best to attach the screwdriver shaft to ground via an alligator clip. Be sure to discharge each large capacitor several times because most capacitors will still store some electricity even after you have discharged them the first time. This method has been used at TV repair shops for decades, but some people say that it causes slight damage to the capacitors each time.

For a more scientific discharge method, cross the leads with a resistor of a value that has been recommended by the manufacturer. This method can be clumsy and annoying because you have to dig up different resistors and shove them into the guts of some equipment without bumping against other components or shocking yourself. Some technicians use a special capacitor discharger, which slowly dissipates the stored voltage without the possibility of damaging the capacitor. Check with some of the large electronics-supply mail-order companies for availability.

SAFETY WITH ELECTROSTATICS

To protect electronic equipment from electrostatic discharges (also known as *static electricity*), you must take almost the opposite mind-set and approach than you did with protecting yourself against dangerous voltages. That doesn't mean that you should stand naked in a puddle of water while groping the insides of a plugged-in power amplifier, but it is still somewhat different from protecting yourself against electrocution.

Many of today's microelectronic components are intended to handle only miniscule amounts of power. Because of the push for miniaturization in electronics, it is better for the parts to be used closer to the damage tolerances than to be forced to build the piece of audio equipment into a much larger enclosure (larger equipment is also more expensive). As a result, it is very easy to damage equipment with levels of electricity that we would have never considered to be harmful to anything just one or two decades ago.

However, with modern integrated circuits, even a small blast of static electricity can melt a tiny hole through the package and destroy one of the microscopic components or interconnecting wires. Blasts of static electricity will either destroy or impair the performance of the integrated circuit. Even the static electricity discharged from your body is destructive. Just wearing tennis shoes and walking across the carpet on a dry day will cause an electrostatic charge that is easily powerful enough to destroy a typical integrated circuit. According to an article in *Electronic Servicing and Technology*, one person (depending on the clothing and other environmental conditions) can build up a charge of static electricity that exceeds 35,000 volts!

As you can see, it is very difficult to handle integrated circuits without damaging or destroying them. To prevent damage, it is important to wear a grounded wrist strap (Fig. 15-5). The grounded wrist strap is a conductive strap that is connected to ground via a wire. This method is effective because the ground bleeds off the electricity (rather than allowing it to suddenly build up), then releases it through the integrated circuit that you are handling.

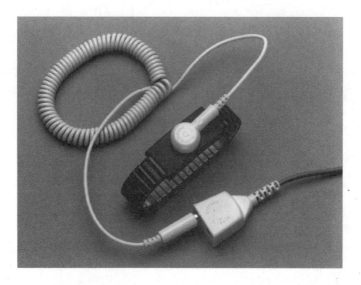

Fig. 15-5 A grounded wrist strap, which is necessary when handling modern solid-state electronics. Plastic Systems

So, if you are working on complicated integrated-circuit-laden units, such as receiver/amplifiers, be sure to use grounded wrist straps. Otherwise, even getting too close to the unit (without touching it) could cause your body to discharge electricity through it (via arc-over) and damage components.

SOLDERING SAFETY

The biggest problem that you'll likely face with soldering irons is not the intensity of the heat, but rather that they don't heat up fast enough. But they're hot enough to melt solder; what more could you want? When troubleshooting and repairing modern miniaturized electronics, it's best to use a soldering gun. Unlike the "pencil" soldering iron, the soldering gun is pistol shaped and is activated by a trigger. These models are typically rated at between 40 and 100 watts, as opposed to 25 watts for a "pencil" soldering iron.

The problem with using a "pencil" soldering iron is that it doesn't get hot enough to quickly melt solder. When you make a soldering connection or desolder a component with an iron, you have to hold the tip in place for a while—heating up and possibly melting the component. I burned up a few surface-mount microswitches within the past year or two using soldering "pencils." With a soldering gun, you can "zap" the connection and move on. In some cases, you might want to connect a heatsink or a pair of hemostats (commonly available at radio hamfests) to the component that you're soldering so that the heat will be transmitted into the heatsink (or hemostats), not the component.

CD PLAYERS

Like all modern audio electronics (except power amplifiers), compact disc players are very complicated units that are packed with tiny components, some of which are sensitive to static electricity. Thus, these units are very difficult to repair, but it is fairly easy to perform some easy maintenance tasks that will keep your discs running properly. The compact disc player troubleshooting information included in this book is limited. For much more information (nearly 500 pages worth), read *Troubleshooting & Repairing Compact Disc Players (3rd Edition)* by Homer L. Davidson.

SAFETY

Compact disc players of all sorts can be very dangerous to work on, both because of your own safety and the delicacy of the player itself. The compact disc player operates somewhat like a record player, but rather than using a needle to pick up vibrations from the disc, a laser beam is used to read the underside of the disc. You can disable the mechanism that turns off the laser and put your hand in front of the beam for a long time. You won't suddenly cut through your hand and you won't feel any pain. For that matter, you won't feel anything. And you thought it was going to be like the scene in *Goldfinger*. Bummer, man. Despite the first impression, this laser is not totally harmless. It can severely cause damage to your eyes if you look at it. So, don't! And to keep your eyes safe when working on a powered-on disc player, place a CD in the machine if you need to poke around inside. The CD will cover the beam. Obviously, your eyes are very important, so be careful.

In addition to the hidden potential for physical bodily harm while working on compact disc players, they also present a potential for self-destruction. As mentioned earlier, compact disc players are prone to destruction from static discharges from your body. Be sure to use a grounded wrist strap and ground your soldering iron, too, to prevent dangerous levels of static electricity from damaging the fragile integrated circuits. Some references also state that you should use a grounded electrically conductive mat under yourself and another under the compact disc player that you are working on.

CD OPTICS

Some of the components that are most prone to failure in a CD player are the optics and the disc-placement assembly (my generic term for the door, drawer, etc.—don't learn this phrase for the repair people, or they will look at you for a moment dumbfoundedly). The optics are prone to failure because they easily become dirty or scratched from wear or the user's botched attempts at cleaning (Fig. 15-6). The disc-placement assembly is

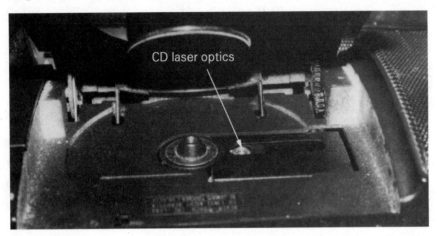

CD laser optics

Fig. 15-6 The optics of the CD player in a portable stereo.

susceptible to damage because it contains some of the only moving parts in the entire piece of equipment.

CLEANING THE LASER OPTICS ASSEMBLY

Aside from a loose head unit or tight suspension, one of the most likely causes of skipping is a dirty or dusty laser optics assembly. Little effort is required to clean the laser optics assembly; it is very similar to cleaning the heads in a cassette deck. Just get some cotton swabs and a bottle of rubbing alchohol. Dip one of the swabs in alcohol and rub it over the glass laser optics assembly. If you see other wads of dust inside the player, clean those up, too, or use a compact disc player cleaning kit. Otherwise, the dust particles might work themselves over toward the laser optics assembly and cause more skipping later on.

CHECK THE SOURCE

Although chances are that any skipping that your CD player is experiencing is caused by the player itself, it's worth checking the

CDs. If your reference compact disc or discs have been scratched or are smudged or dirty, they might be the reason why your player is skipping. I have heard some people claim that if the discs are scratched, they rub nail polish remover over the scratches. I haven't scratched any of my discs bad enough to cause skipping, so I have not been forced to try this method and verify it. However, if you feel uncomfortable using varnish remover on your precious audio, you might want to check out the CD Finishing System from Allsop, which is a disc scratch repair kit. This is the only kit of this type that I have seen on the market, so if you can't find it in a store, you can try writing for information directly from Allsop, P.O. Box 23, Bellingham, WA 98227 USA.

If the discs are dirty, clean them with a plastic-safe, nonabrasive cleaner, such as a common glass cleaner. Or try one of the compact disc optics cleaners that are available from a number of different companies (Fig. 15-7).

Fig. 15-7 A CD cleaner kit.

TECHNICAL ADJUSTMENTS

As stated earlier, technical adjustments are well beyond the scope of this book, especially for compact disc players. For most work on compact disc players, an oscilloscope and other electronic test equipment are required. There is very little that a beginner is able to maintain or repair on a compact disc player.

TAPE DECKS

Cassette tape decks often require more maintenance and repairs than any other piece of audio equipment because they have more moving parts and have to make contact with dirty materials. As a result, it is common for a cassette deck to croak—begin sounding bassy, slow down, or eat tapes after a few years of use. Then, you question why you ever thought the deck sounded great and start looking for a new model. Then, the forlorn deck is sold off cheap or is simply thrown away. Most problems with cassette decks are relatively minor and inexpensive to remedy, so it's a real shame when a deck gets pitched. Again, because of limitations in the scope and size of this book, it is somewhat limited in its trouble-shooting and repairing information. For more than 400 pages worth of information on the subject, read *Troubleshooting & Repairing Audio & Video Cassette Players & Recorders* by Homer L. Davidson.

MUFFLED AUDIO/TAPES ARE EATEN

The most common problems with cassette head units are that the audio is muffled or that the tapes get eaten by the playback mechanism. There's nothing worse than having your brand new $10.99 cassette by the Paul Johnson Trio eaten—especially when these problems have been occurring with increasing regularity over the past few months. You could even make a fist and scream, "When will this lust for ferric-oxide-coated tape ever end?" But the wanton cassette violence won't end until you stop using the deck—unless you choose to make maintenance a habit.

Although muffled audio and problems with the playback mechanism seem thoroughly unrelated, both can be different symptoms of the same problem. Of course, all standard cassettes consist of some mixture of a magnetic substance (usually ferric oxide, chromium dioxide, or metal oxide) that has been very thinly coated onto a synthetic tape. After some wear, these oxides will eventually build up a light coating of residue across the parts that rub against the tape. The residue resembles some form of dirt, and it is exactly that—foreign matter that must be removed to preserve the most accurate sound reproduction possible.

The best way to take care of these problems is to clean everything that is in the path of the tape with rubbing alcohol. With a standard home audio cassette deck, this is an easy task. Just open the cassette door, dip a cotton swab or a cleaning stick into rubbing alcohol, and carefully clean the erase head, the tape head, the pinch roller, and the capstan (Fig. 15-8). If you don't know what

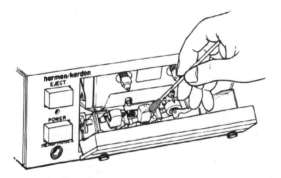

Fig. 15-8 Cleaning the heads of a cassette deck with cotton swabs.
Harman/Kardon

the tape head, capstan, and pinch roller look like, see Fig. 15-9. All of these parts look quite similar between units that have been made by various manufacturers.

The capstan and tape head should be easy to clean; just rub them with the dipped cleaning sticks a few times. The pinch roller is more difficult because it is rubber and you must put some pressure against it to remove the oxide residue. After the tape deck has been used for some time without being cleaned, you will notice that there is a stripe of tape residue running through the middle of the pinch roller. When you clean the pinch roller, you must turn it as you rub it clean. Otherwise, only one spot of the pinch roller will be clean. By the time you are finished, you should

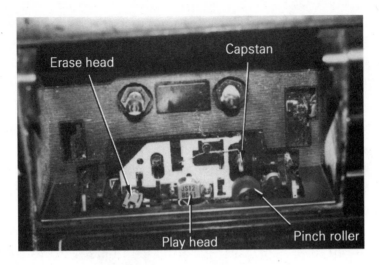

Fig. 15-9 A view of the tape transport in a portable cassette player.

barely be able to see any of the residue stripe. Cleaning the heads is a common part of audio maintenance, and it is recommended that you clean your cassette heads for every 40 hours of use, although few people adhere to this advice. A clean playback mechanism is essential for the deck to perform up to its capabilities. When I worked at a radio station, we were required to clean the heads on the cassette decks and open reel decks at every use. I have to admit that I have slacked off considerably since that time, but a clean playback mechanism is still essential to achieve good cassette performance.

I recently talked to one of my friends about the wonders and difficulties of cleaning the playback mechanism. He said, "Why don't you just use a head cleaner cassette?" Some head cleaner cassettes use abrasive tape to clean the heads. These abrasives can wear out the heads if you played them constantly. Frankly, after paying several hundred dollars for a new cassette unit, I would much rather pull out the rubbing alchohol and the cotton swabs than risk the life of that precious magnetic head. Also, some head cleaner cassettes only clean the heads, not the capstan or the pinch roller, both of which really should be cleaned regularly. If you are looking for a head-cleaner cassette, make sure that it is nonabrasive and that it cleans the heads, capstan, and pinch roller (Fig. 15-10).

Fig. 15-10 A cassette cleaner kit.

If the deck has been sounding muffled, it was probably a dirty tape head. If you clean it, but a few stubborn dirt spots remain, try rubbing the tape head very gently with a soft, clean pencil eraser. Don't use older or dirty erasers because they can leave difficult-to-remove smudges. Don't use pen erasers because they can scratch the fragile tape head.

If you mostly just had problems with tapes being eaten, also look around the capstan for any remaining pieces of tape. These pieces can cause further problems with head units getting the munchies. Little pieces of tape are easy to remove from the capstans of cassette decks because you can easily reach inside.

If the sound is still too muffled, try cleaning the heads again. If you still don't have any luck, try using a head demagnetizer. They usually cost about $5 to $10, or you might know someone who will allow you to borrow one of theirs. Most of the time when the tape heads become noticeably magnetized, it's because the heads are too close to a powerful speaker or some other magnetic field. I doubt that you'll be placing any 18" subwoofers on the top of the cassette deck, but demagnetizing the heads is worth a shot anyway. To demagnetize the heads with one of the handheld units, plug in the head demagnetizer and turn it on. While it is running, put the end of it in the cassette slot and put it near the heads, then pull it out and draw it away while it is still running. If you turn off the demagnetizer while it is running, it will magnetize the heads—possibly even worse than they were originally.

If you have tried everything and the sound is still too muffled, check the speakers. It is possible that you have overdriven and blown the tweeters in your system. Try listening to the tweeters. If you are sure that they are working (i.e., they are producing sound), then leave them alone and move on to the other speakers. If you aren't sure, try disconnecting any other speakers (such as subwoofers) in the system.

If, after all of this, the speakers seem fine, chances are that the heads are wearing out. At this point, it is best to take the deck to a reputable audio repair shop to have it inspected. Heads and the labor for head replacement can be quite expensive, so if this is indeed the problem, be sure that you get a quote so that you can either get an estimate from another shop or you can decide whether the replacement is worth the money. For most of the decks that originally cost less than $200, you will probably be better off just buying a new deck.

WRONG OR VARIABLE TAPE SPEED

The most common cause of problems with the tape speed is the drive belts. The drive belts are fine black rubber belts that look much like thin rubber bands. They drive the various moving parts in the cassette deck, such as the capstan.

If the cassette deck is running slow, chances are that the belt is too loose. If the deck is playing back at faster-than-normal speeds, the belt might have slipped around the flange of one of the pulleys. If the deck is playing back at variable speeds, the belt might be slipping—either because it is loose or because the pulleys have gotten in contact with some light oil or grease.

In all of the conditions, the only recourse is to open up the case and replace the belts. First, you have to try to find the appropriate belt for the deck. Check the owner's manual to see if a part number is listed for the problematic belt. Chances are that it won't be listed, so you will have to look elsewhere. Look up the telephone number for the company that manufactured your cassette deck. After a few telephone calls, you should find someone who can tell you the dealers that are authorized to distribute the parts for their equipment. Then call this company to see if they can either provide the part or at least give you the part number. Otherwise, check with some of the electronics mail-order companies that handle parts for various types of audio equipment. Even if the exact part number is not available for your particular model, the salespeople might be able to provide a replacement belt that has the same dimensions. If you have looked everywhere but you still can't find a belt with the right dimensions, you could try buying a smaller belt and stretching it enough that it will fit and run properly. It's not the best solution, but it beats buying a new cassette deck.

But how much tension is appropriate for the belts? You can skip this question if you have a strain gauge (by which you can measure the amount of tension on a belt) and if you have pried the privy information on belt tension from the manufacturer. Of course, few people have strain gauges, and they would be impractical unless you had a small electronics repair business.

Unfortunately, you might have some problems just accessing the drive belts, let alone being able to test their tension at your leisure. With the cassette deck in Fig. 15-11, the drive belts cannot be removed without first removing several other parts. This is supposed to be a common, simple maintenance task, but I think that it might be necessary to remove all of the circuit boards, etc.

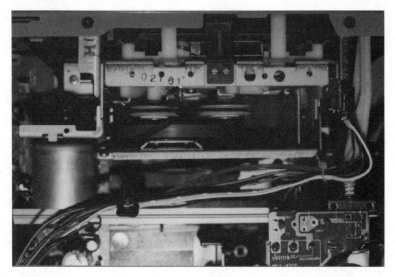

Fig. 15-11 A belt is off the the flywheel (center) in this cassette deck.

from the chassis, just to be able to fit a belt on. I bought this deck from a guy at a hamfest who said, "It works fine; all you gotta do is put some new belts on it." The price was great, so I went for it. I opened up the deck and couldn't figure out how to access the belts, so I put it back on a shelf.

Other problems can result in fitting those thin belts through tiny little nooks and around a few pulleys until they fit properly. I have never read about anyone who seemed to think that this task was difficult. Usually, the toubleshooting and repair books just say something like, "Replace the belts and move on to..." Depending on the cassette deck, the belts can be very difficult to replace.

TURNTABLES

From a troubleshooting and repairing perspective, turntables are entirely different from the other components in the audio system. Nearly every other component is primarily electronic (or, entirely electronic, in the case of the power amplifier). Except for the cartridge, turntables are entirely mechanical. Instead of being in the mind-set of looking for burned resistors or leaky capacitors, you simply want the platter to spin consistently at the proper speed while the needle in the tone arm travels effortlessly through the groove. Except for rusting, most of the severe problems in a turntable occur from physical damage (getting dropped, etc.). Nearly anything else could just be covered by routine maintenance.

CARTRIDGES

The cartridge assembly, as covered in Chapter 4, contains the needle and the magnets and coils that transmit the information in the grooves of the record into electrical signals. The section on cartridges mentioned that the needle must be perfect—not too hard or too soft—or the playback won't be accurate. The problem is that because a needle can't be too hard and is so small, it is subject to wear from constant traveling through the grooves. Once again, a worn needle will alter the playback, but worse yet, it will damage the grooves of the record. The worn needle will rub against the walls and strip out particles from the groove. The record will then be permanently damaged.

Because most records are no longer in print and are difficult to find used, you must be especially careful to prevent your collection from being permanently damaged. How often you need to replace your cartridge depends on how often you use your turntable and how roughly you handle the needle. In most cases, a cartridge will operate satisfactorily for at least several years. However, such actions as dropping the tonearm on the record or platter, or allowing the needle to "skate" onto the record label or onto the platter will quickly stunt the life of the needle. If you are buying a used turntable from a questionable source, such as the Dual turntable that I picked up from a junk dealer, be sure to replace the cartridge immediately after testing the turntable on a record that you don't really like.

Replacing a cartridge is relatively simple. First, check what type of cartridge your tonearm requires. If you don't have the paperwork for your turntable or if that information isn't listed within, just carefully disconnect the cartridge and take it along with you to a local stereo shop that sells turntables and turntable supplies. Most turntables require either standard or 1/2-inch mounts, so although chances are good that you could guess and find a cartridge that fits your turntable, it's better to know the information beforehand.

Instead of going to the expense of replacing the entire cartridge, in many cases you can replace the needle separately. The Shure cartridge, for example, uses a sliding stylus assembly to make the procedure easier (Fig. 15-12). If you are taking this route, just

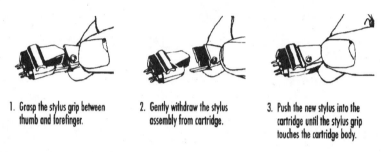

1. Grasp the stylus grip between thumb and forefinger.

2. Gently withdraw the stylus assembly from cartridge.

3. Push the new stylus into the cartridge until the stylus grip touches the cartridge body.

Fig. 15-12 The steps to cartridge replacement. Shure

grab the sides of the stylus assembly (at the front of the cartridge) between your thumb and forefinger. Gently pull the stylus assembly out from the cartridge. Then push the new stylus into the cartridge until the stylus grip touches the cartridge body. Most of Shure's stylus assemblies are a different color from the cartridge, so it is easier to determine what to pull out. Most of the stylus assemblies cost about half as much as a standard replacment cartridge, so just replacing this section will save you some money, but probably not a fortune.

BELTS

After years of use, the belts of a turntable might begin to slip, stretch, or crack. They might even break, but the speed problems typically become noticeably long before this occurs. Turntable belts present an interesting problem. They can easily survive for years without any maintenance, which is a good thing. However, because they will last so long and because fewer people are using turntables these days, it is much more difficult to find the proper belt for your model than it is, for example, to find a replacement cartridge.

Although it can be tough to find turntable belts, if you look around long enough, you might find a few companies that specialize in turntables who sell replacements. One such company is Elex Atelier, which specializes in turntable replacement belts! They have replacement belts for dozens of different turntables—everything from Linn Sondek and Rotel to Edison Cylinder Phonograph belts. In addition, if you have a belt that isn't listed in their catalog, send them the belt and the turntable information, and they will try to find a replacement. Check out their Web page at:

http://206.42.176.16/cdrome/atelier1.htm

Most belts are between $6 and $15, so it shouldn't break your bank account to get your old turntable sounding great again.

AMPLIFIERS

Dedicated amplifiers are a difficult fix for the nontechnician. There are no moving parts and no belts or motors to maintain. Everything is entirely electrical, not mechanical. Because of the lack of moving parts, amplifiers rarely fail (unless they have been driven too hard) and as a result, the better manufacturers have warranties of several years on each amplifier. Normally, when something goes wrong, the amplifier fails entirely. Then, chances are that you're stuck. You must take the amp to a factory service center because if you open up the amplifier to see what failed, the warranty will be voided.

If your amplifier no longer operates and the LED indicators don't even light, first check the plug or surge protector to be sure that nothing has become unplugged or that the surge protector has been turned off. In a rare instance, the line might have taken a nasty surge and has either shut off or totally blown the surge protector. See if the protector button will reset. If the surge protector is blown and won't reset, try plugging the amplifier back into the wall and see if it works.

If the On indicator is lit but there is no audio, check the audio lines, connections, and amplifier front-panel buttons. It's common, especially in systems where you do lots of recording or switching components and audio cables, to have the cables switched around or not plugged in. My systems, for example, confuse most people; I don't have a multi-input A/V receiver, so I either use a mixer to switch between audio sources or I just switch cables. Then, I set my cassette deck on record and feed any audio into it, then to the amplifier. Most people who try to listen to something on my stereo don't realize that the cassette deck is controlling the audio for the whole system and they can't get it running. This type of problem probably won't occur in your system, but if you have a family member who toys around with audio, look out!

If your amplifier appears to be dead or not working properly and you plan to take it in for repairs soon, wait a few days first. Check everything over a few times and give it a few days so that you can think of any simple means that you could use to correct the problem.

Unlike compact disc players, cassette decks, and turntables, which have moving parts and are subject to dirt and wear, dedicated amplifiers generally will not break down unless they have been abused. However, the next few sections cover a few problems that can occur.

MAINTAINING TUBE AMPLIFIERS

To most people these days, electronics parts and systems either work or they don't. There is no in-between. For the most part, that's how modern, solid-state electronics operate. If a transistor, resistor, capacitor, or IC is electrically damaged, chances are that it's toasted. Even if it still operates (which is doubtful), chances are that it might be physically weakened but still operating within its electrical operating specifications.

Working with electron tubes (often just called *tubes* or *vacuum tubes*) requires a totally different mind-set. If you buy a new tube amplifier or retube an old amp with new tubes, the tubes are all starting off at 100%. From the first time that you turn on that amplifier, the quality of the tubes is gradually decreasing. After years of use, you might notice that the amplifier is no longer capable of putting out as much power as it had when you first bought the tubes (or maybe the amplifier will stop working or the audio will become distorted). The tubes haven't blown out, like a dead transistor would, but they are gradually weakening.

If you are really into tube gear, it would be wise to pick up an old tube tester from a hamfest or from the Internet. Tube testers are used to test just about any kind of electron tube (cross-referenced either right in the tester or in a separate booklet) with a variety of tube sockets. My small Heathkit tube tester came from a hamfest for $12 about seven years ago (Fig. 15-13). To use one,

Fig. 15-13 A Heathkit tube tester.

simply plug the tube in, adjust the settings to match the particular tube, and see if the tube tests "good" or "bad." If the tube is either borderline or near-borderline, you should buy a replacement now for when the tube finally causes noticeable problems.

Because tubes were in such widespread use for so long, millions of them are still in existence. I've seen a number of references that advise readers to stay away from tube equipment because the tubes are so hard to find. "Rubbish!," as Thomas the Tank Engine would say. A number of companies deal specifically in selling tubes, and thousands are available at most every hamfest. Tube audio equipment has become so popular as of late that some companies have even started manufacturing them again.

This leads to the next dilemma: What kind of tubes do you buy? This is easy: buy those that match your original tubes, right? That much is true, but you can also buy used tubes that still test good: new old stock (NOS); military (W) tubes; precision high-end audio tubes; or new tubes manufactured in the Czech Republic, Russia, or China. First, some history. For decades, most of the world's tubes were manufactured in the United States, United Kingdom, Netherlands, and Germany. When transistors replaced tubes in the 1960s, most of these companies stopped making tubes, except for a few military applications (in the 1970s and 1980s). The demand for tubes picked up in the late 1980s and early 1990s, so companies in some of the emerging economic countries began to pick up the load. Because these tubes were low-cost alternatives to the old U.S. and Western European tubes, in the 1990s some entrepreneurs began to manufacture high-end units, specifically for exclusive audio systems.

Because of the specifications, the best tubes for the application would probably be the new high-end tubes. However, these are fantastically expensive—as much as 20 times more expensive than an equivalent NOS tube or recent foreign-manufactured tube. If price is a concern, your best bet is NOS or military tubes that were manufactured in the United States or Western Europe. Some of the well-known brands include RCA, Eimac, Mullard, Amperex, Philips, GE, and Tung Sol (Fig. 15-14). The Russian

Fig. 15-14 A variety of electron tubes from different manufacturers.

and Czech tubes are priced right, but are considered by some people to be a bit less reliable. Chinese-made tubes are by far the least expensive, but are rated poorly. I've heard numerous stories of these tubes failing completely (popping like a blown light bulb) several hours after use. Avoid the Chinese-made tubes!

GENERAL REPAIRS

The following repairs apply to a variety of audio equipment. For example, any piece of equipment that has a potentiometer knob could become scratchy. The last two problems, leaky capacitors and burned resistors, occur most often in tube amplifiers and old radios. These electronic repairs are all very simple and are intended for general hobbyists or audio fiends, not for those with an electronics background. As a result, the repairs require no equipment, aside from a soldering iron, some solder, and your senses. If you are really interested in repairing audio equipment, get some test equipment, such as a good DMM (digital multimeter), with a capacitance tester, transistor checker, etc., and check out some more in-depth troubleshooting and repair books.

"SCRATCHY" KNOBS

Sometimes knobs will become intermittent and make scratching noises as you turn them. For example, sometimes no sound is audible as you turn up the volume control. Then, suddenly, you might hear a loud scratching sound and the audio starts blaring through.

The problem is that the potentiometer (a variable resistor) contains metal contacts. These contacts slide against each other as you turn the knob. If the contacts corrode, tarnish, or become dirty, the potentiometer will become scratchy sounding and/or intermittent. The cure is simple. Spray some cleaning fluid inside of the potentiometer and turn the knob back and forth. If the spray is thoroughly worked over the contacts, they should become clean.

NONFUNCTIONAL BUTTONS

Buttons sometimes fail after years of use. One common ailment is that a pushbutton will no longer stay set. These buttons are typically power-on/off buttons, which receive quite a bit of abuse over the years (although other pushbuttons, such as Noise Reduction buttons, can also be similarly damaged). If these buttons fail, you have two options: Go into the innards of the equipment and by-pass the switch (effectively "hardwiring" the equipment "on," in the case of an on/off button), or try to find a replacement pushbutton that will fit the cabinet.

The problem with the first option is that you no longer have control over the equipment button. That's no big deal if the pushbutton is an on/off switch; you can turn it on or off via a surge-suppressor switch. The problem with the second solution is that you probably won't find an exact replacement pushbutton for your application. With luck, you'll find one that fits the hole, but you probably won't find one that matches. This is no problem if your listening area is in a grungy room in the basement, but you will probably want to be more careful with equipment in a living-room audio system.

If your particular piece of equipment isn't too old, you might be able to order replacement parts from the manufacturer's parts depot. Aside from this option, if you want to fix your equipment so that it looks "presentable" for your living room, you can search for an identical (but nonfunctional) piece of equipment at a hamfest or in some of the audio newsgroups on the Internet.

LEAKY CAPACITORS

Aside from the constantly degrading electron tubes that were used in 1930s through 1950s electronic equipment, most are also loaded with paper tube capacitors. These capacitors consist of a paper or bakelite tube that is filled with rolled sheets of aluminum foil and wax paper. In general, you can dig up just about any unrestored radio or amplifier from 40 years (or longer) ago, and at least one of the paper capacitors will be problematic (possibly causing the equipment not to work at all, or as is often the case, you put a severe hum on the audio). Because of these problems, most equipment restorers suggest that you replace every paper capacitor with mylar capacitors. If you use the equipment regularly, it will save you lots of time to replace them all at once (Fig. 15-15).

The next dilemma is equipment restoration. Many antique radio buffs do not believe that modern mylar capacitors should be seen within the case of a piece of antique audio equipment. Rather than make a wholesale replacement of these parts, they will place the much smaller mylar capacitors within the empty shells of paper capacitors. The techniques vary, but some people will place the old capacitors in boiling water to remove the old wax, then will push out the "guts" of the old paper capacitor. If you plan to use the old capacitor shells, be sure to check the types of capacitors and work with rubber gloves. Capacitors have used lots of

Fig. 15-15 Always prone to failure: paper capacitors in an old radio.

different chemicals inside; many contained acid solutions or PCB-laden oil. Although paper capacitors aren't filled with oil, it's best to check with some knowledgeable antique electronics restorers before tearing into some of these components.

Aside from the paper capacitors, you also need to look over the old electrolytic capacitors. These capacitors are large metal or paper cylinders that contain a chemical solution (often nitric or sulfuric acid). These capacitors will often either dry up inside and fail or will begin to leak. Either way, they render the equipment useless. Look for spots under the electrolytic capacitors on the chassis; they will either look wet or leave a light, powdery white residue. If you find capacitors like these, immediately replace them, of course, with components that have the same values. And remember that electrolytic capacitors have polarity (a positive and a negative lead), so connect any replacements following the original polarity.

BURNED RESISTORS

A sure way to find failed components in a piece of equipment is to find parts that have burned. If it's burning, there's a problem, right? The two most common burn failures in a piece of tube electronic equipment are resistors and transformers. Transistors and ICs will fail in newer equipment, but you don't typically see the smoke or flames associated with resistor and transformer failures. Transformers fail with smoke or arcing sounds, but that's about it. Resistors are much more dramatic, so that's what is covered here.

Most resistors in electronic equipment are inexpensive carbon-composition units. If they receive too much voltage or suddenly fail, they will often smoke. I've even seen some resistors that had burned in half! To find these failures, look the chassis or PC board over for burns or ashes, and look for burned resistors. If a resistor has burned up, the unit will most likely not work at all. Be sure to replace it with a resistor that has a similar resistance and power rating. Then test it. If it works, leave it on for a while to see if the resistor blows again. Burned up resistors are often signs of other component failures.

CONCLUSION

Although the electronics layperson is severely limited by what he or she can do to repair an audio system, it is possible to perform some simple maintainance and repair procedures that can save quite a bit of money and prolong the life of your system.

INDEX

INDEX

INDEX

INDEX